Beyond the Strandline

Beyond the Strandline

Linda L. Zern

Beyond the Strandline

Copyright © 2015 Linda L. Zern

All rights reserved. Except as permitted under the U.S. Copyright Act of 1976, no part of this publication may be reproduced, distributed, or transmitted in any form or by any means now known or hereafter invented, or stored in a database or retrieval system, without the prior written permission of the author, Linda L. Zern.

This book is a work of fiction. Names, characters, places, and incidents are the product of the author's imagination or are used fictitiously. Any resemblance to actual persons, living or dead, business establishments, events, or locales is coincidental or used fictitiously.

Cover Design by T. J. Lorance
Cover Photography by Rejoice Photography (www.facebook.com/RRejoiceGPhotography)
Editing by Sarah J. Johnston (Bachelors of Arts in English, Brigham Young University)

ISBN 10: 0975309870
E-book ISBN-13:978-0-9753098-8-9
Print ISBN-13:9780975309872
Library of Congress Control Number: 2015946155
Linwood House Publishing, Kissimmee, FL

Dear Reader,

While *Beyond the Strandline* is a work of fiction, the atmospheric events leading up to the establishment of the S-Line Ranch as an oasis of prepared safety have been and might yet be very real.

Solar storms are a documented part of earth's history. In 1859, a solar coronal mass ejection (a geomagnetic solar storm or solar flares) hit the earth. What little power grid existed at the time, mainly telegraphs, largely failed.

Our modern world, with its complicated power grids and systems, has only grown more vulnerable to the massive influence of our closest star. According to some in the scientific community: EMP's, pandemics, dirty bombs, nuclear attack, global economic collapse, and all the rest are statistically less likely than the storms that we cannot stop but can only try to prepare for.

In the character of Colonel Kennedy, I wanted to show the potential for all of us to be able to think ahead and prepare (prep) for whatever the universe or mankind might have in store.

Curious readers have asked me, "How did he [Tess's grandfather] know what to do to get ready?"

I rejoice at the question. Thinking about what might happen is the beginning. I like to imagine that Colonel Kennedy looked up **emergency preparedness** on the Internet and started reading. Something any of us can do.

This is a story of possibilities and hope and courage and love and survival. In my mind, it's better than a fairy tale because it's a story about the best fairy tale of all—life—in all its unpredictability.

Linda L. Zern

www.zippityzerns.com

. . . And the dearth was in all lands; but in all the land of Egypt there was bread.

Genesis 41:54

Before...

TESS SMILED WHEN Ally and ZeeZee started bouncing on the backseat of the car and holding their arms in the air when they hit Wandering Creek Bridge. They laughed at the hollow thumping noise the tires made on the wooden slats. That sound was like a signpost. They were almost to Grandma Mabel's house.

The car was all the way to the middle of the bridge when Mother screamed, "Oh God. Jon, don't stop. Don't!"

Brakes squealed, the Volkswagen Beetle shimmied to a stop, and it was too late.

Peeking around Mother's seat, Tess watched the man who blocked the way wave the gun, and point it at Father.

"Back up. Go back." Mother grabbed at the steering wheel and yanked. But it was too late. Tess saw it in the horror on her mother's face as she turned to look at something behind them.

Two more men stood behind the car, blocking their escape. They were trapped.

"Jon, why did you stop? What can they want?"

Father didn't answer. He sat frozen and stared straight ahead, his hands a funny color on the steering wheel—as if all the blood had leaked out of his knucklebones.

The man with the gun had eyes the color of muddy water and clothes that flapped around him like torn flags. He walked to the car while Ally and ZeeZee huddled in a terrified cocoon of wrapped arms and silent tears on the seat next to Tess.

Slamming the ugly gun through the open window, he told Father what he wanted.

"Give us the woman," he said, "or I shoot those girls, and then I shoot you."

The window next to Ally and ZeeZee suddenly exploded, and chunky glass covered the backseat like fat ice.

Tess covered her ears, but it was too late. She couldn't hear anything, not even her mother screaming something at Father, at the man with the gun and the ugly eyes. But that couldn't be right, because their mother didn't scream. Ever.

She watched Father nod once and the men pulled Mother out of the car by her long, curly, blond ponytail. They dragged her off the bridge and up Grandma Mabel's side of the mountain. Father never turned, and never looked back.

Tess did. At the crest of the hill she saw her mother yell something down to her family—to Tess—since no one else bothered to look.

"The Strandline. Make him take you. Go to your grandfather's. Go!"

Then the men with the guns disappeared into the West Virginia Mountains with her beautiful, civilized mother, and she realized that the car stank of ammonia, because she'd peed her pants.

Tessla Cybill Lane was ten years old when her world ended. The rest of the world had ended the week before.

CHAPTER 1
Seven Years Later...

TREE FROGS COMPLAINED and grumped from their hiding places out in the woods under the live oak leaves and Spanish moss. Tess buried her head under her pillow to block out their nagging chirps. She heard her name hissing out of the night. Had the frogs learned to croak her name?

"Tess."

Tessla groaned as loudly as she dared and flopped to her side, away from the sound of her sister's voice.

"Tess, wake up!"

She groaned again, quieter this time, being careful not to wake the others. The way they lived now, in her grandfather's WWII surplus Quonset hut bolted to a slab of concrete, made everyone living at the S-Line hyper aware of who was a light sleeper, who had bad dreams, and who was the most likely to sleep through a tornado, but that was life in the longhouse, as her sisters called it. It was a forty-eight-foot steel army barracks without walls or privacy.

When you groaned or burped or farted, you tried to be quiet about it.

"Tess, you have to wake up now."

She rolled farther away from the hiss in her ear.

The tired mattress sagged under her sister's bony, fourteen-year-old body as ZeeZee crawled onto the sleeping platform.

"Are you awake yet?"

"I'm trying so hard not to be." *Come on, take the hint ZeeZee. Take the hint and figure out a way to make peace with Ally,* Tess silently hoped.

"Just face it: she hogs the covers and you snore. Work. It. Out," Tess snarled.

Pulling the frayed quilt over her head, Tess tried burrowing in tighter. Her sister grabbed her shoulder and started to shake her.

"Ally's gone, Tess. Ally's gone off, and she hasn't come back."

She could hear the tears now and the razor's edge of panic. She jackknifed awake and reached for her sister's hand in the dark. Outside, tree frogs sang in the thick canopy and possums scurried from one hiding place to another, hunting and being hunted.

"Hush. Be quiet now; you'll bother Grandfather. Hush, baby, hush." She pulled the trembling girl into her arms. "What do you mean Ally's gone off?"

ZeeZee gasped and shuddered, struggling hard for quiet, for control. Tess could feel her sister's panic and tried to remember the last time she'd seen Ally, ZeeZee's carbon copy. The twins were always dragging around full of teenage troubles and moods, except when there was work to be done, then good luck finding them.

That was it. Two mornings ago she'd sent them to the river to check the trotlines for catfish.

After that they were supposed to have come and helped her butcher and skin rabbits. It was filthy, bloody work that Tess did at the river's edge, close to the water, where their rabbits lived in open warrens: old truck beds that Grandfather had buried and filled with dirt.

She'd needed the twins help, but they hadn't shown. No surprise there. It was a grim job and no one's favorite. She hardly blamed them for ditching, but without their help it had turned into an all-nighter. It hadn't helped that the rabbits hadn't been hydrated enough before hand, making the job harder. Watering the rabbits, that was Ally's job, of course. What was that girl up to now?

On the other side of the longhouse, someone mumbled in their sleep, restless. It sounded like one of Gwen's two boys, Blake maybe.

"She left when you went to butcher the rabbits. She was supposed to be back before the sun went down yesterday."

"That's two days. Back from where? What are you talking about?" Tess scooted closer to her sister. It got harder to keep her voice to a whisper.

Beyond the Strandline

ZeeZee started to cry harder. She reached out and gave Zeez a little shake and then a quick hug.

"Hush. I mean it. You need to stop or you're going to wake up all the grumpy lumps."

She hugged her sister tighter, hoping she'd laugh at the funny nickname they'd given the others when they were asleep. She glanced at Gwen's sleeping platform next to the kitchen. The darkness was solid, hugging them all inside the longhouse. Gwen slept like the dead.

"You know how Ally can be; she's just gone off to the barn loft again to let us know how sorry we'll be if she gets terminal cramps and dies."

Still too dark to see ZeeZee's face, Tess only felt the faint shake of her head and the teardrop that broke against the back of her hand.

"I don't think so. She left a note."

A note? That was new. A prick of fresh worry crept up the back of Tess's neck.

"Show me?"

ZeeZee pushed a wad of paper into her hand.

"Wait. Hold on. I need light."

Tess fumbled for her flint and striker, using her fingertips to feel for the crumbling end of the candle she kept next to the bed. Forget it. She didn't have time to fiddle with it. She reached for one of her precious matches and lit the wick.

In the tiny pool of light she took the note, recognizing Ally's backward-slanting handwriting. She'd crammed as many words as she could on the back of an old cash register receipt. It was a note full of dramatic teenage defiance and bravado. The note got hard to read when her hands started to shake.

"Oh, Ally . . . what were you thinking?"

CHAPTER 2

Tess buttoned up a clean pair of jeans and dragged her hand-me-down hunting vest from one of the pegs next to the bed. She pulled it over the worn Henley t-shirt that she'd slept in. Saved time if she slept in a clean work shirt—no big fashion choices to think about in the mornings.

She could wear the men's hand-me-downs because she was tall and lean like her mother. She never had to spend time hemming the jeans that she scrounged from her grandfather's Levi's stockpile.

Tess didn't waste time with a mirror. She wouldn't even if she'd owned one. She hadn't wanted one for her seventeenth birthday when the twins had tried to give her theirs. Mirrors were a waste of time, that's what she'd told them.

She wasn't like her sisters. ZeeZee and Ally took after their father's side of the family with their straight, fairy-light hair and blue eyes. They looked into a mirror and saw a soft, feminine fantasy.

When Tess looked into a mirror she didn't see her sisters' prettiness. It was her mother's face she saw: her mother's wide gray eyes, her honey-blond hair that liked to curl, and a mouth too stubborn and too big to be pretty. It was her bad luck that when she looked into a mirror she saw a face that made her sad. She made it a policy not to look.

ZeeZee filled her in on Ally's plot while she stuffed her pockets and tried to keep her brain from grinding into paralysis mode, trying not to forget anything. Her grandfather's voice came to her mind, calming her and helping her focus: *Concentrate, Tess. Get prepared. Think it through.*

She could hear her grandfather's instructions and commands over the sound of her sister's voice:

Don't let the crisis have you, gir. Listen. Focus. Plan. Follow the details.

It wouldn't do to panic ZeeZee and let her see the way her hands still shook.

She concentrated on her sister's ragged voice in the dark and what she needed to pack in her vest pockets. How long would it take to travel eight miles on the back of a mule? Should she tell Gwen?

"She said she was going to walk all the way to the Marketplace. That was her plan. She talked about how she was going to dress like a boy and have a look around, that she was tired of being a prisoner here, and she just wanted to see the fountain. Tess, I should have said something, but you know how she can be. I didn't think she'd really go. You know how Ally can be."

Yeah, she knew Ally. ZeeZee sniffled. Outside, the owl in the big oak called to its mate.

"Hush now. Stop crying."

It came out harsher than she'd intended and she knew she wasn't being fair, but the grinding knot in her belly made it hard to be patient.

"It's not your fault."

It wasn't. Not really. If anyone was to blame . . .

Grandfather had warned Tess time and again about filling her sisters' heads with stories about the world before, before the sun had rained solar fire on them, before the collapse. It was her fault that Ally had gone.

He'd warned her, but she hadn't listened. They were always begging for fairytales and ghost stories and to tell them about how wonderful the world had been before the sun had reached out and slapped the earth, collapsed the grid, crashed the government, and pushed the world all the way back to a time of skinning rabbits and riding mules and living like pioneers.

Besides she'd liked it, telling them the stories. If it was anyone's fault it was hers. She shoved her skinning knife into a top pocket of the vest.

"She doesn't have the first clue what being a prisoner even means. How was she even going to find the old Oviedo Marketplace Mall?"

She asked the question, but she knew. She'd been the one describing the road to Oviedo to them since they were little. What it had been like to drive into town, to get ice cream, to see a movie, to shop. Well, she'd described the way Highway 426 had looked seven years ago, the last time any of them had been off S-Line property.

She dropped to her hands and knees and reached under the bunk, pulled out the box where she kept her .45 caliber Ruger pistol. She pushed it into the back of her jeans.

ZeeZee continued apologizing, "I should have told. She promised me that she'd be back. She absolutely promised, and then I promised that I wouldn't tell. I thought she would be back by now."

"Stop. I'll get her back. But you have to stop blaming yourself and help me get ready to go."

She'd take Goliath, the mule, eight miles to Oviedo, another mile across town to the Marketplace, or what was left of it, and nine miles back, four miles per hour riding at a walk. Neither one of the twins had the faintest idea how long it would take to walk there or what might be waiting at the old mall.

She'd never told them those stories, the horror stories.

On the ranch every destination was a prescribed time worked out through years of experience: to the river, a short cool walk through the woods; to the goat meadow, an all morning trudge; to the Spanish bayonet hedge was a trip that could take a little girl past noon and into early afternoon, if she goofed around and didn't start right away. But all the way to the Oviedo Marketplace Mall, who knew? Was there anything left of the road between the ranch and Oviedo?

ZeeZee inched up next to her. The sun rose. Light poked at the leaves outside, finding holes in the slats of the shutters. When they kept the shutters up during the summer, mornings had a way of sneaking in from outside. The gloom in the longhouse started to shrink and soften.

"Are you sure you have to go? Maybe she'll be back soon. Maybe we should just give her some more time?"

Tess didn't have time to argue. She needed to be gone before the others were up and asking questions.

"What's the gun for Tess? She's only just gone to look at the fountain." ZeeZee's voice was strained to the point of squeaking.

"The gun is just in case. I'll have my tomahawk with me and bullets are . . ."

"Too loud to use and too few to waste."

"Exactly. And I'm going because Grandfather can't. You know that, and Father is . . . he's busy with his newsletter and . . ."

ZeeZee snorted.

"And . . . hush . . . they'll be up soon."

Besides, who else could do it? Gwen had her boys to take care of, and the old men, Kilmer and Jess T, were barely able to shuffle through their chores most days. Richmond Parrish, the young man that lived down by the river in their fishing shack, was a ghost. By the time anyone tracked him down it wouldn't matter.

Finding Ally was on Tess.

Her stomach clenched as she wiped suddenly damp palms against her jeans.

Roman, their old rooster, crowed, to let everyone on the S-Line Ranch know that he was still in charge of bringing up the morning.

She blew out the candle and knelt next to the bed again, reaching into her footlocker under the sleeping platform. Tess pulled out her grandmother's sewing scissors.

"ZeeZee, I need you to help me, okay?"

Giving her younger sister an assignment would perk her up, help stop the tears. Zeez was like that—quick to do, loyal, eager: the softer, easier twin, happier to please, easier to lead. It was good to see a spark of interest replace the misery in her eyes.

She scooted closer to the edge of the platform, legs dangling.

"What?"

Tess handed her the scissors and turned her back to the bed, pressing against the mattress. She sat so that ZeeZee wouldn't have to stretch.

"My braid. Cut it off."

There was a gasp and a faint vibration behind Tess from her sister's shocked nod.

"Now, Zeez, hurry."

Tess closed her eyes when she felt the sawing start at the thick twist of her heavy braid of hair.

When ZeeZee handed Tess the waist length hunk of hair, she threw it under the bed. It was too much trouble anyway, all that hair: hard to wash, impossible to dry. Better not to show off long hair out there in the unknown. It was too easy to grab and yank.

"Listen to me: I need you to tell Kilmer and Jess T that I've already gone to the river pasture to double-check the trotline, and that I took Goliath. I packed my bedroll, and I may not be back tonight. Can you do that? I don't want them worrying. Father won't even notice that I'm gone, and it's Gwen's day to make sure Grandfather's okay."

"I hate secrets. You know I stink at them. What should I tell them about Ally?"

It was a good question; the twins were like a matched set. Where you found one you found the other, unless Ally was off pouting.

"You tell them she's with me for skipping out on chores again."

ZeeZee dropped her head and looked miserable. She hated lying, but Tess didn't have time to handhold right now. She pinched her little sister's knee.

"Can you do it?"

She nodded and then scrambled off the bed. Ignoring Tess, she reached under the platform and dragged the hunk of dark blond braid from the cement floor. Tess sighed.

"Don't tell anyone about Ally."

She turned from ZeeZee and kept cramming everything she could think of into her vest: an extra pocketknife, an extra magazine for the pistol, the binocu-lars they used for hunting, hardtack to keep from starving.

She needed a cover story.

What about taking something to the Marketplace to trade? That would give her as good a reason as any to be there. Hadn't Parrish said that there might be trading going on there? Maybe he'd have a stringer of fish that she could take. And Ally would have had to go by his place on the river. Surely he'd be able to give her something she could use: trade goods, information, something. That was if he was anywhere near his shack at all. She could hope. She'd grab a bag of Epsom salts to trade in case Parrish was MIA.

Beyond the Strandline

ZeeZee leaned against the edge of the bed, watching Tess, holding the hunk of braid against the off-white of her muslin nightgown. Tess could feel her short hair already whirling out of control, curling around her ears. It tickled. ZeeZee stared, her blue eyes full of questions and worry.

"I cut it off to make it harder for the big bad wolves to catch me."

"And because of Mom."

Tess felt the shaking start again. She had only been seven when their mother had been taken.

"Yeah, that too."

Tess shook her head; she wasn't going to make it easy for anyone to drag her away screaming.

In the barn, she pulled her grandfather's Boonie hat over what was left of her hair, saddled Goliath, and filled her canteen.

It meant something important to him, the stained floppy hat, because he'd worn it in some old jungle war a long time ago, Vietnam. He'd learned a lot in that jungle, or so he'd told her, mostly to keep his head down and out of the way of bullets.

It meant something to her too, that her grandfather had trusted her to do things right. And now she'd failed him. Ally was gone—gone to see a fountain that no longer existed, in a world ruled by butchers and thugs.

Richmond Parrish would know something about that kind of world. She was sure of it.

CHAPTER 3

THE FISHING SHACK sat next to the Little-Big Econ River like a lonely outpost. It was the color of old Spanish moss, gray and faded. She dragged Goliath straight to it, praying Richmond Parrish was inside.

The river cut through her grandfather's four thousand acres like a brown ribbon, stained almost black by the tannic acid that leached from the cypress trees. The dark water gave them catfish, frogs, and sometimes gator tail. The young man who lived there next to the water watched the river for them, fished it, traveled it, and kept his secrets there in private.

They only saw Parrish once, maybe twice a month in the beginning, when he would come to talk to Colonel Kennedy. *The Colonel*, that's who he'd asked for, when he had shown up at the longhouse. Once or twice a month was the norm until the sweltering day the old man had stumbled to his knees, unable to speak or communicate or walk again.

Since Grandfather's stroke, Parrish came more often, sitting and watching over the fading old man, giving the others a break from caretaking—almost as still and quiet as the man he watched over.

Hollow-eyed and hungry, Parrish had shown up the year Tess had turned fifteen. Grandfather had put him up in the shack at the edge of the river—no explanation, no details. One day he was just there—a part of their lives.

Gradually he'd gained weight, looked less and less like a starving scarecrow. Instead of asking for haircuts, he kept his dark hair long and tied back. Most of the time, his face stayed hidden behind an unshaven scruff, even after his haunted eyes had softened and taken on a warm green and gold light.

To her sisters, Richmond Parrish was a wildly romantic figure. They had fun making up all kinds of stories about him. He was the son of a gypsy prince or a spy or a displaced famous person, or the dead president's son. Tess figured him for one of the men and boys running away from the countless militia groups roaming the country looking for bullet catchers and warm bodies, but she didn't ask.

It felt wrong to pry and Parrish never offered. He caught fish while Tess skinned rabbits and milked goats. They took turns hunting the Sambar deer that now ran wild through the swamps and hammocks that surrounded them.

Once she'd tried to talk to her grandfather about the stranger living in their fishing shack, not because she was like her sisters, of course—half-fascinated, half-thrilled—but . . . well, he did have beautiful green eyes and a way of watching her that made her feel itchy and interested and irritated, all at the same time. Why would he watch her like that? Quiet and careful. Did he watch the others like that?

She just wanted to know about him out of curiosity. Sure. Because it was hard to guess how old he might be. Gwen's boys were younger than the twins. Kilmer and Jess T were older than her grandfather. She guessed he was probably close to her in age. But not close to her in experience, her grandfather had made sure she understood that much about him.

"Not too many more birthdays than you Tess, but a big, bad world of experience older. You just leave him to himself."

The fishing shack was closed up tight when she got there.

"Parrish, I need you," she hollered, tying Goliath to a tree limb. The hardwood hammock dipped into jungle here, pushing up against the shack like a green, leafy zipper closing.

"It's me, Tessla Lane, Colonel Kennedy's granddaughter."

Good grief. That sounded pretty silly. Who else would she be? There weren't that many human possibilities. When no one answered, she shivered, thinking that he was off on one of his hunting or fishing trips.

She pushed through the rickety screen door of the shack, its screen patched and re-patched against the swarms of bugs that shared the river and woods with them, making bug control a very big deal. It was a job that kept Gwen busy mixing up new and better concoctions of essential oils, herbs, and witch hazel.

"Richmond Parrish, I need you," she said, already knowing he wasn't there, but it felt polite and hopeful. She was stalling and she knew it.

She wanted him to be there, ready to help, ready to take her hand, ready to tell her that Ally was just having a temper tantrum, that he knew where she was. She already knew that it wasn't going to happen that way.

The inside of the shack was a surprise: a cot with a moth-eaten blanket, a nightstand with a stack of books, and a table covered with bits of wire, feathers, and fishing line. The few clothes he owned were neatly folded in the corner. It was Spartan to the point of dismal, and there was no Parrish in sight. It didn't seem like he lived here, not really. Just slept here when it rained. She knew he spent his days wandering the limits of the hammocks, swamps, and woods that surrounded them, moving through the forest like one of the animals he hunted.

She was pretty sure he was the only one that could have told or shown Ally the way off the property. It had to be him. Grandfather had never said that there was a way through the labyrinth of scrub brush and Spanish bayonets, those needle-like spikes that he'd allowed to grow up around the perimeter of the ranch. She knew there had to be a way out. And Parrish was the one who would know.

If he wasn't here, maybe he was with Ally. She latched onto that thought like a drowning woman grabbing for a channel marker. Her hands clenched to fists.

Please, let him be with Ally.

It was hard to believe that he would show Ally how to cross the boundary line. It was a rule. No, it was THE rule. No one was supposed to leave. If no one knew they were there, they were safe.

She ran her finger down the spines of the books: *A Long Way Gone: Memoirs of a Boy Soldier*, *The Art of War* by Sun Tzu, *Black Hawk Down*.

There was a theme here. She didn't recognize the titles, and something about that bothered her. She'd read all the books from the main storage shed. There were hundreds of paperbacks, all secondhand library books, next to the dehydrated onions and the lemon pepper spice, but not these. She'd never seen these books before.

Beyond the Strandline

The screen door creaked open behind her. She whirled. Her heart slammed behind the cage of her ribs.

"Dad!" she said. "You scared me."

"Did I?" He looked at her with confusion and hurt. His pale blue eyes darted and shifted, never really landing on her. He clutched his briefcase against his chest. "I'm sorry for that, Tessie. I saw the mule."

He hunched his shoulders and flinched as if he expected her to strike him. It was a gesture she'd come to hate.

"Don't, Dad, it's okay. I was looking for Parrish. I . . . uh . . . I have something to ask him."

He looked relieved to have a topic to focus on.

"Me too. But he's not here. He roams."

That was funny coming from her father. It was hard to know where her father spent his days and most of his nights. He was like a phantom that drifted from one haunting to the next: a bleached shadow of a man, who wandered the hammocks and woods of the S-Line hauling his briefcase full of notes and handwritten drafts for the newsletter he perpetually slaved over—a newsletter no one ever read.

"What did you want to ask him?" he said, looking at her with a droopy half smile. "Maybe I can help . . ."

She shook him off with a wave of her hand.

"No. Nothing for you to worry over. I need to get moving," she said, brushing by him on her way to the door. "So, do you have big plans for today?"

She could feel him perk up at her fake interest.

"Well, yeah, I thought I'd rewrite an op-ed about the enormous employment opportunities there'll be when the lights come back on . . . I thought I might interview Mr. Parrish. As a young man, he'd be interested in job opportunities."

"Okay, sure. That sounds fine." She pushed past him. The screen door hinges squealed. Morning sun warmed the leaf mold surrounding the shack; its spice sharpened the air, a familiar woodsy perfume.

She looked back at her father through the screen door and saw Ally's soft blond beauty.

"Dad?"

"Yes?" His eyes had jittered away from her face, again. He was already rewriting his pointless article in his head.

"Sounds . . . great. Can't wait to read it."

He didn't answer her.

"Okay then. Hey, I'm going to be out for a bit, probably over night. I'll finish up with the rabbits when I get back." She knew that he wasn't hearing her anymore. He stood in the frame of the closed screen door, his eyes glazed and dreamy. Sighing, she walked down the porch steps.

She didn't turn around until she hit the bottom step. It was silly really, the way she suddenly needed him. She felt ridiculous crashing back up the steps, wanting to hug him, needing him to hug her, the way he had when she was little. She threw open the screen door.

His eyes narrowed to slits when she threw her arms around him. He stood like a tree trunk made of dry bark, the briefcase wedged between them. She patted his shoulder.

"Okay, Dad, okay," she said. "Check on ZeeZee if you think about it, and Grandfather while I'm gone."

He frowned down at her, looking confused. She knew he wouldn't remember.

"Don't be gone too long. I'll need you to read over this." He pushed the briefcase at her.

"Okay."

He didn't respond. She didn't really expect him to. She left him there on the rickety front porch of the fishing shack, pulled Goliath free, and went to break her grandfather's number one rule: NEVER LEAVE THE S-LINE.

Grandfather had turned his ranch into a castle keep because he'd seen it all coming: the avalanche of destruction that had swept her mother away and crushed her father's heart and mind.

He'd started preparing years before the end: stockpiling food, ammunition, books, Levi's, and plotting their invisibility in plain sight, letting the boundary lines of fence and pasture slowly fade into a ragged, unrecognizable

Beyond the Strandline

wall of thorns and underbrush. Fences rotted where they stood. The ranch road dissolved. He'd burned down his beautiful ranch house.

Now the S-Line was a fortress and they were three princesses surrounded by an actual wall of thorns. How many times had she told her sisters stories about princesses tucked away behind the protection of enchanted briars?

Except that now, one of the princesses had found the hole in the wall and wriggled her way out.

CHAPTER 4

THROUGH THE SCOPE of his rifle, Parrish watched a pair of ducks disappear over Puzzle Lake, frightened off by the crashing and thrashing behind him. He sighed and lowered his rifle.

"I know you're there. You sound like a yeti riding an elephant through the woods," he said, staring at the now empty sky. "What do you want?"

One of those girls, the twins, popped out from behind a scrub palmetto like a seed out of a watermelon. It was a game with those two girls, stalking him, spying on him, giggling at him behind trees. He tolerated it for the old man's sake.

He tolerated a lot for Colonel Kennedy's sake because he was grateful.

"Which one are you?"

"Zeta," she said, using her real name, not her nickname.

Growing up, he guessed. How old were they anyway? Fourteen, almost fifteen, maybe? They looked older, the way some girls did at that age. He crushed the thought of what his sisters had looked like at that age out of his mind.

He noticed the tears when she stumbled closer, tripping over a knot of pine tree roots. He caught her arm before she went down into the heavy white sugar sand at his feet.

"Is it the old man, your grandfather?" He tightened his grip on the rifle and her elbow.

"What?" she said, but confusion soon cleared to understanding. "No, no, that's not it."

"Kid, you almost gave me a heart . . ." he paused, studying her face.

It was dirty; tears had washed clean tracks through the dust on her cheeks. She rubbed at a smear of mud on her chin.

"What then?" He jostled her a bit. "What is it?"

It came in a rush.

"Ally. She's gone and Tess is gone . . . to find her. She left. She's gone."

"Which one?"

She looked at him like he was brainless, the way teenagers looked at grown-ups. Surprised, he realized that he *was* the grown-up in this discussion.

"Both!" she yelled. "Ally went to the Marketplace to see the fountain and Tess's gone after her, to bring her back. They've left the ranch. They've left! Both of them."

The kid looked horrified. She should have, if it were even true. Probably just more teenage drama that Tess was having to sort through.

A quick vision of Tess as she'd crossed the sheep pasture a week ago, her unbraided hair a loose tumble of curls, flashed through his memory. It had looked like warm honey in the sunlight. She'd been hurrying on one of her endless errands, not the least of which was keeping her younger sisters on task and out of trouble.

He found himself doing that more and more, watching her from the shadows, telling himself that it was to help Colonel Kennedy keep an eye on her. Great. When had he become as bad as those silly girls?

Parrish dropped the kid's arm and glanced back at the soft ripples of water on the lake. He tried to ignore the way his gut twisted up at the possibility that she was right, that Tess and Ally were gone.

"And you want me to do something about it?"

She tipped her head to look at him. She made him think of a woodpecker looking for bugs on a tree.

"But I thought you would . . . want to . . . go after them, I mean." She looked shocked now. "That you would want to help me."

The wind picked up, a fidgety gust, hinting at rain. Maybe a storm was coming. It was about time.

"A false alarm. That's what this is." He pushed down the poisonous dread that clawed at his throat. Time to dump the kid off on Gwen Dunn. She'd have the straight story. He needed to get back to the real work around here: keeping food on the table.

"But Mr. Parrish!" she gulped. "Mr. Parrish! Tess took her gun. She left this."

At first he thought she was holding a horse's tail. It was a hunk of hair, the color of old honey, shot through with hints of sunset. Tess's hair. She'd cut off her hair.

"But why? Why would she cut off her hair?" He was surprised when the girl answered him. For a second he'd forgotten she was there.

"Because of the wolves. That's what she said. And the men that took our mother."

Parrish took the braid away from her and tried to ignore how soft it felt in his hand. He thought about the wolves who ran the Marketplace Mall and shuddered with rage.

Lucky, that's what it was.

The rains were late, and the river was still shallow enough for her to ride Goliath along the bank toward the main road. The farther she went, the smaller and tighter the river ran, bottoming out and finally spreading wide into marsh and bog. Tess hit the wall of Spanish bayonets just as the river became an impassable marsh.

Sand dunes and slash pine edged out the wetlands on her right. The bayonets waited like soldiers on guard as her luck ran out. Smart old Grandfather. There was nothing here: no trail or path, no hint of a way forward. There was only the hedge of Spanish bayonets, planted by her grandfather for years and as effective as concertina wire. She pointed Goliath toward the dunes and the wall of spikes.

Goliath was a big mule, rawboned and rangy, but even he was reluctant to push through the six-foot-high barrier of slender, spiking leaves tipped with three inch needles when they hit it. There was a reason they called the yucca plants "bayonets." He balked until she cut a switch and smacked him with it.

She tried clearing a path with her tomahawk, but the green leaves folded under the blade. Getting close enough to the trunks to cut the plants down was a death wish. As tough as Goliath's hide was, she worried about his soft muzzle and eyes. Before they'd gone ten feet she'd been stabbed a dozen times, blood streaking her pants and shirtsleeves.

A few more feet in, he jammed on the brakes and refused to take another step.

Thorns closed in around them. She slid to the ground and longed for body armor. A thorn stabbed her neck. Blood dribbled. Hot tears threatened. If only she'd thought to wear heavier clothes, something to protect her face and neck, not to mention Goliath's eyes and face? How could she have known it would be this bad?

No way Ally had pushed through this. No way.

Goliath snorted, nostrils flared in misery and pain, as he stamped at the ground. She wiggled around to his head. She had to smack his nose when he nipped at her.

"Come on, Buddy, this should help."

She pulled a strip of terry cloth, the last of a bath towel reduced to rags, out of a vest pocket and threw it over his head, covering his eyes. It gave him a bit of protection and seemed to calm him. Hunching inside her vest she dragged him forward, pushing the bayonets back with the flat of the tomahawk, trying not to cry when they stabbed her.

Yeah, Grandfather had been a smart old prepper, planting rows and rows of the yucca cactus, not just for defense, but for food and fiber too. By the time they hit an open space—a cow pasture gone to sand, palmetto, and goldenrod—she wanted to curse that smart old man.

"Good boy, Goliath." She used the towel to wipe the worst of the blood off the mule's head. He snorted at her and tried to nip her again. Blood slicked her fingers.

She didn't have time to figure out how much of it was hers. Sweat stung as it ran over the needle pricks. Too long, it had taken too long to get through. The sun was closer to its zenith than the horizon. She'd forgotten the windup pocket watch in her hurry, of course, and had to guess how long it had taken to push her way through the bayonets.

Worse than not knowing the time was the feeling that they were probably lost. The pasture was a maze of tufted grass and clumps of scrub. How could Ally have had the guts to try this on her own?

She looked back at the interlocked wall of spikes that had closed in behind them as if they'd never come that way. Good thing. If it were easy, Goliath would have probably turned around and bolted back for home and safety.

Who was she kidding? She'd have led the way.

Ally had to have known another way or someone had helped her. But who? Add that to the list of discussions she'd have with her wayward sister when she found her. It was Tess's turn to snort.

A vague memory of going "to town" dragged Tess forward, across the relative open space of grassland. She led Goliath through the maze, heading west, away from the river, away from home, ignoring the tightening knot in her gut.

What if it was all gone? Surely seven years hadn't been long enough to erase the roads, all those ribbons of asphalt that crisscrossed Florida. That's what Tess counted on, hoped for. She'd never seen the ruined roads for herself, but she'd heard her father and her grandfather argue about it often enough: What the world might look like after the collapse. Back when her grandfather could still argue a point and her father wasn't so . . . pre-occupied with his endless scribbling, they'd held many a late night debate.

How long would it take for the old world to completely fade away—the roads, the power grid, the bridges?

Her father had argued that the ruins would never completely disappear, because he wanted so badly to believe it could all be saved somehow, brought back from the grave. That's why he wrote that silly newsletter of his on reams and reams of old computer paper, front and back, by hand.

Grandfather's theory had been that it would all be brittle bones in ten years and gone in twenty. America's infrastructure had been rotting for years even before the solar flares, he said. Now here they were into year seven after the event horizon.

Tess didn't have a theory, just the first tightening knots of panic. She didn't need theories or arguments; she needed a clue, a hint, something to help her know which way to go to find Ally in all this ragged, broken wildness.

If you're stuck, Tess, try moving forward. Forward usually works.

"Get on the mule and ride, Tess," she said to no one in particular, but she thought her grandfather would approve.

CHAPTER 5

Riding Goliath worked. It helped to slow the prickles of fear that threatened to paralyze her. He picked his way as daintily as a ballerina through the tearing vines and saw grass clumps. Eventually they stumbled onto the moth-eaten edges of Highway 426, the two-lane road from Geneva to Oviedo. The ragged edges of pavement were little more than crumbling chunks of asphalt picked apart by roots and rain. Holes gaped in the center of the road, filled with slimy water and cattails. But it was there, and she could see it, the faint broken white line of paint that had once separated the coming and going of traffic, the coming and going of other human beings.

She dismounted and squatted next to the road, light-headed. She clung to the reins of the bridle, the only thing connecting her to the here and now and the highway in front of her, as she fought the memory of another road and her mother being dragged away, forever gone. And now, Ally was gone too.

Stop this! Get up! But she couldn't move.

The blood of a dozen bayonet stabs dried on her jeans—blood and sweat and more blood. Her empty stomach revolted against the instant flood of fear-drenched adrenaline. She dry heaved into the sand in front of her. She pulled the Boonie hat off of her head and wiped her mouth with it.

The road to what was left of Oviedo and the old Marketplace Mall lay like a scarf of rotting lace in front of her. Once, she and her mother had traveled back and forth this way without a thought on summer vacations, to go shopping, to get ice cream, so they could escape the verbal fistfights between her mother and grandfather.

Her hand cramped around the bridle reins. She forced her fingers to relax and watched the blood rush back into her hand. The big mule sniffed at her hair. He had good timing and a pretty decent bedside manner. She slapped the hat back on her head.

"I know. My hair, it's pretty short," she said. She stood up, patted his bloody nose, and realized he'd already brought them both pretty far.

"But I have a hat. And I've got you." She scratched under his chin.

He blinked. His long ears ticked forward, listening to something she couldn't hear, something on the ruined road ahead. At the edge of the field, lamb's ear grew in fat, mounded clumps. She stooped and picked a fist full of the big, wooly leaves, wiped her mouth again, then rubbed at the smears of blood on her hands with the velvet leaves.

Maybe it was the feel of silk against Tess's cheek that brought the quick, light memory back: Ally, by herself for once, tucked up in the hayloft of the barn during one of their summer visits to the S-Line, humming little girl music punctuated with the delicate mewing of new kittens. Tess found nothing but a mound of hay and the sound of humming when she climbed the ladder. She'd called her name and out of the haystack poked the face of a four-year-old Ally, a yellow tabby kitten balanced on her golden head. "Come on, Tess. Come sing with these tats." That was Ally, sweet and wild and surprising and now gone.

Love and misery swamped her. If only she could keep away the memories that made her weak. But now was not the time for "if onlys." She crushed the soiled leaves of lamb's wool in her hand and threw them away. Bending, she picked more and stuffed a pocket of the saddlebag full of the handy plant.

"And now I've got some cowboy toilet paper. Good enough, Old Man," she said, pulling herself back into the saddle. "There's not much you can't do with cowboy toilet paper."

Goliath lifted his block of a head and trumpeted an enthusiastic bray. The sound echoed and banged through the motionless air.

She jabbed her heels into the mule's gut.

"Shut up! Geez, why don't you just announce, 'Dinner's ready, come and get us?'"

She pushed him into his trademark gangly walk, keeping the faded white line of the highway on her right, weaving through the shrub at the edge of the asphalt, and staying as close to the protection of the big trees as she could.

Beyond the Strandline

Parrish forced himself to focus on the rifle in his hand: the weight and heft of it; the feeling of control it gave him. The kid next to him swiped at her nose and sniffled.

"Don't. You. Cry. Stop it. Your sister decided to cut her hair. That's all there is to it. Hardly worth crying over."

It felt like ashes in Parrish's mouth, telling ZeeZee not to cry. How many times had he said it—told some homesick, terrified kid that same thing, used those same words? Then sent those same kids, unprepared and crying, to their deaths. He crushed the memories, the horror, making note of the sound of cicadas and the smell of distant rain that teased at the air. Don't go back there. Don't.

"But I thought you would want to help us."

She gestured to the length of hair in his hand. The cut end of the braid had begun to unravel. He should give it back to the kid.

Because she'll want it, would need it if this thing with Ally and Tess turned out to be true . . .

But he didn't hand it back. He tucked the braid into the pocket of his sleeveless hunting jacket.

The birds and frogs had stopped talking to each other because of the kid and the way she'd smashed her way through the woods. The quiet of the forest was over—the kind of quiet he craved. It was the part of hunting he liked best: the absolute need for silence, for stillness.

When she started to cry without making a sound, he was grateful. Okay. Fine. Cry then and get it done.

Ignoring her big eyes all glittered up with tears, he slung the rifle onto his shoulder and started back through the pine scrub that grew like a fringe around Puzzle Lake. He followed a game trail through the tangle of underbrush, having to duck more often than not. He'd gotten tall those last few years in the militia. How tall? Who knew? There hadn't been a lot of time for keeping track of that kind of stuff, what with trying to stay alive and all.

ZeeZee trailed behind him like a noisy dog.

To her credit she didn't beg or whine or nag. Smart kid. It wouldn't have helped her cause if she had. That other twin was always causing some kind of drama, and he didn't need it. The Ally kid had probably crawled off to some corner of the ranch to hide and pout. No way she and Tess had left ranch boundaries. No way. He wouldn't let himself think beyond that denial. Couldn't.

He slowed his retreat long enough to hold a branch back and out of the way for the girl. He didn't think she noticed the gesture when she plowed ahead of him. When she started to drift to the north he stopped walking and watched as she went about getting herself good and truly lost.

Sighing, he called to her, "Hey kid, back this way or you'll wind up somewhere you won't want to be."

"No I won't." The words might have cut glass.

He watched her walk past a thicket of saw palmetto and disappear behind it. Palmetto fronds rattled and shook as she moved. At this rate he'd be able to hear her all the way to the Atlantic.

"I mean it. You're heading toward the sinkhole clearing."

Serve her right if she ran into the feral hogs that were tearing up this part of the ranch. Coyotes, bobcats, black bears, feral pigs, and panthers—he'd heard the panthers but not seen them—fought for territory and food, taking back the land when the humans had faltered.

"Seriously, kid. Come on back." He stopped, turned, and plowed through the underbrush after her.

Tess had turned left. It had been as simple as that and easier than she thought it would be.

There was a faint path here close to the road that reminded her of the deer trails back on the ranch. Others had traveled this path, not often, but enough to leave a faint trace in the quick grass and sand spurs.

Enough to mark the coming and going of someone between what was left of Oviedo and what had once been a happy spot on the map, the village of Geneva.

Was this how it began again? Civilization? A faint line worn in the dirt between survivors? People finally saying, "I need what you have," and wanting it badly enough to leave their fortresses to get it: the militias, warlords, child soldiers, slave traders, tribes and survivors?

Goliath's ears stayed forward like furry antennae. Thankfully, deer fly season had passed enough to keep Goliath from being eaten alive. And once the haze of morning had burned off, the mosquitoes and biting flies died down.

They plodded along, slow and steady. She stroked the rabbit skin messenger bag where the tomahawk thumped against her chest, a nervous habit she'd picked up since she'd had to kill a feral sow down by the green spring swimming hole last year. She'd come close to being gutted by the sow's six-inch tusks. The hogs grew bolder every year.

The adults had argued about teaching the girls how to use guns, knives, and tomahawks. Her grandfather had insisted. Her father had been horrified at what he saw as the hardening of his baby girls into Amazonian warrior queens, killers. His words. But they'd learned and they were good: pistols, knives, tomahawks, you name it. Tess and her tomahawk were inseparable and lethal. Ally could have won prizes with her pistol shooting once upon a time. ZeeZee wasn't far behind her. Desperate times called for desperate measures and Amazon warrior women.

After the sow, she'd quit even trying to listen to her father, realizing he hadn't been right in the head since long before that day on the bridge in West Virginia. He'd somehow managed to get them down the East Coast, past the roadblocks, the car thieves, the marauders, and the mobs of the starving, to Central Florida. Even so, nothing could change the fact that he'd lost the battle and the war when he'd lost Mother—both in his own mind and in Tess's.

Better to have guns, knives, and tomahawks than to let a bunch of pigs tear you to pieces.

Tess made herself drop her hand from the rabbit skin bag so that she could take up Goliath's reins with both hands, steady and strong.

CHAPTER 6

GOLIATH STOPPED IN his tracks as if someone had bolted him to the ground.

She didn't have time for stubborn mule attitude. She rammed her heels into Goliath's side. He didn't flinch. She'd just started to take the end of the reins to his backside when he lowered his head and wheeled around on his hindquarters like a five-year-old quarter horse. He tried desperately to escape, turning back the way they had come.

Tess smelled the hogs before she saw them. In the rising heat of the morning, they'd burrowed up under a stand of cypress bordering a marshy area where the road made a hard right turn toward town.

"Oh no you don't. No self respecting mule would let a bunch of pigs keep him from finding Ally."

She yanked his big head into his side, spinning him in a circle.

"You big coward, let's go!"

She dug her heels in when she heard piglets squeal. A boar erupted out of the underbrush, plowing forward like a tank, going for the mule's belly, slashing upward with razor sharp tusks. She didn't have to do any more convincing. Goliath lunged forward with a grunt and a bellow.

Tess bent over the saddle horn and hung on. The boar snorted behind them as the other hogs crashed away through the woods, squealing and grunting their outrage. Staying tight in the saddle, she tried hard to avoid getting brained by low hanging limbs and let Goliath run it out. Four miles per hour—hardly! At this speed they'd be there in twenty minutes.

Hanging on she let him run, straight into the first signs of civilization she'd seen in seven years.

Beyond the Strandline

It was a camp of sorts that had grown up like a poisonous mushroom where the highway and Van Arsdale Street intersected. A place that was hard to comprehend or imagine, unless a person saw it, smelled it, and even then . . .

As she blasted through the ruins at a dead run on the back of a frightened mule, Tess had the wild thought that she'd found Peter Pan's lost boys—only a lot more filthy.

The stink burned Tess's throat—rot and despair. She didn't see anyone as they blasted through the camp, but there were eyes on her; she could feel them.

Goliath thundered through heaps of garbage and twisted car wrecks that looked like the bones of butchered animals draped with poorly cured hides. A partially collapsed barn as big as a warehouse flashed by on her right, sitting off to the side of the camp like a collapsed tin can. Goliath snorted and blew at the assortment of stinking obstacles. At the edge of the pitiful collection of hovels and wrecks, she pulled the frothing mule back into a one-rein stop. His big feet skidded as she pulled him into a smaller and smaller circle. Heaving like a deflating balloon, his sides thundered against her legs. She felt woozy from her own huffing and puffing.

He finally stopped, dropping his head almost to the dirt.

The only other human being Tess saw was a little boy, naked, dragging something through the dirt behind him. Filth streamed down the back of his legs. He stared at her. No one seemed worried by the threat she might pose to the child, since no one came for him.

They were the John and Jane Doe Kids. That's what her grandfather had called them. Kids without names, the little ones that were left, orphaned, abandoned, pushed into filthy places like the Van Arsdale Camp, trying to care for each other—or not.

She stared at the little boy in front of her. He dragged the hind leg of a deer behind him. The deer's hoof left a neat groove in the dirt as the boy wandered in and out of the maze of garbage. It was just how Ally and ZeeZee would drag their blankets and toys around with them when they were little.

The boy smiled. His front baby teeth were brown where he'd fallen or been hit. Zeez had fallen and browned out her baby teeth. Everyone had been so happy when her permanent teeth had come in to replace the ugly ones.

"Hello."

He didn't answer.

An older kid, about the age of the twins, stepped out from behind one of the shrouded car chassis. This kid had a wooden club in his hand. The club bristled with nails and spikes. Impressive, if you were a caveman. He pointed at Tess.

"We're taking that horse. This is our place."

"Direct. I like that."

Children of various ages and states of nakedness crept out of the rubble.

"It's a mule, and seems I still need him."

"Don't care." He shook his head. His greasy hair flopped into his bleary, blue eyes. Their color screamed out of the dirt on his face.

The camp was filled with a low, droning hum. Flies. The entire camp hummed with the sound of wings. The boy shook his head again, shooing flies that gathered at the corners of his eyes and mouth. Goliath stomped as flies cruised in for the attack.

"What makes you think that I'm going to give you this mule?"

The boy cocked his head at her and smirked. It was that smirk more than anything that worried her.

Leaves trickled down as tree limbs overhead rustled and then shook. There were more Doe Kids, as skinny as monkeys, scrambling through the branches over her head.

They pushed what looked like a wad of rags and ropes out of the tree over Goliath's big head—a makeshift net. Tess had to admit it would have been a good enough plan if Goliath weren't still skittish over the big, mean, feral pigs. He lunged sideways, away from the falling netting. Tess lost her balance and grabbed for the saddle horn.

She wheeled Goliath away from the monkey kids in the trees. Something bounced off of her leg. The little brown-toothed boy had dropped his deer-leg trophy long enough to pick up a chunk of cement. Another piece of pavement flew by her face.

These Doe Kids were serious.

"We want that horse."

"You're not eating this horse—I mean mule. Come on Goliath, we're out of here." Goliath bolted at Tess's familiar touch.

Goliath slowed to a canter when they came to where Van Arsdale Street should have curved into Florida Avenue. They came after her, howling and spitting. The crumbling road curved ninety degrees to the left. Goliath made the turn like a champ. The kids made the turn as well, but then the howling mob of children stopped as if they'd hit an invisible force field.

She didn't have time to worry about invisible lines they refused to cross.

In the end, Parrish walked the ZeeZee kid all the way back to the longhouse. He told himself it was to keep her from plotting some crazy, pointless rescue plan and winding up lost too. He wanted to tell her that Tess and Ally were probably already home. That it was all some kind of silly misunderstanding, some incomprehensible girl drama. He wound up saying nothing. Let the Dunn woman deal with it.

Besides, anything he said would be bogus. When they'd crossed the river, he'd seen the hoof prints in the mud. Evidence that Tess had ridden the big mule up river and into the marsh. It was the first real proof that the unthinkable might be true. A hunk of hair was hardly a clue of anything, except a kid's wild imagination and story telling. Didn't girls do that kind of stuff? Cut their hair, fuss with their clothes? But those hoof prints . . .

The woman, Gwen Dunn, rushed outside to meet the kid at the door of the longhouse and wrapped her in a bear hug. Her eyes lifted to him as she hugged ZeeZee, looking for answers—as if he had answers.

"She's . . . it's the kid . . . she got worried." He couldn't think of anything else to say about it. He knew he sounded like an idiot.

By now wouldn't Gwen have noticed three whole girls missing from their tight, little lives? What else was there to say except I brought this one back?

She shook her head, patted the girl, and sent her into the dim interior of the longhouse. He could smell oatmeal and cinnamon—breakfast. It was late morning.

The woman pushed a piece of paper at Parrish and looked at him with liquid brown eyes in a face the color of caramel. He always thought of coffee and cream when he looked at Gwen Dunn. He stared at the paper in her hand.

There was expectation in her eyes, a simple hope.

"Lady, I just brought the kid home. She'd wandered all the way out to Puzzle Lake. Someone needs to keep better tabs on her."

He turned away from Gwen and tried to imagine ZeeZee's story a different way, because if Ally *had* left the S-Line and Tess *had* gone after her . . . God. There would be nothing for them but blood and butchery out there beyond the ranch. Nothing.

"Because of this," she said, shaking the paper at him. "She came to find you because of this note. Won't you look at it?"

He shrugged, making no move to turn around and take the paper from her; he felt numb just thinking about it. He resisted the urge to reach into his jacket and touch Tess's braid.

"How is he today?" They both knew who he was talking about.

"That's all you have to say? What about this . . . this note?" She rattled it at him again. "What are we going to do about this? Those girls are his granddaughters. How do you think he would feel if he weren't sick, knowing that you don't care?" She slowed down, took a breath, and then added, "Parrish, I know something of what you've lived through. "

He rounded on her. The rage must have broken through; she fell back a step at his look. He'd scared her.

Holding her palms up, she said, "Ease on down. I know some, not all of it . . . but some."

"Don't."

Parrish pushed straight out through the door. The screen door smacked shut behind him.

He could picture it. Inside, Gwen's boys were busy stirring the pot of oatmeal on the wood stove at the far end of the hut. Jess T and Kilmer, two gray tumbleweeds already dusty, would be sitting at the picnic table they used for family meals, waiting in front of empty bowls as they watched the boys get breakfast ready. In the corner, next to the stove, Colonel Kennedy would be slumped inside a summer quilt of bright yellow sunflowers, propped up in his rocking chair, if it was one of his bad days. The old man's head drooping almost to his chest, his hands twitching softly in his lap. All of them pretending they hadn't just heard the "discussion" Parrish and Gwen had had moments earlier.

"Parrish?" Gwen called, walking quietly to the door of the longhouse.

He wasn't used to hearing the sound of his own name said so much. It made him uncomfortable. He didn't want to answer the demand in her voice or face her pity. Turning, he walked back into the longhouse, past Gwen, and headed toward the old man. ZeeZee stood next to her grandfather, tucking and smoothing at his blankets.

It shocked him when he passed the rumpled mess of Tess's bunk. Her nightstand drawer gaped open. Clothes spilled out. He couldn't remember a time when her space wasn't always perfect, orderly, soothing, and in a sad way, anonymous—no photographs, no drawings, no keepsakes.

This was panic. He pushed passed the mess, not allowing himself to hesitate. He didn't want Gwen to see him notice.

He squatted at the feet of Colonel Kennedy.

ZeeZee kept her head down, doing meaningless, patting things to her grandfather. She hadn't accused or blamed Parrish when they hadn't found Tess and Ally sitting safely at the breakfast table waiting for oatmeal with the others. Gwen's boys peeked at him, the way they always did, too shy to stare outright. He concentrated on the man in front of him.

When Parrish visited now, it was as if the dying man was disappearing. He told himself that he would have already moved on if it hadn't been for the Colonel, but he owed the man, all the way owed him, down to whatever sanity he'd managed to scrabble back together after surviving the youth militias.

Even before it had all gone to garbage, Colonel Kennedy had been there, running the Junior ROTC program at Oviedo High School. He'd cared, been one of the good teachers. For a lot of the cadets he had been their first real taste of high expectations and discipline, their first real father figure, and they had loved him for it.

Back then, Parrish wanted the leg up that the Junior ROTC program would give him in becoming an officer. It was just a bonus that the Colonel had taken to him, worked with him, trained him, and tried to warn him.

A lot of people thought the old man one part conspiracy nut and one part crazy prepper, always talking grid collapse, or EMP attack, or Wall Street melt down.

To his credit, the Colonel had tried. He'd tried to get them ready.

Too few had listened.

When the military trucks—old, beat to death, pre-computer chips or circuitry— showed up, with the government military screaming martial law, the Colonel hadn't been the only one who'd objected to the U. S. Army dragging his boys and girls off. But he'd been one of the first ones to shut up when he saw the firepower they'd brought with them.

They'd shot one man that day, Brian Rolland's dad. He'd objected, claiming his kid wasn't going to be the pawn of any government takeover. Parrish had been fifteen when he'd watched his own government splatter the blood and brains of Brian's father under the skylights of their community gathering spot, the commons area of Oviedo High School.

Parrish's world ended that day.

Except that Colonel Kennedy—this shriveled, crippled man in front of him—had given him something to hang on to. Just before they'd thrown Parrish into the truck along with a weeping Brian, the Colonel had managed to get to him, to whisper, "Stay alive. That's an order. Head to the ranch when you can. When you can. I'm ready. It's all ready."

It had taken him five years to follow that particular order.

But he'd made it when a lot of them hadn't. None of the Brian Rolland types lived. They'd died by the thousands: fighting each other, insurgents, starving civilians, gangs of kid soldiers, and finally the dozens and dozens of warlords that sprang up in the vacuum of grid collapse. In the end, they'd died fighting just to stay alive—long after their families had disappeared into the hellfire of what they'd come to call the Flare-Out Wars.

Parrish reached out to pat the man's withered hands. Because of Colonel Kennedy he'd had somewhere to go, a goal to focus on, when most of the others had no one and nothing; all their families, communities, friends drained away, swirling down the open sewer of a burned-out world.

Something wet splashed against the back of Parrish's hand. Tears. The girl again, Colonel Kennedy's granddaughter, was crying. God. Not begging or nagging or demanding, just big, silent, splashing tears. He wiped the back of his hand on his jeans and pushed away from the man and the crying girl.

He walked to Tess's bunk and stopped, wanting to straighten out her blanket or pick up the pillow with her name printed on it in faded pink letters. The jumble was all wrong. He'd come to find steadiness and peace at the S-Line, not the awful chaos he'd experienced in a fallen world. He'd found a sanctuary… he'd found her.

Gwen came to stand next to ZeeZee, the note still crushed in her hand. The rest of them stared at him with hungry eyes, waiting and watching.

Why couldn't they understand? He wasn't the silent hero they hoped he was.

Gwen, a dental assistant in another life, was someone else the Colonel had rescued. She frowned at him.

"What should we do? What's the rule for helping people who break the rules, Parrish? Ally was stupid and dumb and made a bad mistake and Tess's gone to get her back. What *can* we do?"

Gwen pushed the note at him one more time.

"I'm sorry," she said. "I am."

He reached for the note.

"Yeah, sorry is how it always starts," he told her.

CHAPTER 7

EVEN WHEN TESS recognized the lonely collapsed heaps as houses, it was hard to put any kind of human beings into the picture. Nothing alive had stayed behind, nothing human. A couple of times she saw the flash of a raccoon or a feral cat lurking in the gutted garages or roofless living rooms. The ruins looked like cardboard cutouts melted by rain and time.

She rode passed them, the neighborhoods with streets that had once had lovely, happy names: Sweet Violet Drive, Starlight Court, Lake Charm Avenue. She twisted in and out of saplings and clumps of ligustrum gone wild, ducking under the heavy drape of low-hanging tree limbs, into the center of Oviedo where Broadway Street stretched out—buckled, blocked, and weed choked.

Circling the giant blasted shell of the Baptist church on the hill in the center of town, she saw that here someone had tried to take a stand, to fight back. Who knows, maybe they'd tried using the church as a refuge or a headquarters?

She rode Goliath through the stringy grass around the building that had been gutted by fire. Four partial walls, darkened by heat and flames, leaned awkwardly to different sides, barely erect at all. In the front of the church, two crosses stood tilting at drunken angles.

One of the crosses had fallen, pushed over maybe. They were metal; otherwise they'd have rotted away too, like the town. The crosses looked unchanged, except for the corpses wired to them. It was like a bad Halloween display, those remaining crosses, bones and rags hung flat and still under the noon sun.

Goliath didn't take much notice. The bodies were so old and desiccated that there was no smell. Head down and listless, he plodded through town.

Beyond the Strandline

She rode around to the back of the burned-out church, stopped at a small retaining wall, and dismounted. It was as good a place as any to leave Goliath. Out of the direct sun and off the beaten path behind the ruins of the church. Didn't need to take any more chances that someone might try to take him from her, not that anyone was around.

She tied him to a scrap of chain-link fence and patted his sore nose.

"My job is to go get Ally and your job is to be here when I get back, okay?"

He closed his eyes. When she left him, he was already asleep, one hind leg cocked.

Throwing her saddlebag over her shoulder, she headed along Broadway. It took her another hour to navigate the stripped frames of abandoned cars and overgrown weeds. When she finally hit a major trail, a trail made by a lot of feet coming and going, she remembered those crosses in front of the church.

Dried rattling bones that hadn't crawled up on those crosses by themselves.

The trail widened. The view took on a shape filled with memories. She knew this place; it was the entrance to the mall, the old Oviedo Marketplace Mall. Now it was another place of public execution. They'd used one of the last light poles still standing. A corpse twisted in a slow waltz of brutal warning—a girl, her face puffed and black from strangulation. The sign around her neck read, "Thief and Raider."

The dead girl wore a dress, once pastel pink and covered with daisies. It was fouled with black stains. She dangled barefoot and dirty over Tess's head.

For a brief, heart-stopping second, Tess thought the girl might be . . . but no, the rope twisted back on itself. This girl had been younger and smaller than Ally.

"Oh my God, Ally. Nothing is worth this."

The rope creaked in answer to her whispered words.

Traffic in and out of what was left of the Marketplace was slow to the point of non-existent. Cicadas hummed in the swelter while the air shimmered. Tess lay in the dirt at the edge of the pockmarked parking lot. She could feel the heat of the day leaching from the ground into her belly. Hidden, she lay watching, trying to understand what kind of people left a child hanging from a lamppost as a welcome message.

It had taken her twice as long to travel the eight miles from the ranch as she'd planned. Seemed there was no such thing as traveling a "straight shot" to anywhere, not anymore.

Standing up, she adjusted the saddlebag with the Epsom salts over her shoulder, and then adjusted it again when it slid down. The salt made the bag unbalanced, and it kept dragging at her shoulder. Since she hadn't found Parrish, she was counting on the Epsom salts to be her cover story: something to trade, an excuse to be here.

Ally couldn't have had much of a cover story; she'd probably blabbed the location of their hidden ranch oasis to the first person who had asked where she was from. Hopefully Epsom salts would be a big enough, valuable enough distraction to hide behind. She needed to get in, find Ally, and get them both home again before the questions started.

The parking lot was surprisingly full of vehicles, pulled by a collection of bony horses, mules, and one cow. Was that a cow? She almost laughed when she saw it strapped to a hay wagon. She wandered, keeping her pace lazy and slow, trying not to stand out, trying not to stare.

Pulling the Boonie hat lower, she wandered through the strange assortment of vehicles: flatbeds, wagons, and carts. One truck had what looked like a giant boiler and gutter piping strapped to the back; a steam engine on a truck, maybe? It looked like some kind of Dr. Seuss contraption.

Finally, she spotted the people she'd been expecting. Most of the vehicles parked in the lot had a guard of sorts, children with ancient rusted machetes or women veiled against the hot sun or angry dogs with heads like cement blocks.

The dogs were the worst. The length of their chains were impossible to judge when they were curled up in the shade under their property. The women and children barely registered Tess's existence, except to follow her with tired eyes. The dogs were a different matter. More than once she had to jump back to escape snapping teeth.

Beyond the Strandline

She could hear a hollow drumming sound coming from inside the building. It was an unrelenting thrum, like a command. Something about it clawed at her. She started to walk faster, not caring if she stood out. She had to get to her sister.

When she stumbled against a flatbed wagon hitched to two broken-down horses, a brindle pit bull the size of a small deer lunged out from the shadows of the wagon's wheels. His jaws snapped shut just short of her right kneecap. Dogs erupted into a panic of barking and growling across the lot. She flung herself backward against a truck without tires next to the wagon.

A woman's round face popped up in the passenger window, followed by a man, cursing the interruption. They were naked.

A rasping cackle greeted Tess's confused retreat.

"What's got you walking around out here in the heat?" An old woman, her mouth a collapsing hole where her teeth had been, stared down at her. Someone had tied the woman to the front seat of a flatbed truck with a loop of chain. The truck had no roof. She couldn't see any harness traces for mules or horses, and there was no engine. She couldn't imagine how they moved the truck from point A to B. The woman pointed at Tess as the barking faded.

"Lose something did you?"

Her skin looked a little bit like the patchwork of asphalt that surrounded them. Darker than the gray of her skin, a brand scarred her left cheek: a black diamond.

It wasn't just the heat that made so many women cover their faces now. She'd overheard them, her grandfather and Parrish, talking about what he'd seen on his way to the S-Line. At fifteen she'd been eaten up with curiosity about the stranger and what he'd seen and where he'd been. She'd pretended to be asleep, listening with horror and fascination to their whispered conversations at the kitchen table.

Parrish couldn't say when it had first started, but he'd seen it, the branding. Brands to identify members of families and tribes and clans. Government marks when there'd still been one. Brands to advertise professions or punishments. Brands to indicate ownership. She had no idea what a black diamond meant. Hadn't really believed it until now.

"Could be I lost something, how about you?" Tess said, curious, trying not to stare. This old woman was the first adult she'd talked to other than her S-Line family in a long time.

"Had a hat. One of those palmetto ones, you know?" The old woman pointed to her naked head.

Tess nodded. What was she supposed to say to that?

"Can't remember where it got to."

She started to walk by the woman with no hat, making sure the pit bull had given up, then hesitated.

"What if I had lost something? What could you tell me about that?"

"I'd tell you to get inside to find it. Nothing out here but us dogs," she said, laughing through the empty hole of her mouth.

Pulling a scrap of muslin from one of the pockets of her vest, Tess walked over and handed it to the old woman.

"It's not a palmetto hat but . . . "

She didn't look to see if the gesture was appreciated. She pretended she didn't care what the woman thought. She just needed to find Ally.

At the far entrance of the mall, where the word SEARS could still be seen silhouetted against the stone, she pulled the Boonie hat farther down, angling it over her face, and marched inside.

CHAPTER 8

EMPTY. PARRISH KEPT to the empty.

He moved through the lonely, overgrown landscape, skirting the edge of the Van Arsdale Street Camp and a cluster of homes that showed some evidence of care just off the highway.

He was careful to stick to the emptiness. The last time he'd traveled this way there'd been clots and knots of refugees flooding through the woods, complicating everything, slowing him down, trying to drag him into their misery and confusion. Being alone was better he'd found, always better. Not as many bodies to bury that way.

Passing a burned-out stump, he remembered one young father, desperate, holding the limp body of a woman, his wife possibly, who'd demanded Parrish's supplies and weapon. The man had had nothing but despair and rage to fight with for the dead woman in his arms. He vaguely remembered a couple of kids.

He'd known at the time that he'd been looking at another dead man, another dead family, and he'd thrown the man a loaf of bread, scavenged out of a ruined camp from up the trail. There'd been blood on most of the slices of Wonder Bread, anyway. He remembered blood on the bread.

Dark, haunted thoughts followed him to a pump house that wasn't big enough for more than one person. Parrish wasn't the only one who kept to the empty places. The well inside had been dug to draw water for cattle, back when human beings had time for such things.

Now Jamie Tallahassee used the shed to keep the rain off when he wasn't running the countryside scrounging, bartering, surviving, doing errands for the S-Line, or running interference for Parrish. Jamie was their link to the world. Hopefully, he'd be available for backup.

"Tallahassee! Front and center," he ordered. The old habits of command came back easily, too easily.

He heard a rustling from inside the shed, a grumpy voice cursing his existence, whether Parrish's or the occupant's was hard to tell.

Parrish waited, wondering how he could explain a rescue mission he wasn't sure he understood himself.

Inside the Marketplace, storefronts were hollow openings between the cement columns. Glass windows and display cases were long gone. In a few spots a faint outline of the original paint for the store names drifted up through the grime: The Gap; Dillards; Bed, Bath, and Beyond. It was like seeing hieroglyphics from another world.

Most of the stores were empty holes. A few had heavy quilts and curtains across their entryways. Living quarters maybe? The quilts and curtains rippled as she passed, and she felt curious eyes peeping at her from behind the patched drapes. She headed toward the sound of pounding in the center of the building.

The people were there, in the middle of the building. It felt like a lot of people.

Tess felt ready to jump out of her skin. Could they tell that being near this many people had her heart thundering? And they smelled. She wanted to hold her nose, but forced her hands to hang still and quiet at her side.

It felt dirty. The air inside of the mall hung heavy and stale. Designed for air conditioning in another time, what was left of the building had no airflow. The shops without a roof or back wall were a relief; fresh air drifted into the interior of the building in blasts of light and afternoon breezes.

The other shops, the ones curtained off, had to be where people lived, worked. A few men wandered the long center hallway armed with crossbows and machetes.

The drumming pounded out of the central atrium of the mall like a giant heartbeat. She kept walking.

"Come on Ally, help me."

One of the men turned, looked at her, and frowned.

Out loud, she'd said Ally's name—out loud. Talking to herself was a habit that hadn't mattered on the ranch.

Beyond the Strandline

The man's face was almost invisible behind his bristling, black beard. He kept his hand on the hilt of a machete slung across his chest.

Tess dipped her head and hurried to the center of the building.

The drumming noise was the thumping compressor of a generator. They had power, electricity—kind of.

Tess looked up and stared at the shocking sight of twinkling Christmas lights, actual lights, ringing the open atrium. The arched glass overhead had shattered and collapsed in, but plywood patches across the roof covered the open holes, cutting off the sun, the air. The lights were nice, though. Cheerful.

The old Regal Cinemas had been on the upper level of this section of the mall. Parts of the railing were still there, like the balcony of a king's palace. An escalator led to the upper level—jammed and frozen. Guards, at the top and bottom of the serrated steps, scratched or leaned in boredom. Important people lived at the top of the escalator, celebrated with Christmas lights; that was easy enough to figure out.

The buying and selling happened under the twinkling lights, under the watchful eyes of the important folks above. Long tables made of planks and old doors stacked on cement blocks lined the walls of the big, open central hall.

The old fountain, Ally's fountain, a wall that had once poured water into a pretty artificial stream that cut through the building, was as dry as she'd known it would be.

Traders lined the basin of the fountain and the dry streambed. As she walked she was able to look down on the sellers and see the trade goods. Instead of water, it was a river of odds and ends: dented pots, cups, plates, rusted links of chain, broken bits and pieces from old appliances, homemade tools.

She didn't want to admit it, but the tools made her hungry to make a deal. She really needed a new rubber mallet, but what she'd rather trade for was information.

Pulling the bag of Epsom salts out of her saddlebag, she wandered among the tables, looking for someone who might be willing to talk to her for a bag full of magnesium sulfate.

CHAPTER 9

"Haven't seen Epsom salts for some time. Had some witch hazel come in last month, but that was home distilled and pretty weak. You don't have any witch hazel do you?"

The woman, with a bony, narrow face, one cheek scarred with a fancy curling *F*, lifted the bag of Epsom salts and hefted it in one hand. "There's a lot here." She looked at Tess with tired eyes. "More than I've seen in maybe two or three years."

Her face hardened with suspicion. She looked Tess up and down more carefully.

"Don't remember you around here."

The Epsom salts were a mistake. Tess had made herself unusual, memorable. She'd picked the woman out of the dozen or so traders standing behind the tables, partly because she was one of the few women. She was dealing in small jars of lotions and potions, running a card table pharmacy of sorts.

The longer the woman stared, the more uncomfortable it got. Tess kept her head down, wanting nothing more than to yank the trader across the table and demand the whereabouts of her sister.

"You're smart to keep your face to yourself around here," she said. "Since you're not marked."

There was more wrong with Tess than owning too much magnesium sulfate, she realized. The face brands had become a major form of identification.

"No, not marked. Are there a lot of . . ." she hesitated, "people . . . not branded?"

"Women, you mean. A few. You're not from around here? That's obvious."

This time the woman tipped her head and stared at Tess like a bird looking for worms in the dirt. Pulling her stringy hair back from the side of her face, she displayed her cheek. The brand was old and long healed, dragged down by gravity as her face had sagged and settled.

"Better to be marked. Better to belong some place. Otherwise . . ." She glanced up, her eyes darting back and forth, assessing the others in the atrium of the mall, mostly men. "You can wind up fair game. Fair, fair game."

It wasn't hard to mistake her meaning.

"Your brand, it's an F."

"The Fortix family of First Street. They own this place now. All of it. I've pledged to them, and they let me buy and sell. And that's the way it works everywhere," she said, suddenly sounding less sure of herself. "Well, at least around here. F for Fortix. Sometimes it's a diamond for purity, but that's for the young ones who get passed around, the girls not sworn to any one tribe or clan. Eventually, it's a black diamond—not so pure, not so pretty. You get me?"

Tess did. Too much talking, not enough answers. Tess needed answers.

"So, I was hoping to trade for Chapstick if you have it."

"Chapstick." She laughed and smirked, her scared cheek jiggling. "Where've you been, under a rock? Folks around here have been using fat and a little beeswax. I got a nice mixture here," she said, handing over a small metal tin that said *Altoids*.

Opening the tin, Tess sniffed the balm. It smelled faintly of bees and honey.

"Lady Wendy brings it to me to sell for her."

"Lady Wendy? Like Lord and Lady? Is she a Fortix?"

"Something like that. Yes, that's Wendy Lamont Fortix. She's the big man's lady." She pointed to the upper balcony of the atrium. "Marco Fortix's woman is up there, along with all the women they like the looks of and decide to keep. They stay up there at the top of those stairs."

Tess followed her pointing finger and saw one of the guards watching them. She didn't take her eyes off the curious guard as she said, "The balm, it's good. I'll take it for the salts."

It was a poor trade, and they both knew it, but Tess hoped the avarice in the woman's eyes might buy her some time.

"Anytime, Honey. Anytime you need to make a trade," the woman said, laughing.

Turning toward the frozen steps, Tess tried to calculate how hard it was going to be to get up that escalator.

"She looks like you, you know, not color wise, but through the nose and mouth," the woman said. "You're a lot more peaches and cream. Honey gold instead of blond. That's what we used to call it, you know. Back when I ran the cosmetic department at Dillard's. You're an autumn harvest."

Tess didn't say anything. She couldn't. Ally was here after all, and Tess hadn't fooled anyone.

"But you won't be getting her back. You can't." The woman's voice dripped venom. "Even if she's still here, which she probably isn't. They sell them, you know."

Turning, Tess looked the woman straight in the eye.

"We'll see."

CHAPTER 10

Tess turned and marched to the guard at the bottom of the broken escalator.

"I want to see Marco Fortix."

The guard at the bottom of the steps, a big man with more bone than muscle, looked at her like she'd asked to see God in his underwear. Another guard stared at her from the top of the escalator, a bookend to the goon at the bottom. Brothers, if she had to guess.

"He runs this place, right?" She wasn't loud or obnoxious. She didn't need to be.

Her obvious breach of protocol stopped business as usual. Everyone froze, except for the woman who'd traded lip balm for an entire bag of Epsom salts. Tess knew that the woman wasn't going to keep her good fortune to herself for long. She had just made the trade of the century with an idiot girl who obviously had no idea what she was doing. She might as well use Tess's presence to her advantage. Tess saw her nod to the guard. Yep, she had just become a valuable asset the Fortix's were sure to want.

"What makes you think that you can just ask to see Mr. Fortix without an appointment?" he asked, frowning. "That's not the way it's done, not around here."

"He'll want to see me," she said, raising her voice.

"Yeah? Who are you supposed to be?" He leaned forward, squinting at her.

She wasn't about to tell him the truth. "Martha Washing—"

"No. That's not right. Her name is Tessla Lane, for the famous scientist, right? Nikola Tessla. And your sisters' names are Alpha and Zeta for the Greek letters. All very smart, right Tess? Your parents were real eggheads."

He knew her name. No one knew her here. No one. She looked up to see who knew so much about her and worse, her sisters. The weak glow of Christmas lights around the balcony cast more shadows than light from where she was standing. Whoever was speaking was little more than a voice above her.

"Come on, Tess. It's me, Jerome," he said, suddenly sounding like a kid.

He practically skipped down the escalator. The goon at the bottom of the stairs reached out to grab her arm.

"It's okay, Micah. I know her. She was in my Sunday school class. Weren't you, Tessla? With your grandmother. Sure. Remember?"

She must have looked as confused as she felt, because he kept right on, pouring out details and information that left her breathless. He even knew the name of her childhood dog and favorite book.

"Don't look at us," he screamed at the curious stares they'd attracted. There was a collective hunching of shoulders and backward shuffling.

She jumped when he barked at the others, shocked at the change in his voice. One minute he'd sounded like a long-lost pal and the next minute the words "pit bull under a wagon" came to mind.

When he smiled at Tess, she saw that he was wearing a retainer, *a retainer*, for goodness sake.

She recognized him then: Jerome Fortix, from her grandmother's Sunday school class. From back when they had come to spend summers at the ranch and life had been swimming in the creek, milking goats for fun, and church on Sunday. She could see it all: the children in their neat row of chairs and her sitting in her prim, pleated skirts, and the scrawny, grubby, buck-toothed boy sitting next to her who'd liked to pinch and tease.

He'd called Tess the "teacher's pet" and got in trouble with Grandma when he tried to take her crayons. Grandma had talked about praying for people like Jerome and his unfortunate family. It all seemed so far away and small.

"I know you. From before." She watched him puff up at her recognition.

"Forget before," he smirked. "I like now. Now is working just fine." He pointed to the Christmas lights.

Beyond the Strandline

He'd grown up and wasn't terrible looking. Dark hair spilled over his ears, and his pale brown eyes measured her up and down. He was still thin, but not quite as scrawny as before.

Jerome was a Fortix, of the Marketplace Fortixes, the important family at the top of the escalator.

"Come up here and see us, Tess." He said it like they were old, dear friends. "There's someone here who'd like to see you. And my mother's here too. You remember my mother, Wendy, and my father, Marco."

An older, heavier version of Jerome appeared at the top of the steps on the balcony, drawn by the fuss, starring down at her with a thin-lipped smile. It had to be Jerome's father, *the* Marco Fortix.

The older man smiled at her with a strong white overbite, no braces or retainers for him. "I knew your grandfather, girl," he began, "and the S-Line ranch. How is your grandfather and the ranch? Not far, is it? Right outside of Geneva . . . all that property." He sounded almost dreamy. "Sure, I remember, along the river. We heard that it burned to the ground in the beginning, right after the lights went out."

Speculation flooded his face. His smile never changed, but it never reached his eyes either.

Marco waved her up with an easy flip of his hand as Jerome came down to meet her halfway; the invitation was exactly what she'd wanted after all, but instead of hope that she'd find Ally, she had the sinking feeling that she might never come down from the high and mighty world of the Fortix family. She couldn't think about that now; she had to know.

Tess started up the steps of the motionless escalator.

CHAPTER 11

SHE'D TAKEN TWO steps up the escalator when someone else called her name, someone from behind her.

"Tessla Lane, I need you to stop," Richmond Parrish said. "Do not take another step. Come down now."

She froze. All those times she'd eavesdropped when he'd talked to her grandfather. She knew his voice, from her dreams if nothing else. Parrish was here, sounding like he was asking her for a cup of water: calm, controlled, almost polite.

Looking over her shoulder, she was shocked when their eyes met and she saw a hot, bright flash of relief on his face. He was glad, *glad* to see her. Heat burned up her throat and into her face. Her heart double-timed. He was happy to see her, and he was here to help. Relief flooded through Tess's body.

She turned back to Jerome, ready to demand to see Ally.

Parrish's voice echoed behind her, turning sharp. It made her think of knife blades and razors.

"She's not going up. Right Fortix? Because she won't be coming back down again."

"Why did you bring *him*?" From above her, Jerome's voice whined, "You brought muscle. Who is he?"

She watched Jerome close the distance between them, eyes narrowed to slits, pinched and mean; it seemed that not much had changed from Sunday school. His father stared down at Parrish, past Tess, dismissing her. The guard at the top of the stairs shifted closer to Marco.

"Tess. Now," Parrish repeated.

Beyond the Strandline

"But, Ally, I need to find my sister. She's here," she said, turning her back to Jerome and his father. She was about to tell Parrish to back off, to give her a chance to find her sister.

But Parrish wasn't looking at Tess anymore. He had an AR-15 semi-automatic rifle jammed into his shoulder. His eyes had turned to stone. He stood halfway between Tess and the entrance. She saw the way everyone looked at him, at the rifle in his hands, the traders eyeing him like field mice spotting a gliding hawk.

She could see that none of the traders was carrying anything more lethal than a machete. His assault rifle must have looked like a cannon to them.

"What are you doing?" Tess snapped. "Have you lost your mind? She's here. I know she is—"

"Shut up, Tess. Start back down now, before they bring out the big guns."

Something crashed to the ground next to her, off to her left, and Jerome jumped backward up one step. She reached for the Ruger that she'd shoved into the waistband of her jeans, pulled it free, and two-handed it as she turned to take another step up the escalator.

She wasn't going to let Jerome slip away. Not now. He knew about Ally. He had to. She heard voices, several men and at least one woman, asking questions from the dark shadows over her head. Next to Marco, the guard fumbled at his waistband. A gun. He was going for a gun.

"Jerome? What's happening? Marco?" a woman yelled.

Jerome inched backward. "Mom. It's the sister."

"Come back here, you jerk! Jerome!" Tess screamed, lunging for the sleeve of his shirt as she shoved the gun at him. "Where is she?"

"You're going to shoot me? Really? Can't tell you anything if you do that." The words were tough enough, but his voice shook when he said them.

He slapped at Tess's hand. If she caught him, she was going to shake his teeth and that retainer out of his head and make him tell her about Ally. His eyes widened when he stared into the black hole of the pistol in her hand. A second later he looked over her shoulder at Parrish and the rifle in his hands.

"Don't look at him. I'm here. Right here," she said, yanking at his shirtfront, trying to pull him closer. She pushed the barrel into his chest.

Panicked, shaking, he spit at her.

She let go of him to swipe the spit off her face. He slapped at the gun in her hand again.

Spinning away, he ran straight up into the lump of bone and muscle at the top of the escalator. The lump had managed to pull a wicked short-barreled pistol out of his pants, pointing the pistol at Tess over Jerome's shoulder as Jerome retreated to cower behind his father.

The roar of the AR-15 boomed and echoed off the remaining walls inside the atrium. A bloody flower bloomed in the guard's shoulder.

The man collapsed and fell back as Tess pivoted on the stair. Heading down, she stared straight into the rusted gun barrel of the guard at the bottom of the steps, Micah as Jerome had called him. Micah yelled something to the wounded man at the top of the steps. Hate and rage pumped from his eyes as he swung his gun from her to Parrish and then back to her.

He aimed. She lifted the Ruger and shot him. His face disappeared in an explosion of blood and gore. Obscenely, he continued standing as his hand convulsed, sending his shot wild.

Above her someone screamed. Tess flew down the remaining steps. At the bottom of the escalator, the body of the dead guard lay in a heap.

Dead. She'd shot a man. She couldn't drag her eyes away, couldn't think beyond the sight of the crumpled body in front of her.

Screams and crying pulled her back. She looked to the top of the escalator and saw blood drip down Jerome's face onto his chin and then down his shirt. He and a woman next to him wailed as Marco collapsed into Jerome's arms. The exit wound from his father's neck sprayed blood onto Jerome as they fell.

The man she'd shot had shot Marco Fortix.

The woman's scream stripped the air, the sound a raw wound. She was all long arms and trailing black hair as she leaned into the bleeding man.

The big man's woman, Wendy Fortix, met Tess's eyes above the dying man in her arms.

She didn't see sorrow. What she saw was rage—the blistering white rage of hate. Tess wanted to explain, to shout that she'd only wanted her sister back. That she hadn't meant for anyone to die. But there was nothing in the woman's eyes but an invitation to come and bathe in the blood at the top of the frozen steps.

It had been that guard Micah that had shot Jerome's father, but now Jerome looked down at Tess, white faced under the gore—bleak, accusing, and vile.

In shock, Jerome shoved his dead father into his mother's arms and braced against the side of the escalator, a howling mess.

He screamed down at her, "You did this! You did it! She's not even here, you witch!" He took a step down and fell, rolling toward the bottom of the escalator. When he crashed into her, he went for her throat. She was trapped wrestling Jerome on top of the dead guard, fighting for her life against Jerome's mindless rage.

The collar of her shirt cut into her throat as someone yanked her up and over the body and away from the clawing Jerome. She managed to kick Jerome as she tripped backward, hitting the ground butt first; she lost her grip on the Ruger. The gun skidded across the ground. In disbelief, she watched the woman with the lip balm scurry out, pick it up, and tuck it into her waistband before she ducked down behind an upended trading table.

Parrish dragged Tess away from the escalator across the floor.

She batted at the hand on the collar of her shirt. "I have to get to her. Let go of me. I have to get to Ally!"

"Get off your ass and on your feet," Parrish ordered. He pulled her up, and gave her a quick shake. "I'm going to say run, and when I do you are going to run."

He hadn't looked at her as he dragged her to her feet. He'd kept his eyes on Jerome, kept checking the balcony. The dead man's body blocked the way down. Jerome looked unconscious. Men at the top of the stairs wrestled Marco's body out of the way. Panic and confusion swirled over their heads. There wasn't much in the way of tactics or organization from the defenders of the Marketplace. Hanging kids must be easier than facing one man with a rifle.

To her left, a table crashed forward and the man behind it propped a sawed-off shotgun on the upturned edge. Probably full of rusty nails and screws. She felt rather than saw Parrish swing his gun toward the shotgun muzzle. He popped off a couple of shots in the general direction of Mr. Shotgun, who dropped back out of sight.

Wendy Fortix screeched, "Shoot them!"

"Run, Tess. Now. Run! I'm behind you."

More shots rang out. She covered her ears and ran.

Tess didn't have to look back to know that they were in trouble. Someone cursed at her. Parrish answered it with another series of *pop, pop, pops*.

From outside, beyond the gaping entrance of the atrium, Tess saw the flash of another rifle muzzle. A guard from the parking lot? Someone else joining in the gunfight? Either they were terrible shots or they weren't trying to hit them. More shots. She ducked and ran for the entrance. It was cover fire! She'd heard enough talk of tactics and strategy over the years to know it when she saw it.

Whoever was shooting was trying to help them, not hit them.

When had Parrish come up with a rescue team?

Tess headed through the door, grateful for any cavalry they could get.

"Go." Parrish's voice slapped at her. "Keep going!"

She didn't have to be told twice. She bolted for the parking lot.

"Which way?"

Parrish yelled, "To the woods, edge of the parking lot, now! Don't wait for me."

The few men that patrolled the parking lot scattered as shots ricocheted. Children and dogs scrambled under trucks and wagons to be anywhere but out in the open as she thundered past.

Dogs went off in a frenzy of barking from shadowed hiding places, snapping at her when she got too close.

Taking a chance, she stopped and ducked behind a flatbed, trying to see Parrish. He'd stayed back to cover her flight, draw their fire. Him and whoever was backing him up.

What if he didn't make it out of there? She'd killed one man and might be responsible for the death of another, and she was no closer to finding Ally. Panic screamed in her ear, threatening to deafen her.

More shots boomed inside the mall. She ducked out of reflex and ran by the old woman with the scrap of muslin wrapped around her head.

Beyond the Strandline

Tess scurried around the back of the truck. Hopefully, the woman would return the favor of the muslin.

"Please help me! I need to look for my friend up there. Can I come up? Will you let me?"

"Why, sure thing, Honey Girl. Come on up beside me."

Tess scrambled into the seat beside the woman, trying to catch her breath. Slumping against the woman's side, she hid in plain sight. They would be looking for someone running, someone panicked. It was a smart spot. Tess could see above the labyrinth of carts and wagons. She searched the parking lot for any glimpse of Parrish and whoever might be helping him.

The old woman reached over and patted Tess's cheek. The woman's sour smell burned her nose, settling in the back of her throat. It was hard not to lean away and cough.

"So pretty, your skin. Being marked won't be too bad if they do it right. It's quick if they do it right," she said, her breath reeking. "First they'll check you out, make sure you're clean for the boy." Her laugh was a bark.

Tess pulled away from the woman's calloused hand and stood up. The woman's eyes were a little mad, a little empty. She hadn't noticed before.

"Don't touch me, please."

The woman clawed at her.

Without warning, the woman grabbed at Tess's vest, trying to drag her back down. She pulled a whistle from her withered cleavage, puckered her mouth, and tried to get enough breath to sound an alarm. Luckily her lungs were as worn out as the rest of her.

Reaching over, Tess grabbed the whistle, and yanked. The chain snapped. She stabbed at Tess's eyes with bony fingers.

"Stop that, you nasty old bat."

Slapping the wrinkled hands away, Tess forgot the real threat: the men wandering around what was left of the parking lot.

"You fool girl. You're worth more than you can possibly know. You and that sister—unmarked, untouched, probably virgins—diamond types." She pointed to the black mark on her face. "You have no idea what this means, idiot!" She sucked at her withered lips. "And I need a hat, not some crap piece of rag."

Someone grabbed Tess around the waist and dragged her from the truck seat.

Terror and momentum pulled her to the ground. She went crazy, slugging and thrashing.

"Oof... are you demented?" Parrish choked out, then gagged. "For God's sake, stop that."

He grabbed her by the shoulders and thumped her once against the ground.

"It's me. Stop kicking and start crawling. Roll, now. Under the trailer. Crawl!"

She rolled to her knees and crab crawled underneath a rusted utility trailer. When she hesitated, he shoved her butt to keep her moving and then slid in next to her, pressing against her side. The heat of his body reassured her. She glanced away from him and saw boots next to the old woman's truck, heard her cracked voice as she answered the man's questions, filling him in, mumbling about crappy rags and a crazy girl with crazy hair.

"Keep going," Parrish mouthed to her. She heard the old woman asking about a reward, heard the sound of fist hitting flesh. Too late, she thought, there wasn't going to be a reward. They were going to be long gone.

She belly wiggled under the next jalopy, a station wagon up on blocks, and kept crawling, until she scrambled straight into the face of a snaggle-toothed mutt chained to the axle of a hay wagon. The dog snapped at her face. She yelped before she could stop herself and then stuffed her fist against her mouth to prevent any more outbursts.

It was too much: the dead men on the stairs, the vicious old woman, and no Ally. She did the first thing that came to her mind; she slugged the dog in its ugly, snarling face. It was the dog's turn to yelp.

The dog whined and crawled its way behind the closest wagon wheel. She kept crawling and only stopped when she felt the iron grip of a hand around her ankle.

CHAPTER 12

ON HER STOMACH, her face full of dirt and gravel, Tess concentrated on his fingers around her ankle; his hand was a tether that kept her from floating away on the wave of adrenalin. The dog's whimpering behind the wheel got worse as another group of men walked past, their boots kicking up dust. Boots obviously meant something other than going for walks to this dog.

She would have bolted; the men were too close, panic swamped her. Parrish squeezed her ankle. He knew before she did that she had been going to move. It unnerved her, those knowing fingers digging into her leg. Tess curled her fingers into the crumbling asphalt of the parking lot. The men stopped next to the wagon, their boots next to her face. She closed her eyes and waited.

The dog crept away from his hiding spot and wiggled up against her leg. Great. She'd made a friend.

The men shuffled away.

"I'm done," said one of the men. "They're not out here, probably headed down to the old trail to town and gone. Let Jerome come and look. " He sounded less than motivated.

His partner mumbled something and then laughed. She thought she heard one of them mention Marco's name, but she couldn't be sure. They walked away, back toward the mall. She moved her leg so that she could scoot back, the dog clinging to her like a tick.

Parrish squeezed her ankle again and then disappeared back the way they had crawled. She followed, worming her way out from under the wagon. The dog followed, grunting.

When she reached the edge of the wagon, Parrish reached down and grabbed her by the arm, pulling her to her feet.

"We are leaving."

"Not without Ally, we're not." She pulled her arm free and turned back to the mall.

"You're not a dope, Tess. What makes you think Ally is even here?"

"Because it's where she told ZeeZee she was coming. Where else could she be? And that woman said she'd seen her, the one I traded with. She knew what she looked like. She's been here. I know that much."

"Maybe," he said. "Maybe not. But we aren't going to find out this way."

She snorted and would have walked away from him, but froze when she saw another group of armed men coming around the corner of the building. They looked more determined than the others. She squatted out of sight behind the truck.

The old woman yelled to the men. Tess had forgotten about her.

Grabbing her arm, Parrish pulled her toward the edge of the parking lot. This time she didn't argue; he was right, and she was right behind him, bending low to the ground, hustling. The dog gave a yip. She spun back and yanked at the chain that held the dog. It came free with a clod of dirt. Holding the dog's chain like a leash, she dragged him along.

The old woman's holler turned into a coughing fit. Served her right.

Somebody should smack the shrieking old witch silly, but Parrish was right, it was time to go.

CHAPTER 13

Hesitating, Parrish glanced back to make sure Tess was still with him, and watched as she slipped the collar off the dog's neck, rolled the chain into a ball, and slipped it into one of her vest pockets. A chain might come in handy. You never knew about things like that. Odds and ends were a big deal now. He got that. She looked chagrined when she caught him looking. He led her deeper into the forest.

He stayed low in a crouching run, a dozen steps ahead of her, his rifle loose in his hands.

He could tell that she was struggling to keep up as they headed straight into what looked like a wall of cabbage palms. He slowed his pace as the forest spun out into low trails and paths that wandered and twisted. He kept pushing forward, winding through the maze of trails like one of the animals that had made them in the first place.

He didn't plan on giving her much choice except to follow. There was no way he was going to let her find her way back to that viper pit of a Marketplace.

He expected the dog to run off, but every time he checked it was still running on Tess's heels, a big dopey grin on its brutal pit bull face. The dog acted like it was on some great adventure and Tess was his best friend.

Some adventure. The men of the Marketplace weren't going to give up, not when they started adding up the dead bodies.

Parrish kept going, running low and fast, until the air hung like a wet blanket over them under the heavy weighted limbs of a hardwood hammock: big oaks and tall maples.

"Stop. We've got to go back," she gasped out. "Ally's back there . . . please . . . we have to . . . Parrish you have to stop."

He stopped, spun around, and grabbed her by the shoulders, breathing as hard as she was. He didn't talk or explain as he pulled her against his chest. He had to touch her, to assure himself that she was here—safe, with him.

Shocked, she froze and started to pull away from him. Every cell of her body went rigid, rejecting him. He didn't care.

"Tess," he whispered. A long, slow moment passed. He felt her relax.

Her name was all he could manage. He didn't have the words to tell her what had gone through him when he'd seen her on those stairs already halfway to the top—already halfway lost to him. He couldn't have described the despair that had washed over him when he'd thought of her disappearing into the world of butchers and barbarians that ruled now—lost, sold, or worse. So much worse.

Her hands hung still and easy at her sides as he wrapped his arms around her more tightly. He didn't care. Thinking of the braid of hair he carried in his jacket, he pressed his cheek against her curls, damp with sweat. He felt her breathing against his chest.

It surprised Tess how good it felt when he hugged her. Safety and comfort and strength. Carefully, she lifted her hands and wrapped her arms around him, feeling the rigid muscles of his body relax under her hands.

She sighed as he exhaled.

As quickly as he'd pulled her into his arms, he pushed her back, awkwardly trying to recover from his moment of raw emotion. He turned to glare at the dog, watching it slink carefully out of arm's reach.

Shock turned to surprise turned to confusion.

"Get out of here, you mutt!"

"Hey!"

He glared at her. "A dog? Really? You couldn't have stolen a bag of white flour or a new stock for my shotgun? A dog? That was your big plan?"

Confusion and frustration made her clench her teeth. One minute he was hugging her and the next he was accusing her?

"Don't be ridiculous. You know perfectly well I didn't come to steal a dog. I came after Ally. If you don't know that, then why are you here?" Her voice sounded ragged and a little squeaky even to her own ears. She gulped air. It still hurt to breathe.

Beyond the Strandline

Annoyed, she saw that he'd already caught his breath. Of course he had.

Looking up at him in the gloomy half-light, all she registered was how tall he seemed as he glowered down at her. She couldn't remember him ever saying her name until today. She hadn't known that he even knew her name.

What was he even doing here? If he wasn't here to help her find Ally, why had he come?

"I didn't steal the dog. It just followed us," she gulped. "I thought it would go away. I only wanted the chain." She patted the front of her vest and stood up. "Forget the dog. We have to go back and get my sister out of that place."

When the dog heard her voice, it belly crept up behind her and flopped down next to the tree trunk where she sat.

"I'm going back." She could finally breathe again. "If you don't want to go with me, I understand." Spinning around, she tried to decide which way they'd come.

The dog stood and shook, turning to follow as she took a step back toward the Marketplace—at least she hoped it was back. She pushed past Parrish.

He grabbed her again, spinning her around to face him. His fingers were rigid on her shoulders.

"I'm here because your ZeeZee brought me this," he said. He yanked a hunk of hair out of his jacket—her braid—and shook it at her. "And because it wasn't too much of a stretch to imagine you trying to storm a slave-trading warlord in his own stronghold. Do you have any idea how dangerous that was? How lucky you are that I found you when I did?"

It was the most words she'd ever heard him string together at one time, and he was calling her stupid.

His voice dropped to a whisper. "Besides, she's not there. Didn't you hear them say that?"

"And you believe those people? Those . . . what did you call them? Warlords? How could I know anything about that place? The way my grandfather kept us in the dark. And you too. You could have said something. You should have said something."

"Me?" He looked at her, shock widening his eyes. "It's hardly my place to keep you up to date on current events."

The dog whined and sniffed at the back of her leg. The air around them grew darker. She could smell rain. They were about to get soaked. He finally let her shoulders go.

"Not *your place* to say? What is that? Your place? I mean other than the occasional offering of fish and frog legs. I needed your help, and where were you? How did ZeeZee find you? Because I couldn't. I looked. And what about Ally? Did you help her do this? Leave her home?"

A crack of thunder punctuated her last question. The violence over her head felt strangely satisfying. She started to turn, to get back to Ally, even if she had to chop her way through the woods with her tomahawk.

He stared at her with his mouth open, looking like he didn't know which question to answer first. He clamped his lips shut and looked at her with glittering green eyes.

"We don't have time . . ."

He lifted his gaze, searching the woods again.

"Tess!" It wasn't an order; it was a roar. "Go!"

He shouldered the AR-15. The muzzle flash blinded her. He fired again. The noise deafened her. She didn't have to turn to know that someone had found them. Panic pushed her toward Parrish and farther into the woods.

She ducked under his arm and then flung herself into a clump of scrub oak. There was no game trail here, no visible path, just the tearing slash of wild sweet potato vines as they wrapped around her neck and shoulders. Irrationally, she was suddenly more worried about a banana spider in the face than getting shot in the back.

Another shot sang through the leaves, hitting a tree trunk next to her. The tree bark splintered. The gunfire behind her pushed her farther, faster into the tangle of vines and brush. Somehow the pit bull kept up, crashing through the brush as fast as she did.

Tess heard Parrish yell, "Keep running. I'll find you!"

She ran.

And didn't quit until she couldn't run anymore. She collapsed into the curve of a massive, live oak root just as the storm broke.

Beyond the Strandline

The sky churned, a black mass of thrashing leaves over her head, as the oak tree shuddered with the violence of the wind. Lightning exploded, the flash bouncing around the wet streamers of rain as it poured off the palm fronds. *Like a fountain*, she thought. Like Ally's fountain. She had come to find her baby sister and now she was as lost as Ally. The dog whined against her leg and buried its head under her thigh.

CHAPTER 14

THE STORM MOVED with the wind and the wind headed toward the coast. When there was no lag time between the flash of light and the explosion of thunder, Tess hoped she wasn't sitting under a tree destined to become a lightning rod. And wasn't this the luck? No rain for months and now a tropical gully washer.

She'd lost her hat a long time ago. Rain blinded her.

She didn't see the lightning bolt that hit a palm tree, but she heard the tree explode with a sound like paper ripping, followed by cracking and the shattering of wood. It came down on top of her, a confusing rush in the rain. A fork in the oak stopped the palm tree's free fall inches from her head. Flattening out like a spider, her heart banging away inside her chest, Tess wound up with a mouthful of wet leaves and dirt.

In the gray downpour, the boy was nothing more than a ragged outline at first. She saw him standing near the snapped base of the palm tree, the stump a smoking ruin.

The rain kept the lightning strike from turning into a wildfire. There was no way to fight fire now, not a big one. It destroyed everything.

The kid didn't say anything. It was hard to tell how old he was—maybe Ally and ZeeZee's age. His clothes were a collection of soppy odds and ends: some kind of cutoff jeans, a jacket with the sleeves hacked off. His hair streamed down his face and neck. It was the big kid, the one who'd demanded she hand over Goliath.

He watched her with big, dark eyes under the fringe of his dripping hair. He was close enough to smell. She suspected this rain shower was the first bath he'd had in a while. His gaze made her think of the way a squirrel would watch a cat.

Darting straight at her, he reached out, snatched the bag with her skinning knife and tomahawk, and dragged it over her head, yanking hard enough to break the strap. The dog snapped a warning. The boy snapped back, maybe growling too, and cowed the dog with a perfect imitation of a vicious snarling bark.

Then he was gone, disappearing into the dripping woods.

"Hey, you brat. I know where you live!" Tess yelled after him.

The race was on. She was up and after him. She might be lost in the woods, wet to the bone, and worried out of her mind about her missing sister, but she was not prepared to lose her last line of defense. He was as quick as a hummingbird, darting through the woods like he'd had it all planned out—the snatch and grab. He was good.

She felt the rain slowing as she ran. Adrenalin pumped through her legs like fire. The forest here changed—the trees got bigger, the underbrush thinned, palmettos disappeared. He was quicker, but she was madder.

She stayed with him until he headed into the overgrown yards of some long abandoned subdivision. He vanished into the maze of crumbling garages and living rooms.

She stopped running in the kitchen of someone's ruined home, huddling under what was left of the roof. Pausing, she tried to catch her breath. On the wall, under the mildew and rot, someone had drawn some kind of countdown calendar, black slashes marking off days and weeks, the lines barely visible now. Lower to the ground she could see children's scribbles—a stick family next to a stick house.

Someone had been counting down the days until . . . What? The lights came back, law and order returned, the city started picking up the garbage again? But it hadn't. It still hadn't. She wondered what had happened to the family, afraid she already knew.

The rain stopped. Water dripped from what was left of the eaves of the broken home.

A palm print against the wall in the hallway was fresh with wet mud. He'd been here. She walked to the gaping frame of the front door and saw muddy prints leading through the wreckage of homes called Sunny Estates; she followed the trail left by his bare feet in the leaves that formed a carpet over the road. Time to get her mule, find that kid, and take back the only weapons she had left.

CHAPTER 15

SHE HEADED BACK to the ruins of the big church and Goliath, but every step seemed harder and heavier, like being dragged through deeper and thicker quicksand. Dread threatened to swamp her. Ally was back *there*—at the Marketplace.

The dog padded behind her, or beside her, or crashed through the woods just beyond her sight, running here and there, enjoying his first taste of freedom.

Why hadn't Parrish come after her? The possibilities weren't pretty, and ran through her head in a depressing loop. She'd never be able to backtrack and find him.

She tried to shake off the feeling of doom. *He had come after them.* He'd left the S-Line and he had come. And the other shooter, someone else who'd had their backs, had come after them too. Someone she didn't know about—a friend.

She couldn't think about all that. Tess had one goal in all this craziness: Get Ally and get home.

The horror of that place crept into her skull: the dead girl spinning in the wind, the women and children tied and chained in the parking lot, the strange greeting she'd gotten from Jerome, as if they were friends. But she'd handled it, hadn't she?

If it hadn't been for Parrish pulling her off that broken escalator, maybe she and Ally would be on their way home by now.

The broken walls of the big church loomed. Afternoon shadows stretched out, stroked the ground like giant, dark fingers. The dog came crashing out of the woods at that exact moment with his big, stupid, grinning, dog face and his big, goofy, dog attitude. He scared her and she tripped, going down on one knee. He came over to lick her face.

"You are one dumb creature." She reached out to touch him.

He skipped out of her way—a fun game.

"You idiot. Get. You're free—isn't that enough? Get away from me. My mule is not going to like having you around."

The dog jumped and frisked away from her efforts. He was big and senseless and infuriating.

For a long moment, they stared at each other. He almost had her smiling, and in the end, she let him win.

"Come on, but don't blame me if Goliath kicks your block of a head off."

At the church, she whistled softly, expecting Goliath to answer her with his trademark snort. There was no stomping, no swish of his stringy tail. Her heart dropped. She powered through the leftovers of a hedge, saw that the ground was trampled and pawed, but no Goliath.

A pile of manure, still warm, told her that she hadn't missed him or whoever had taken him by much. He was gone. Losing Goliath was closing in on the last straw.

Footprints in the dirt next to Goliath's screamed clues—small, child sized. Those kids from Van Arsdale. They had her mule *and* her bag, because they'd been following her every step of the way, watching her.

Great. Back to confront the land of the baby spear chuckers and their sticky-fingered leader. The sun tilted off center, toward the west, but if she hurried she might be able to get Goliath and her stuff and make it back to the Marketplace before nightfall.

Tess started to dogtrot the mile or so back toward the highway.

Almost home. Tess realized that Van Arsdale was halfway between the hell that was the Marketplace and everything that made Tess feel safe. Van Arsdale was halfway to home and safety.

There was no order she could see among the clump of ramshackle hovels, no obvious pattern. Tess studied the setup from a depression in the ground, a collapsed drainage ditch. Rain had pooled in the shallow bottom. The muddy water reminded her that she was thirsty. She gulped water from her bottle. Luckily, the water bottle had gone into a vest pocket and not around the horn on Goliath's saddle.

Being still, she felt the fatigue and hunger settle into her head and stomach. She sipped more water. It helped, some. When her stomach growled, the dog whimpered in sympathy.

"Hush. I don't need your help getting caught. If they catch us they'll probably eat us both."

The dog plopped his head onto his front paws, which were braced on the lip of the ditch next to her.

She peeked above the rim of the ditch. Everything was quiet. The air after the rain felt light and clean.

Her right boot had started to leak. Her sock was soggy.

She watched a kid crawl out from under a pile of rotted boards, then another. Ducking down she watched another child, one of the younger boys, crawl out from under the splintered wood and wander around. Then another child, a bit older, maybe a girl, wearing a long, filthy T-shirt like a dress, came for him. She dragged him toward the wreckage of the collapsed metal barn. One minute she could see the boy and the girl and the next they disappeared like moles down an invisible hole.

Nobody seemed excited about a stolen mule.

Tess studied the barn, the only place she could see to hide a mule. It was an old metal building, collapsed in the middle, perhaps looking in worse shape than it actually was. It didn't pay to let people think your life might be better than their life. She got that now. They might be children, but they were survivors first.

There were no guards that she could see. She skirted the piles of jumbled metal and garbage until she was in the back of the building where huge intake fans had hung. The empty holes had been covered up with a patchwork of wood and brush. It was easy to peak through the cracks.

Inside, the partially collapsed roof was propped up in spots with piles of twisted metal—the blades of the big fans and broken car axles. From the outside it looked like a pile of rubble, but inside there was a crazy kind of order. Open holes in the ceiling acted as skylights. There was an assortment of ruined tables, cots made of strips of wood, some shelving propped on piles of concrete. They were hiding in plain sight.

Smart little monkeys. Something hard jabbed her in the back. Tess turned.

"You want something we got?"

She stared into the muzzle end of an ancient shotgun. She counted the fact that she was still breathing as a good sign. Holding up her hands, she tried smiling, but it was the face of the same smart aleck kid who'd snagged her tomahawk bag staring back at her. Great.

At some point the ugly brindle dog had slipped away, maybe for good. First smart thing it had done since she'd punched it in the face. Time to stop messing around.

"My mule. I want him back. And my weapons bag."

"When you were here before, I told you what I wanted."

Goliath brayed loud enough to rattle the loose wood propped against the outside of the barn.

The kid tipped his head to the side and said, "Come on and you can tell him goodbye." He gestured with the end of the shotgun, "Under there, under that road sign." He pointed at a twisted piece of metal, hardly recognizable as anything useful, let alone a sign. She looked closer. Under the grime it read, "Greenway. Sanford. Orlando." Words from that other world.

She put her hand against the sign and felt it swing to the left. Ducking underneath, she stepped into the maze inside the building. The room was full of big eyes that followed her, watching from corners and cubbies everywhere she looked.

She recognized the little boy from earlier that morning. Someone had put pants on the kid and taken away his deer-leg play toy. He had the vague, sightless look of someone not altogether in the game.

The building was stuffed with scavenged junk. Paths cut between the piles. The kid followed her with the gun. There was a scabby goat that watched her from under a slab of tree bark. The smell was close to toxic: urine, mold, and rotted food. She coughed and tried not to gag.

Beyond the Strandline

Still, they were trying. She could tell. A girl that looked about eight had what was left of a broom in her hand.

"Keep walking. All the way to the back."

He nudged Tess through the heaps and piles of junk, pushing her forward with the muzzle of the gun. It was hard to tell if the rusted gun would even shoot, but better not to test her luck.

She kept walking.

Rounding a stack of crumbly cardboard boxes, she walked into an open area, sort of a family room. Surprise knocked the wind out of her. There in the spotlight of the late afternoon sun, under a hole in the gaping roof, was Richmond Parrish and Goliath.

CHAPTER 16

Parrish, filmed with mud, stood with one hand on Goliath's rump and the other wrapped around his rifle. Sweat streaked his face. There was an alert tension in his body, an energy that radiated from him. They weren't safe yet.

"What happened to you? I couldn't wait, that kid took—" Tess started to say.

He held up his hand to stop her and then glanced down at a girl sitting behind him, behind Goliath, on a pile of heaped rags. Tess forgot what she'd been about to snap at him.

The girl could have been any of the other grubby kids inside the barn, but something about the way she sat, balled up in misery and pain, slumped in the half light, made Tess look closer. She knew the curve of those shoulders and the sheen of sunlight on this girl's bowed head.

"Oh my God, Ally. You're here! You're really . . . are you okay?" Hot, hard tears choked her. But Ally's cowering stopped Tess from running over and flinging her arms around her. Instead she moved carefully, the way she would around a newborn fawn.

Going to her knees in front of Ally, she reached for her hands and stroked each familiar finger, unable to speak. Ally's nails were bitten to the quick and bloody. What she had done to her hands made Tess afraid to look into her eyes. Ally kept her head down, her hair falling across her face like a tangled, blond curtain.

"How did you get here? How did you get away?"

"Easy, Tess," Parrish said. His voice was quiet and insistent. "She's safe, but . . ."

Beyond the Strandline

There was muck on Ally's shirt, a man's shirt, one that Tess didn't recognize. Still, her sister's hands were warm and she could feel the comforting thump of blood in her wrists. She ran her hands up her sister's slender arms.

"I know what you're doing. You can stop. Nothing is broken," Ally said, and then stopped, her voice cracking at the end. She pulled her arms free and curled back into herself.

Ally was here. She was alive. Tess couldn't stop the avalanche of emotion. Tess threw her arms around Ally and looked over at Parrish. "How? How did you do this?"

"Not now. Later. We should move out—now."

"What makes you think *he* did anything?" It was the kid. He sounded pleased with himself. She ignored him.

For a moment, Tess had forgotten everything but Ally. She reached for Ally's clenched hands again, stroking the backs with her thumbs, careful not to touch the tips of her bloody fingers.

Parrish knelt next to the filthy bedding, forcing Tess to focus on him. "We need to get her back. They'll be coming."

The barrel of the shotgun pressed again into Tess's back. Parrish exploded to his feet, grabbed the gun, and ripped it out of the boy's hands. The boy stepped back and pouted.

"Hey, this is our place. We had a deal."

Parrish shook the rat's nest of tacks, nails, and gravel out of shotgun. He flipped the safety on the rusty, corroded weapon and held it over the kid's head, out of reach.

"You're liable to blow yourself up with this piece of crap. Back off."

Ally's hands started to tremble. She still hadn't looked up.

"Yeah, whatever," the boy said, unfazed. "We had a deal."

Parrish pushed the shotgun back at him. Other kids crept out from the shadows and corners, drawn by drama and curiosity. He ignored them and reached out and touched Tess's arm.

"Tess, these kids. They got Ally back."

"That's right, and we want our payment."

The boy's voice broke, became a teenaged squeak, ruining his attempt at playing a tough guy. Someone giggled. He hushed them with a murderous look.

Tess could hardly make sense of his demand for payment. She didn't have any money.

"We're keeping the mule," The kid said.

At first it didn't register. Then she looked over at Goliath, his hind leg cocked, his ears flopped forward as he dozed in the corner of the barn. Someone had brought him water in a crumpled bucket.

"The mule. We want it; we're keeping it. We won't let anyone go, unless we get him—"

Parrish cut him off. "Yeah, we get it, little man. Ease back." He cut a look at Tess out of the corner of his eye. "These kids had already rescued your sister when I came to them for help. They said she was a friend of theirs. If they'd known you were her family, I doubt they would have attacked you and Goliath in the first place."

The crowd of children had grown—almost a dozen, maybe. They were dressed in an assortment of muck-covered clothes, if they were dressed at all. She could see sores and bug bites covering them. One little girl swiped at her swollen eyes.

"Tess, this place. These kids here, they're . . ." He hesitated, " Tess, they're starving. When they brought me to Ally, I promised them they could keep Goliath if they kept her safe until I brought you back. I couldn't tell you they had Ally until we were far away from that hellhole and any goons they might have sent out looking for her, or us."

She took a moment to look beyond Parrish and the kid who carried a busted gun bigger than he was. She could smell their despair. Goliath lifted his head and his tail and produced a pile of steamy, hot manure. It added another fresh layer of stink to the mix inside the building.

She looked at him. "I get it."

"Tess, I don't think—"

She cut him off.

"I get it."

Turning back to Ally, she pushed at her sister's hair, sweeping it back out of her face. Ally wasn't crying anymore, but she had been. Tear tracks had cut through the dirt and blood on her face. Tess tipped the point of her chin up with one finger. It was a miracle they'd gotten her back at all.

But not soon enough to prevent the raw wound on the perfect skin of her cheek.

The brand they'd burned into her cheek screamed ownership, possession. They'd had no intention of letting Ally go.

She reached up to touch the cursive F burned into her sister's cheek. Ally flinched. Tess balled her hand into a fist. How much would it hurt to be held down and have a hot iron smashed into your face? How much would it hurt your heart to be marked like an animal, to be someone's belonging?

"Oh, Ally."

"I want to go home." Ally sounded exhausted, empty. She came off the lump of rags, throwing herself into Tess's arms. "I just want to go home. Now. Please."

"Parrish?"

He watched them with those eyes of his, his head tilted. He stood still, quiet, and intense.

"Tess, please, " Ally repeated.

Tess nodded.

"I just need my tomahawk bag back, and then we can go."

Parrish nodded too. There were a few minutes of back and forth between Parrish and the boss boy with the gun.

Ally flinched when Tess raised her hand to stroke her hair. Tess dropped her fist against her thigh when Ally shook her head and pulled away, her hair falling forward again, a curtain to hide behind.

Parrish handed the rabbit skin bag to her. She slung it across her chest.

"Can you," she began, "I mean, will you help me with her, you know, get her home? Without Goliath, Ally might get tired."

He might have nodded. She didn't check.

"Geez, Tess. I'm not a baby. I can walk."

Tess pulled Ally closer. She trembled against Tess's side for a brief second but shook off any fussing or concern, straightened her spine, and marched back through the jumble. She didn't look back.

Watching her sister walk away made Tess feel so tired she couldn't move. It was a wall, the sudden exhaustion, the feeling of being paralyzed.

"Come on. You need to eat and be still for a while where you feel safe. Not here," Parrish said.

He reached a hand out to her. She took his hand without thinking and let him start to pull her through the maze of garbage. His hand swallowed hers. She tried to ignore the jolt of heat when he gave her hand a quick, light squeeze. Did he feel it too? They were just holding hands, and now wasn't the time to worry about how happy it made her feel.

"Don't look back, and don't think about him until you're home," he said. He let her hand drop and then reached up to touch her. His big hand on her shoulder made her feel small and thin like one of the kids. She must feel like that to him under her man's shirt and vest.

She stumbled, hesitated, and started to pull away.

"You're not going to fall out now, soldier," he said when he felt her hesitate. "You're not. Let's go."

She shook her head. "I won't. I need a minute."

"Tess, we don't have long." His frown was part disapproval, part sadness.

"Just a minute."

He gave her shoulder a squeeze and followed Ally out.

Goliath stood against the back wall of the building, a slumbering giant. How had they managed to stuff him into the building? He looked huge and dusty and tired.

"Old man," she said, brushing her hand over his muzzle, "thank you."

Then she whispered in his ear, knowing that the children were watching her. Pulling the saddle from Goliath's bony back, she was surprised to see that they hadn't ransacked her saddlebags.

"I'm not leaving the saddle or the bridle. If you try and eat the leather it'll make you sick." She looked at the semicircle of big eyes staring at her. The kid with the gun smirked.

She turned to him and said, "Be quick. He's been a good friend to me."

CHAPTER 17

HIS MOTHER HADN'T cried—not really. Jerome knew that she wouldn't. After the initial horror and screams of rage, she'd spent hours wiping Father's blood from her hands onto the front of her favorite white blouse. She'd stood with blank eyes, restless hands moving over and over the soft, once-pure fabric. When Willet had come to help her change, she'd slapped the foolish woman and kept wiping, over and over again until the front of her shirt had dried into a red-crusted sash.

He was dead. Jerome could hardly process it. Dead. The Great Marco Fortix shot dead on the escalator leading to the high rooms over the atrium. And now his mother was in her room, obsessed with the endless ritual of trying to rid her hands of his blood.

Jerome knew that he should be devastated, heartsick at the very least, but it was hard to feel anything bigger than the shock . . . and worse, the first glittering sparks of relief.

They'd murdered him. They'd murdered his father in front of him. Well, not by her own hand, but it was Tess's fault and those others with her. Jerome wanted to be angry, even furious.

But it was just shock and relief.

The old man had been such a ball buster sometimes—always pushing, always planning, always wanting more.

Sure, he'd made the Marketplace work, but at what price? Mother needed her obsessive rituals to feel secure and, if he were being honest, there were days he'd been tempted to head toward the coast and just keep walking.

Jerome watched as the men wrapped his father's body in the quilt from his parent's bed. A few of the men had started to dig the grave out in one of the potholes in the parking lot. It was too hot to wait. They'd bury him quick.

Quick or not, he wasn't going to be around when they buried the old man.

Jerome shoved a change of clothes into a backpack. He had somewhere to be. Father had already sent Arnold, his goon, after the girl Ally, before that fool Tess had come looking for her.

Ally Lane. She'd proven to be the last argument Jerome would ever have with his father.

She'd shown up out of nowhere, her hair tucked up under a grimy ball cap, thinking that no one would notice a perfect, unmarked stranger. She'd asked him to see the fountain, just like that. He could barely remember when the water worked in this place. What a joke.

He'd pulled her cap off then and all that glorious, clean, blond hair had spilled down her back. She'd seemed like a diamond in the dirt. Perfect.

His father had scooped her up, had wanted to sell her to the coastal men, claiming her value equal to a year's worth of fuel for the generator.

They'd argued then. Jerome had wanted her so badly he'd stood up to the old man for a change. He'd fought for her, deserved her.

Then those wormy Van Arsdale kids had taken her. God he hated them, everyone did. They were like rats, rustling through their garbage.

Still, Arnold was about as smart as a hammer and about as subtle. Jerome worried he'd hurt Ally, mess up her pretty face. He needed to get Arnold back to the Marketplace anyway, since they'd been attacked by . . . what? Twenty plus armed men, who'd murdered his father and helped kidnap his girl. That was a better story than losing Ally to those rat kids and his father to Tess and her sharp shooter.

Should he tell Mother he was leaving? Probably. Hadn't she examined the girl and pronounced her clean, pure, untouched, good enough for her son? Argued for keeping her? Hadn't she helped Jerome burn the mark into her cheek?

He thought about his mother and the blood on her hands and shirt. He left without telling her.

He'd find Arnold. He'd find his girl, Ally. He'd fix things.

CHAPTER 18

ALLY WALKED AHEAD of them, not talking or hesitating. She stared straight ahead, unblinking, like a sleepwalker. Parrish reached out and pulled the saddle out of Tess's hands and slung it on his shoulder.

Ally tripped over a clump of palmetto stumps and almost went down. Tess jumped to go to her, but Parrish grabbed her elbow, held her back, and shook his head when he saw the question in her face.

"Give her space. For now."

His attitude of superiority when it came to her sister was starting to get old. What made him an expert on how much space to give someone, anyone really? Tess pulled free of his hand, shrugged.

"She's back. We got her back. That's all I care about. It's going to be all right." She said it as much for herself as for him.

Tess fell in step beside him, watching her sister's rigid, tight posture, how she never turned to see if they were following or how close. Ally might as well have been walking alone.

"I'm sorry," he said.

She thought of the vicious burn on Ally's cheek. What it might mean. What it might still mean for all of them.

"She's back."

He glanced at Ally and then scanned the woods as they followed the trail. They'd made good time.

"Yeah, that too, but I meant about the mule."

She shrugged again, dismissing his concern. She was tired and didn't want to think about that gang of hungry faces with their greedy eyes and swollen guts. She needed to get home as much as Ally did. It was all that mattered. She changed the subject.

"Who was it? Back at the Marketplace—the shooter, covering us? We would have never gotten out of there otherwise."

She chanced a quick glance away from Ally to search his face.

Now it was his turn to have a question stamped on his face. He looked down at her, frowning.

"Come on. You really didn't notice? The guy covering our butts? I didn't know you knew anyone but us. I didn't know there was anyone but us."

He made a noise—part snort, part grunt—and continued to ignore her questions.

He knew, but he wasn't saying. She watched him and decided to let it rest. There was a scar on his chin near the corner of his lip. Funny, she hadn't noticed it before. It made the stubble on his face patchy in that spot. She watched him scan their surroundings, alert and ready. Curiosity filled her.

"Mister Parrish?" she began.

His snort, this time, was close to being a laugh.

"What? It's what my grandfather tried to get us to call you. Mister. I think he thought it would make you less interesting to my sisters. He was wrong."

"Mister Parrish? Really? It makes me sound like an old man or my father."

"Your father?" she said. "Are you like him then? Were your parents from around here? How do you know my grandfather?"

The questions exploded out of her before she saw the pain move across his face at the mention of his parents. The pain was like an open wound or brand. She knew better. Everyone had lost someone or everyone. She should know better than most about picking at the scabs of the past. She felt her face get hot. She hadn't realized how thirsty she was for information—about him, about the world.

About everything, she told herself.

"Sorry. That was . . . dumb."

He shrugged and looked down at her; as tall as she was, she still had to look up at him.

"No. It's okay. Yeah, they were from around here—once."

Beyond the Strandline

Then he got quiet.

She went back to watching him out of the corner of her eye. He carried the rifle in one hand, his other hand balancing the saddle on his shoulder. His skin was the deep brown of someone who spent all their time in the sun. There were faint hints of lines at the corners of his eyes. His heavy, black lashes framed the way his eyes glowed an impossible green in the fading sunlight.

"How old do I seem to you?" he asked quietly. The mockingbirds in the underbrush were so loud she almost missed the question.

"What? Oh, older than me. That's for sure . . ." she said, letting the observation trail off. "Mister Richmond . . ." She mumbled the next bit, "Old Man Parrish."

"I can still hear, you know. Old man that I am. And it's Parrish—just Parrish. Only my men called me . . . never mind." He flashed her a quicksilver grin. It stunned her the way the smile changed his face. Something inside of her thrilled at that glimpse of him. It was her turn to snort.

"You never answered me, you know. You think I didn't notice. Who do you know back there, at the Marketplace? How could you know someone we don't? I thought we weren't supposed to leave S-Line property? The big rule and all."

"A little late for that discussion, don't you think?"

She groaned but had to agree. Ally didn't turn around at the sound.

It worried her the way she never looked back. The little sister of three days ago would have come back when she heard their voices and wedged herself between the two of them like a tick in a dog's ear, all the better to eavesdrop, to be the nosey twin.

"Okay. I left the S-Line. I had to," Tess said. "But what about you? Didn't you agree that you'd never cross the boundary? Wasn't that part of my grandfather letting you stay? When did you leave the ranch and how often? We had help back there, and I think you know who helped us."

The curve of his mouth came close to a smirk. "Better not to know all the secrets, Tess. Besides, if I did break the rules, you never knew about it. Would never have known about it."

He stopped walking long enough to hold a branch back for her, to keep it from smacking her in the face.

"Don't do that. Don't try to be nice and distract me. How can you say that about secrets? Look what's happened to Ally. That's what secrets have gotten us." She stomped by him.

His hand closed around her arm as he pulled her back. Heat and electricity ran through her skin where he touched her. She wasn't used to it, being touched. That's all it was, nothing else to it.

The woods around them were filled with the tittering and chirping of cheerful finches, all the little daytime birds, the lizards darting through the leaves; the sounds of home. She let their busyness soothe her.

"Tessla," he said.

Nobody used that name, besides her mother. She wasn't used to hearing it. His hand tightened on her arm.

"I know you're worried about Ally, but you need to let her come to you about what's happened. Will you do that? Don't push too hard. And don't blame yourself. Don't waste time doing that."

"Wow, my full name *and* sage advice. You sound like my mother." Now it was her turn to think about the sad past. *Good job Tess.*

He just looked at her and waited. She shrugged away from his touch.

"Yeah, okay."

Ally had disappeared around a curve in the path in front of them. It made Tess itchy when she couldn't see her anymore. Dismissing Parrish, she went after her sister.

"I need to get to her," she said. "I need to be able to see her."

This time he grabbed her by the wrist. His grip turned to iron.

"Hey!" she gasped.

"Listen," he hissed, and pulled her off the path and into the darkness of a cascading wild grapevine. The bird sounds were gone and the woods fell to stone silence around them.

"I don't . . ."

He slid the saddle to the ground and put his free hand over her mouth. They were surrounded by quiet. Horrified that she'd let Ally get away from them, she struggled against his hold.

"Be still," he whispered, squeezing her in warning.

Ally's scream jolted through her body like electricity. The next thing Tess knew she was on her head in a clump of grapevines, and he was gone. Rushing away, he stayed close to the heavy gloom of the underbrush along the path, away from Ally's hysteria.

Tess scrambled up, cursing Parrish's panicked retreat. She headed toward the sound of screaming on the path ahead.

When she saw Ally struggling in the arms of an armed man, she didn't wait. Somewhere between the time she'd heard that first scream and seeing Ally thrashing, she'd pulled her tomahawk free. Ally shifted in front of the man, her knees collapsing. The move pulled the man off his feet. They went down, crashing into the mud of the path. Lucky for him, Tess was afraid to make the throw.

Tess flew down the trail and threw herself onto the man's back and did the only thing she could think of; she bit him—hard, raising the tomahawk over her head for the kill.

Yowling, he fell backward onto his butt. Ally scrambled away on all fours down the path away from the wrestling match, jumped to her feet, and disappeared—again, but the wrong way from the S-Line.

"Cripes, you'd better not have rabies," the madman said, clamping one hand against his neck. Blood smeared his fingers. She was on her feet, the tomahawk a comfort in her fist, ready to finish it, finish him, before he could figure out where he'd dropped his rifle.

Standing over him, she waited. He looked up and pouted.

"Seriously, you almost killed me. I just wanted to talk to that girl, and she went crazy on me."

Shocked, Tess realized that she was looking at a young man, a lot taller than Ally, but probably just a teenager. He looked up at her with soft blue eyes full of hurt. His red-blond hair fell over his forehead, emphasizing the freckles on his nose and cheekbones. He looked about as dangerous as a baby possum.

"Get up."

"Are you going to bite me again?" He eyed the tomahawk in Tess's hand.

She shifted her weight to the balls of her feet and settled into a fighting stance.

Sighing, he moved to pull something out of his pocket. She shifted forward, ready to pounce, when he quickly held up his free hand in surrender.

"Ease on down, Pocahontas, I was just going to try and stop the bleeding." He pulled a hunk of cloth from his pocket.

A strip of bleached muslin—she recognized it. She'd given it to the woman back at the parking lot. She met his eyes.

"Yeah, I saw you give it to that old lady. She wasn't using it anymore," he said. "Those men took their frustration out on her when they couldn't find you."

Parrish popped out from behind a fence post. He'd circled ahead of them, cutting them off, and seemed surprised by the sight of her standing over Ally's attacker.

"Tess, where's Ally?"

She heard rather than saw him, refusing to take her eyes off the guy sitting in the dirt in front of her.

"That way," she said, nodding toward the path behind her. "She took off. . . back toward the Marketplace. She panicked. She's headed the wrong way."

She stopped, not wanting to give this fool any more information than he already had. "I've got him. Don't worry. And where were you, by the way?"

"Flanking the fool, but then again," he said, laughing, "that's no ordinary fool."

When Parrish laughed, Tess almost dropped her guard. Almost. Looking up, she watched him start down the path after Ally.

"And making sure the fool wasn't followed." His voice drifted back to them.

"Parrish seems to know you. How is that?" she asked, bending to pick up the rifle he'd dropped.

He dabbed at his neck; he seemed more worried about her biting him than anything else she might be planning. She relaxed. The woods had started to come back from that hard edge of frightened silence, filling up with noises again. Birds chattered. Insects buzzed. He pulled the rag away from his neck. He refolded the muslin and pressed it over her teeth marks.

"Oh for heaven's sake, I bit you. I didn't tear out your jugular."

Looking at her, he grinned.

"Sure. But human bites are dirty. I'll be lucky not to die of scurvy."

She laughed. "You can't get scurvy from a human bite. Scurvy is from a lack of vitamin C."

"What? Does that mean vegetables?" he said, looking suspicious. "I'd rather be bitten. Besides, we'll be lucky if we both don't die of exposure and starvation by the time you're done glaring at me. You look like you could use a hot meal."

"Are you calling me skinny? You're one to talk."

This guy was giving her a headache. She rubbed at the frown lines between her eyes.

"Yep, hunger and exposure, all kinds of exposure, and I'm not talking about to the elements. I just wanted to warn that Ally girl, the one that the Fortix clan had back there, 'cuz they're already planning on finding her and dragging her back."

Hearing her sister's name come out of this stranger's mouth made her mad. Unconsciously, she raised the tomahawk.

His eyebrows winged up but didn't move.

"Who are you? And how do you know my sister's name?"

He looked at her, his jaw clenching just a little, stubbornly refusing to answer her. She thought of Samantha the Goat when she got an attitude.

"His name is Jamie," Parrish offered.

Turning at the sound of his voice, Tess saw Parrish standing close to Ally. He didn't touch her, but stood close enough so that if he wanted to he could reach out and grab her. Ally reminded Tess of a rabbit frozen in a trap. He murmured something to her too low to be heard, and she watched her sister's shoulders relax a bit.

Stepping closer, he reached down and dragged the guy, Jamie, to his feet.

"Come on. We're going to need to make plans. Jamie's been our real-world hookup for a while. Right Jamie?"

Jamie smiled and nodded. "That's me, getting what there is to get—for a price." He paused and considered, "That should be my company motto."

He stood up straight and brushed off his backside.

Open mouthed, Tess watched Parrish walk off, the boy falling into step beside him. On his feet, Jamie was taller than she'd thought at first—bony, all arms and legs. There was something strangely similar about the two of them walking side by side, the same loose, ground-eating stride, the same alert awareness of the surroundings.

Ally drifted toward Tess, waiting. They watched as the two young men walked away.

"Hold up! Parrish!" Did he really think she didn't need more information than that?

They kept walking, ignoring the girls.

Enough, she'd had enough of everyone knowing more than she did. She raised her arm and sent the tomahawk sailing between the two of them. It hit a branch that dangled over the trail, the blade vibrating half buried in the rough bark.

Jamie hit the dirt when he heard the thunk of the tomahawk. Parrish stood frozen, his back a rigid wall. He didn't turn around; instead, he reached up and yanked the tomahawk free. Turning, he faced Tess, eyes narrowed, shoulders locked. He spoke low and slow and steady.

"The Fortixes. They know about you. Not all of it, but enough. They know about you and Ally and they'll guess at the rest. Marco is dead or as good as dead. They'll be coming, and that's all we have time to discuss right now." Then he turned, leaving her standing next to Ally in the dirt of the trail. He buried the tomahawk in a stump next to him. "Now, do you want to stand here discussing this or do you want to get back before we're cut off?"

Ally made a sound that was close to a moan. She grabbed Tess's hand and dragged at her arm.

"Please, Tess, we should hurry."

CHAPTER 19

Tess had never seen that look in Ally's eyes before: shame and horror.

"Come on. We need to go," Ally said, her voice sharpened to a knifepoint. "Now. Now."

She yanked at Tess's arm, pulling her off balance and digging her fingers into her arm.

"Ally, stop. You're hurting me!"

Nothing. She didn't stop. Ally acted as if she'd gone blind and deaf with fear. She dragged Tess forward.

"Ally!" She grabbed her sister's arm and yanked back. "Stop it." Her sister stumbled to her knees.

"I can't. I can't stop. Those people." Tess could hear the tears building in her sister's throat. It made her sound like she was drowning. "Those people. Jerome."

Tess knelt next to Ally. The sand of the trail was warm, almost hot under her knees.

"Tell me. So I'll understand."

"Jerome and his mother, they're . . ." She choked, and started again. "She said she was a midwife, but I didn't know what that was." Ally's eyes glittered with unshed tears and something else. "Tess, she, that woman, examined me. She looked inside me and they talked about selling me, because I haven't . . . because I'm . . ."

Tess reached for Ally's hands. They were cold in spite of the heat and humidity.

"Pure. She said I was clean." She dropped her head, letting her hair fall forward again. "But he wanted me instead. That's it. That's how he said it. He said he wanted me, and she said that she could make that happen."

"Jerome Fortix?"

"Jerome. That horrible . . . boy. They held me down and . . ." She stopped talking, pulled one hand free, and started to reach up to touch her face. She let her hand drop. "That's what they do. They sell people, kids and women. I saw it. I was almost . . . was almost part of it. They changed their mind about me, and then those kids, the Doe Kids, came. Then Mister Parrish found me with them and then you came . . ."

She wanted to smile when she heard Ally call him *Mister*. That word was like an echo from the past when so much had changed . . .

"Parrish. It's just Parrish."

There was a ghostly hint of the old speculation and curiosity in the look Ally gave Tess.

"Yeah, okay." She seemed to think about that for a minute. "Tess, we need to go before he finds me." She pushed against the ground, levered to her feet, shivered as if she had a chill, and started to walk away.

"Jerome?" Tess called after her. "He's a brat, always has been. I owe him a couple punches in the face, but I don't think he's got the stones to . . ."

"Tess, you're not hearing me. That boy . . . Jerome. His mother. They burned my face."

A cough and a discrete shuffling of feet let them know that they had an audience. Parrish watched them. Jamie watched the woods. Ally wrapped her arms around herself, glanced at the two men, and then dropped her arms.

Lowering her voice she walked back to Tess and said, "He thinks we're married. He thinks I'm his wife."

They were all there except Kilmer, who'd headed out to do chores. ZeeZee cried when she saw Ally, and then she didn't cry when she saw the mark on her sister's cheek.

"Oh, Tess, your hair," Gwen said, reaching out to brush at Tess's curls.

Tess shrugged off her friend and nodded to her sister.

"Not me. See if you can do something for Ally."

"What happened, Tess," Gwen started, paused, and then whispered, "out there?"

Tess answered with a shrug and went to check on the others.

"Later. We'll talk later," she said, giving Gwen what she hoped was a reassuring smile.

Her grandfather sat in his chair, an FSU blanket draped across his knees. It was a college that had been his favorite at one time: the team, the school. Father sat quietly at the picnic table in front of the stove, pencil in hand, ready to record the minutes of whatever meeting he thought they were about to have. He watched Tess with foggy eyes.

Jess T sat with his hand on her grandfather's wasted knee, getting ready to take over Colonel Kennedy Watch for the night.

Tess smiled her thanks at him. All she got was an old man harrumph. It all felt so expected and normal she almost cried.

"Good to have you back. You should have asked for help," Jess T said.

"I know."

Gwen sat next to the twins on their bunk, murmuring and making mother noises, trying to get Ally to look up at her. It was another normal sight, Gwen fussing over someone, making her comforting sounds. What would they do without her? Tess looked at her family and tried not to think about what might be hunting them out in the dark. Tess focused on Gwen.

Once, she'd been their grandparent's dental hygienist, and then she and her two boys had made their way to the ranch in those early terrifying days, one of the few who'd listened to that crazy Colonel Kennedy and signed on to survive. And that made her family. She had a steady way of helping and a solid, meaty way of hugging her sisters when they acted up and drove Tess crazy.

Her boys had their mother's big brown eyes in light dusky faces. Now, Blake and Blane avoided looking at the sleeping platform where Ally huddled with ZeeZee and their mother making clucking noises.

As soon as Ally had come through the longhouse doors, the two girls had retreated into their private world of sameness. Except for Gwen, there was an eerie quiet coming from the corner where her sisters, identical to the point of being bookends, were holed up.

Except they weren't identical. Not anymore.

Parrish hovered near the screen door, looking less and less sure of himself, looking ready to bolt back to the fishing shack where they'd left Jamie cleaning his gun and dabbing at the bite mark on his neck.

Looking around, she could feel the fear, the sudden sharp pang of it. They'd all put it together, that Ally had broken the rules and had come back wounded and hurt by hands unknown.

Tess caught their looks with her quick, furtive side-glances when they thought she wasn't looking. They wanted her to say something, to be reassuring, to lead. She knew that and tried to think what she could say that wouldn't sound lame.

She threw her tomahawk bag onto her bed, heard it thump against the wall of the longhouse, and had started to peel off her filthy vest when the world went sideways. She staggered as her head started to spin.

"Tess, get something to eat. And you," Gwen called out. She pointed at Parrish. "You're staying and eating. You make Tess eat too. Be useful."

Parrish looked surprised when he realized Gwen was talking to him. He quit hovering and started to back out through the screen door.

"I should . . . be . . . getting back."

"No. You'll stay," Gwen snapped.

Tess was too dizzy to argue with Gwen over the way she was treating Parrish. He had just saved their lives.

Before he could bristle, Tess added, "Please, stay and eat." She caught his eye and saw him hesitate, just as ZeeZee peeled away from Ally's side and grabbed at Tess's sleeve.

Parrish slid away in that moment with a headshake and a murmured, "Thanks. But I should check on things."

The screen clanged shut and he was gone. Later they would have to talk about Ally and the Fortixes and how bad it might get. Later.

"Tess, I'm sorry," ZeeZee began. "I really tried, but I couldn't make Samantha stand still for me, and Gwen couldn't either. She needs to be milked or she's going to get sick. No one could do it. That rude old goat, she just wanted you."

ZeeZee took it as a personal insult when Samantha, their Nubian milk goat, acted picky and stuck up.

Here was a problem Tess understood.

"She hasn't been milked since when?"

ZeeZee's shoulders sagged. She glanced over at Ally, who had disappeared under their quilt. She resembled a patchwork rock.

"Since you left."

"Don't worry. I'm here. I'm back."

She reached out and squeezed her sister's narrow shoulder. She felt like a bird under her hand—light and fluttery.

"Just look after Ally for me. Can you do that? See if you can get her to let Gwen look at her face. And a bath, maybe? Clean clothes. Her own clothes."

ZeeZee's eyes glittered in the fading light inside the longhouse. Soon it would be time to light the hurricane lamps. They tried to get by on natural light during the day and not waste the oil they used in the lamps. For now there was enough light left to see the tears that spilled down ZeeZee's cheeks.

"Don't cry now, Zeez, please." Tess hugged her and then leaned down to whisper in her ear, "We'll cry later, when we have time. I promise. You and me. We'll cry and cry."

She turned away before she broke down in front of them all. There would be no later and they both knew it. There was always too much to do. And now they had the fallout from Ally's wild adventure to deal with. Tess grabbed her tomahawk bag and slung it back over her shoulder.

"Just stay with her."

Gwen called Tess's name, but when she waved the older woman off, Gwen reached in her apron pocket, pulled out a power bar, and tossed it to Tess. Five thousand calories and they tasted like stale coconut, but in emergencies . . .

"Eat something. Drink some water. There's stew when you get back."

"Okay, sure," she said, pushing her way past the lot of them. She heard her father call her name but pretended not to hear him. The screen door slammed behind her in answer to the thin sound of his voice. Looking back at the longhouse, she noticed how the screen bulged at the bottom from getting kicked. She added that to her to-do list, right under "Prepare for an Invasion."

CHAPTER 20

AT THE SECOND paddock, Parrish stopped and thought about kicking a fence post. Pointless. It was pointless to worry about her, about any of them, but there it was. Shrugging, he turned back in the direction of the longhouse.

Before, at the longhouse, he'd expected crying and hysterics and angry accusations. Instead it had been deathly quiet when Ally had finally made it back to the house full of pale, frightened faces and haunted eyes. Tess's eyes had bothered him the most: gray like storm clouds full of rain, sunken in purple shadows and exhaustion. She'd only given him a glance when he'd left.

She hadn't looked at him when the others had needed explanations, comfort. Even Gwen, who was older and a mother, had looked to Tess for strength, not to him. He understood that. He knew how it was with them—they were a family, and Tess was the head of that family.

It would have made more sense to have one of the adults step up after Colonel Kennedy went down. It should have been her father, but it had fallen on Tess. Sometimes it happened that way. He knew that better than most. Some leaders were born, some were made, and some just happened to still be standing when no one else could or would. He had seen that during the Flare-Out Wars, when everyone and their dog was fighting over scraps. Some of the most unlikely people took the lead, or had to.

He hadn't walked far when he heard the slap of the screen door and watched as Tess headed toward the barn. What now? Hadn't they agreed she should take a break? Get some food? They couldn't even give her time for that?

She was out of sight when he heard a goat bell jangle in response to the sound of her voice.

Goats. She was going to milk goats—now? What was wrong with these people? He remembered the mule's saddle. He'd slung it over the corner of the paddock fence when they'd finally staggered home. Parrish trudged over to the barn and hauled the saddle off the fence, threw it over his shoulder, and headed toward the sound of jingle bells and goat wails.

A big alpha female, her bag swaying side to side, close to bursting, led the happy band of goats into the barn. Tess whistled softly and the big goat jumped up on the milking stand. The goat put her head into the stanchion and waited.

When he walked into the center of the barn, the big doe bawled at him, demanding to be fed. He got her a bucket of millet.

The shadows under Tess's eyes looked carved from ice. She didn't seem surprised to see him—too tired for surprise, maybe.

"We'll be lucky if she doesn't get mastitis after this. We've been milking Sam straight for a year. That's a record for her," Tess said in a dazed, exhausted way.

He watched her pull a milk bucket down, settle against Samantha's side, and shoot the first few jets of milk into the bucket. The splash of milk clattered. A sleek, tiger-striped barn cat appeared at her feet, waiting for the strippings. Tess checked for blood or pus.

He took the bucket of strippings out of her hands and poured them into the cat's dish. When he turned back to Tess, he saw her slumped on the milking stool. She looked like a deflating balloon.

"Come on, get up—I'll do it." He nudged her off the stool.

Shaking her head she started to argue, "She'll kick you."

He reached down and drew her up from the stool.

Tess felt drunk with exhaustion. His hands on her made her remember the way he'd held her in the woods outside of the Marketplace. It had been so nice to lean on him then, to let him hold her, to be held. No one had held her in a long time.

Too tired to worry or think or second-guess herself, she sagged against him and burrowed her face into his shirt. He smelled of sweat and heat and male.

Beyond the Strandline

She felt him freeze when she wrapped her arms around him to steady herself, just for a minute, because she was so tired. He acted as if she was one of the sambar fawns, like he was afraid of spooking her. Then carefully, slowly, he pulled her more tightly into his arms. If Tess hadn't been silly with exhaustion, she'd never have stopped long enough to let this mysterious stranger comfort her, much less hold her. But after all that had happened today, Parrish's strong arms felt like heaven. They stood in the fading light of the big barn, holding each other, listening to the first faint calls of a Whip-poor-will.

"Why?" she asked.

"Why what?"

When she didn't answer, he tried again. "Why what?"

"Why did you hug me after the parking lot, in the woods before we got separated, before they found us?" Tess had never had a free moment to consider that Richmond Parrish was a boy, a *man*, and a beautiful one at that. Romance and crushes and holding hands had never been a part of her life. She'd never expected them to be. But now, all of the sudden, this attractive man was holding her in his arms. Overcome with exhaustion, Tess remembered that she should be nervous. Thankfully, her nerves were too shattered to be useful, and she remained calmly encircled in Parrish's embrace as he considered her question.

Parrish thought about trying to describe the flood of joy that had threatened to swamp him when he'd seen her, standing there safe in the woods after their escape; hot and sweaty and dirty, but safe. He still didn't have the words.

Her hair curled out of control. Her quizzical eyes were sunken in purple smudges. She'd cut her hair to go after her sister: hadn't hesitated, hadn't eaten, hadn't rested. It was one of the single-most foolish and unprepared rescue missions he'd ever witnessed—and the bravest. How could she be simultaneously so foolish and yet so brave?

He didn't have words.

He lowered his mouth to hers because anything else would have been a lie.

He kissed her softly, gently; his mouth a shock of velvet and steel against hers. It felt inevitable. They were home and safe and together. She curled her fingers in the denim of the back of his jacket.

It made her dizzy when he angled his mouth more completely to hers. His kiss grew more demanding, more forceful. In the back of Tess's mind, something screamed for her to stop, that she barely knew this man. But all she was able to focus on in the heat of the moment was that *he* had rescued *her*. He had shot up a mall full of warlords for *her*. And it felt *so* good to be held, to be wanted by someone other than her little family.

Samantha stamped and bleated her impatience, kicking at the milk bucket between her legs. Her bleating complaints became frantic. She needed more grain.

Distracted, Parrish pulled back to look at the girl in his arms; she stood with her eyes closed, her face flushed, and her mouth soft and full.

"Why?" he said. "Because you cut your hair."

She opened her eyes like a sleepwalker coming to life.

"What?" She reached up to touch her hair. "My hair? What does that have to do with anything?

"Tess, I'm . . . never mind. Sorry. You're tired. We're both tired. Forget it."

He pushed her gently away, sat on the milking stool, and turned his back to her. Better to dismiss her, he reasoned to himself. Out of the corner of his eye he saw her touch her mouth with her fingertips.

He could feel her confusion, her embarrassment, as she stumbled back a few steps, then steadied herself.

"She won't let you. She'll kick," she said. That streak of stubbornness and fire in Tess was still there, regardless of her moment of exhaustion and weakness. Her emotional guard was back up and ready for a fight, even if it was just over a goat.

"Nope, she won't. Will you pretty girl?" He threw another handful of grain into the goat's feed bucket. Samantha gave a quick bleat and went back to licking up her dinner.

"If you aren't going to go home, then at least sit down before you fall down. Let me milk this goat and then . . . then we talk. Please?" It wasn't a word he used much or ever. He looked back at her and waited.

She mumbled something about him "not being the boss of her" or some other foolishness, hesitated a moment, and then folded up in the straw next to the goat stand like a house of cards. He'd come into the barn to warn her, to frighten her if he had to, to prepare her for what was ahead for them. Instead he'd confused them both by kissing her. It was selfish and cruel and unfair. Unfair to let her think that he could ever be what she needed.

"Sleep," he said. But she was already out, leaving him alone with a sickeningly familiar twist of tension and fear in his gut, a feeling that threatened to grow and crush him. He shut it down viciously. *Just milk the damn goat*, he thought.

The cat twined through the legs of the stool on its way to Tess's lap. Goat milk filled the bucket in jets and spurts as Parrish worked. He concentrated on working while she slept. The barn smelled rich and alive: the sharp tang of raw milk, the spice of grain, the dry musk of peanut hay. The rhythmic sound of milk splashing against the bucket fell in time to the cat's purring. He let the simple chore calm him; distract him from the moment he'd shared with Tess that he never should have let happen.

Regardless of what had happened to Ally Lane at the Marketplace Mall or after the riot they'd started, there were still goats to milk and people to feed for now. Going to war never left much time for farming.

He watched Tess sleep, trying to work up some good old-fashioned guilt over kissing her. He couldn't. It had already happened countless times before in his mind. Instead of guilt he felt a kind of relief; relief that he wasn't just living in the past and in his dreams anymore. That he was *alive*.

He was shocked when her family didn't check on her. They were ignorant to be so trusting. All of them were casualties waiting to happen. Hadn't Ally proven that?

He smirked at their foolishness and then felt the familiar pangs of worry.

It wasn't their fault that they didn't live inside his head—inside the creepy, crawly reruns that played over and over again and left him drenched in sweat and terror at night. It wasn't their fault that they didn't share his nightmare memories. It was a blessing they didn't.

Lighten up, he thought. The kid had been stupid and Tess was exhausted. So what? And the family was used to Tess spending her nights in the barn or under the stars.

However, stupid and tired was a good way to wind up swinging from a lamppost. Geez. What would she think if she could see inside his head now? Or hear him arguing with himself? He should be glad she couldn't see the way his thoughts had a way of slipping back to those years when he'd fought with and against children—little more than a kid himself. Glad she didn't see the way his past framed too much of his present in a yellow haze of anger.

He finished milking the big nanny goat, set the pail down, and let Samantha hop off of the goat stand. She sniffed at Tess's hair and then strolled off to the goat paddock, taking the other goats with her.

Parrish looked at the pail of milk. Now what?

They would need to scald the milk, or whatever it was they did with it to keep it from going bad. The sight of foaming milk made him think of the soft cheeses and butter Gwen and the girls made, how the longhouse always smelled of yeast bread and boiling stew.

Kicking at the bucket with his toe, he reached for the cat's bowl, dipped the bowl in the bucket, filled it full of goat's milk, and swigged it down. It was warm and rich and tasted faintly of Samantha the Goat, but it hit the spot. He sat next to Tess, settling into the straw at her feet, leaning against the wooden slats of the milking stand.

Someone should be looking out for her, even if it was just to make sure the goats didn't step on her. The idea made him smile. Goat stampede. Wouldn't it be great if that was all they had to worry about?

Fatigue dragged at him. Tess made one of those sleepy sounds—-part sigh, part sob—and time shifted and he was back again: watching over a gaggle of school kids turned toy soldiers as they dreamed their unquiet dreams. He reached for a horse blanket hanging on a peg over their heads and threw it over her.

She twitched in her sleep and curled tighter into herself. He had an urge to smooth the wild mop of curls that covered her head. Her short hair made her look younger and softer. It suited her somehow, not as severe as the heavy braid she'd always worn, not as serious.

Flop Washington, short curly hair, big brown eyes—that's who she reminded him of now. Flop because of his hair. Washington because he'd been conscripted from a middle school outside of Washington, D. C. That's how it worked back then. There'd been no last names, just places where they were from—less sentimental that way, less heartbreaking than a name that reminded you of family and home.

Flop Washington, a kid who'd had no more business carrying a sniper rifle than a baby. What had happened to that kid, anyway?

Oh, right. They'd hacked him to pieces on Interstate 95. One of the machete gangs.

Tess whimpered in her sleep, mumbling something that sounded like "Mother."

He should wake her up, drag her back to the longhouse. Later, he'd make her go later. Instead, he reached down, unlaced her boots, and pulled them off. He eased back and watched as she squirreled down into the hay.

He hadn't bothered to light the barn lanterns. A full moon made him glad they'd gotten back to the S-Line before sundown. Solid darkness was more his speed when he had to travel through enemy territory. If he couldn't see them, they couldn't see him, and that worked for Parrish. Now the moon gave the ground a misty definition and kept the barn from feeling like a tomb. A triangle of silver moonlight painted Tess's cheek. It made her look like something out of *A Midsummer Night's Dream*, some enchanted creature. He'd seen that play at the high school his sophomore year. Not all the memories were of doom, he thought.

He had to shake himself out of the trance of staring at her. Maybe he'd stay and watch over things tonight, but soon he needed to scoop up Jamie and figure out their exit strategy. This wasn't a fight they could win. He'd seen enough David and Goliath fights before, too many, and it was his experience that Goliath was going to win.

Goliath always won in the real world. He looked at her again and made a decision. He would at least tell her what he knew before he left. He'd give her that much—for the old man's sake. She whimpered again, all alone in her dreams.

Suddenly, he remembered the dog and wondered if it had wandered back to the questionable safety of the Marketplace. It was like that with some dogs, some people, too; they'd rather put up with the slaps and kicks than be alone.

Surely, Kilmer or Jess T would come down and check on her. Or were they used to her wandering off in the dark by herself? Did she do that a lot? Were they really that out of it? He settled in to keep watch as the night turned overhead.

There was sand. She was on a beach. Ally and ZeeZee had buried her up to her neck and then made her a mermaid tail—sand and seashells and seaweed. It was fun, letting the twins tell her what to do, feeling the weight of the sand pressing on her.

"Don't move Tessie. Don't scratch your nose. Don't wreck the mermaid's tale."

But then some bully kid had shown up to kick sand in her face, the big brat. She was ready to come up swinging when she realized that "the brat" was making clucking noises next to her nose.

Opening her eyes, she came awake and stared at a chicken's backside. It scratched its way through the main aisle of the barn. She sat up.

She collapsed back into the hay and exhaled, remembering Samantha and Parrish and being more tired than she'd ever been in her life—and a kiss. Had there been a kiss? Heat rushed into her cheeks.

The hen kept scratching toward the clear, bright daylight outside. In the open barn door she saw a dark silhouette against the rectangle of morning light. Her heart jumped. Parrish. He was still here. Embarrassed and then annoyed, she brushed dirt and hay from her Levi's and sniffed herself. Ugh. Not pretty.

He didn't turn when she came up behind him; he was so intent, looking up at the morning sky. His body reminded her of a bowstring: tight, ready, powerful. She wondered if he was one of those people that took pleasure in the glitter of the sunrise, but then she smelled something else—smoke. The acrid smell and taste settled in the back of her throat—wildfire.

She gasped, checking the treetops and the subtle bend and sway of the leaves.

"Where? Where's it coming from?" Before she was done asking she knew the answer.

"Van Arsdale," he said. "But the wind is taking it west, back to town."

He kept his eyes on the sky.

"I think you're going to dodge this one. Look that way." He pointed to the eastern tree line.

Heavy, black, rolling clouds piled up in the distance, heading inland from the coast. More rain.

"About time," she sighed. "It's been so dry this year."

She said it like they were talking about a good time to plant the spring millet, but she knew. She knew that the Doe Kids were paying a terrible price for helping them.

"Parrish? Those kids . . ."

"Are dead unless they were smart and fast and got out."

His hands tensed to fists.

"And that's what you need to think about, Tess. They're going to keep poking until they find you and the kid and the rest. They know you have weapons and ammunition and resources. It's going to keep them coming, and you should think about bugging out—soon. Get them moving down river or to the coast. Head north, maybe."

The way he said "you and the kid" scared her more than the threat of a raging, out-of-control wildfire that could take the whole ranch down to charred dirt.

"Parrish, I wanted to say . . . about yesterday," she started. "About what you did for us at the Marketplace . . ."

He relaxed one fist long enough to stop her with an open hand.

"Don't. For the Colonel, that's why I went. I wouldn't have except for him. You should know that. I know you think we can help. Maybe we can draw their fire, but not if we stay." He avoided her eyes. "I can't stay. I'm sorry. Yesterday. We were tired. I shouldn't have kissed you. People do crazy things when they're tired."

His voice had gone empty and cold. It pushed her back.

"They're going to remember the guys with the rifles and blame us if you're very, very lucky." He looked back to the sky where smoke billowed and roiled. "That's a warning for you and your people."

Finally he looked at her, his eyes roaming over her face, as if he were taking inventory.

"There's hay in your hair."

Confused, she reached up and felt the prick of straw.

She watched him lift his hand to touch her hair and then ball up his fist again. He pushed his hands into his pockets.

"Don't wait, Tess. They won't. They never do. And don't forget your bucket of milk," he said and then walked away, in the direction of the river and a darkly burning sky.

CHAPTER 21

Gwen took the bucket from Tess, reached up, and pulled another piece of hay out of her hair.

"I wasn't too worried when you didn't come back from the barn. Kilmer said he saw you asleep in the barn and that Parrish was there with you, watching." Gwen pushed a curl behind Tess's ear. "He did a good thing, that boy, for you and Ally. He did a good thing."

Tess smiled, recognizing Gwen's mothering voice.

From the start, Gwen had sunk into the role of chief cook, sometime disciplinarian, and keeper of the medical kit. Her husband, Bruce Dunn, had planned to meet up with his family at the ranch in case of a crisis, but weeks and then months and then years passed and no Bruce Dunn. If she mourned her husband, she never spoke of it.

"Sorry about that, but I was so tired. I kind of collapsed. Is my father around?"

They had the longhouse to themselves for once.

"He's around, left here about ten minutes ago, I guess. I'm more worried about that," she said, waving a hand in front of her nose. The smell of smoke and death had drifted and crept into the longhouse. They'd be able to smell it in their blankets and clothes soon. "What are we supposed to do?"

Stepping to the door, Tess looked above the trees at the plume of black smoke that cut into the belly of the sky, an angry exclamation point.

"Parrish doesn't think it's out of control or sweeping this way, but we should keep an eye on it. At least he didn't think that it was earlier."

She neglected to add the depressing idea that the fire was likely a targeted, ruthless warning for the S-Line and that Parrish had talked about leaving, and wanted them to run too. Soon enough. She'd have to find a way to break the news to Gwen, to all of them.

Now, she needed to get a shower. Or at least as much of one as she could squeeze out of the solar shower her grandfather had rigged up.

"Is there any water, you think, for a shower?"

"Yeah, some, after the rain," Gwen said as she shifted the bucket of goat's milk from one hand to the other.

When Tess started to walk to her bunk, the older woman followed. She had more to say it seemed, was working up to it. Gwen usually kept herself moving throughout the day, sending the boys out to do chores, staying focused on the constant cooking and cleaning that having no refrigeration required. But it often took her a while to talk something over. Tess waited.

"Tess?" Gwen set the bucket on the ground at her feet.

Tess saw that the twins' bunk was empty—rumpled, but empty. She touched the blanket they used, full of big pink and red gingham checks.

"Where are they?"

"They said something about checking trotlines, after they helped me with the Colonel."

Gwen glanced over at Grandfather's cot and, for a moment, they both watched the slow rise and fall of his chest under a light summer sheet. Checking on him throughout the day. It was a habit they'd all fallen into.

Gwen started, "I was actually glad that Ally was up and moving. I let them go."

Tess could hear the question in her voice, the need for approval.

"Sure, that's good," she said, finding that someone had straightened her living area, made her bed. "Thanks for fixing my bed." She nodded at Gwen.

"Wasn't me. It was ZeeZee. She was pretty upset while you were away. Blamed herself, you know?"

Sure. There was a lot of that going around. Tess started toward the door.

"Tess, stop."

Gwen made a move to follow. She sloshed milk when she knocked the bucket with her foot.

"Oh damn. Let me move this."

Beyond the Strandline

Gwen never cussed. Better get the report over and done with; she should have asked about the twins—about Ally.

Showering could wait. Should wait.

"It's Ally. She seems better today, but I don't know."

"They're out and about. That's good. You said so, right?"

"Sure. Except I think that it's ZeeZee who's out and about and Ally is following her around like a puppy."

That was different. Usually it was the other way around. But it was probably not all that big a deal, considering.

"Like a puppy who's been beaten," Gwen added.

"I know. I saw it on the way back. But it'll get better, Gwen. They're . . ." She had been going to say tough, but it was hard for her to think of her baby sisters that way. "They're smart . . . smart girls. She'll figure it out."

"Tess, I cleaned and treated the . . . that thing on her face, but she wouldn't let me look her over. Maybe you could talk to her some about it. I'm afraid," Gwen said, hesitating. "I'm afraid for her."

"She told me the strangest thing about some woman at the Marketplace," Tess said. "That this woman, Wendy Fortix, examined her, like a doctor would—a gynecologist. Wanted to know if she was *pure*."

Gwen stepped back, her face a study in confused worry.

"What can that mean? Why would something like that matter?" Gwen's forehead dissolved into worry lines.

"Value. I think it's about value. Listen, I'll talk to her. Then we should all talk."

Gwen's dark chocolate eyes were confused and troubled. She nodded and went to deal with the bucket of goat's milk.

The air inside the longhouse felt humid and warm and rolled with familiar smells: the endless rabbit or squirrel stew that bubbled and steamed, the spice of men who worked hard enough to sweat, all wrapped up with hints of eucalyptus and lavender and the other essentials oils and herbs Gwen mixed and mashed. But over everything loomed that faint, foreboding taint of burning—a funeral pyre, sizzling somewhere beyond their control.

"Don't worry. We'll talk. All of us."

"Okay, you're right. Go, get clean. Eat something."

Tess smiled, turned, and pulled a towel from her dresser.

"Of course. Absolutely. Shower. Eat. But after that."

Gwen walked over to Tess, reached out and touched her cheek with her fingertips.

"Have I told you how glad I am you're okay?"

Tess shook her head.

Smiling, she let her hand drop, her full lips pressed tight. "I know, and I'm sorry. I should have said it sooner. I know how hard it was for you to go after Ally. I do. But Tess, they put a brand on her cheek. I can't even guess what that might mean about what kind of people we're dealing with. What it might mean about what happened to her."

"Okay, when the girls get back. We'll . . . I'll talk to Ally and figure things out."

The screen door slammed behind them, and they both jumped.

"Sorry girls, but I need to find my other set of gloves." Jess T held up a ragged pair of work gloves with the thumb ripped out of the left hand.

Gwen hurried to help him find his other pair.

"They're here. I finished sewing up the last pair you shredded."

Jess T looked at Tess when she walked by.

"Some haircut, Champ. Like your mom. You make me think of your mom, Champ, with your hair like that."

CHAPTER 22

THE TRICK TO getting clean under her grandfather's solar shower was speed and routine. Solar shower: that was a fancy way of saying a trashcan lashed to the top of a four-legged cedar scaffolding. Rain filled the trashcan. Sun heated the water. Pulling the plastic lid open on the bottom end of the can let the water trickle out of the nail holes in the bottom.

The trick was to get wet, close the lid, soap up, try not to go blind from soap in the eye, and then rinse. Rinsing was the best part, especially if the water had cooked long enough in the hot Central Florida sun. If you were careful and quick, there was enough water for two whole bodies to get clean.

Tess heard the rumble of thunder. More rain, and they needed it. Good time to get a shower in. The water should be warm enough for now. Fresh rainwater would be icy.

She pulled the cord and danced under the sprinkle of water, then let the lid flip shut. The wooden platform under the shower and the ligustrum hedge were new additions, added when the twins complained that their feet were never clean when they showered and that they hated being naked out in the open. The hedge had turned out nice—plants dug up and replanted from the ruined foundation of the old farmhouse.

It made Tess laugh. Who was going to see them? Just us and the owls out here.

Still laughing, she tipped her head back as she scrubbed her hair. It was easy now. There was hardly any to wash. The short wet strands that slipped through her fingers brought it back to her: ZeeZee's panic, the sawing sound of the scissors, Goliath and those kids, and now the pall of smoke.

Forget it, she ordered. She gripped the bar of soap, smelling it. Irish Spring. They were so lucky to still have cake soap. Grandfather had always said that stuff like that was the easy part: soap and toilet paper and even tampons—thank goodness he'd known about girls. He'd had a daughter of his own after all.

Probably needed to check with Gwen about making soap, see how their supply of stuff to make homemade soap with was holding up. The Irish Spring wasn't going to last forever.

Soap they could make, but it had been the big stuff that had worried Grandfather: clean water, food, and ammunition.

Still, they were lucky, that's what they were, to have hot water and a shower, such as it was. She pulled the rope, planning to stand there and rinse until the garbage can water tank ran bone dry.

Then suddenly Ally was screaming her name and stumbling onto the shower platform, throwing herself into Tess' arms, knocking her back, almost tipping them both off the far side of the platform.

"Ally, stop. Geez, I'm trying to get a shower here. What are you saying? Are you hurt?"

Her sister wrapped herself around Tess like a wet towel. Tess tried peeling her off, but Ally's fear and panic thrummed through her like electricity.

"Stop, Ally, let me get my towel. I'm soaked. Sweetie, please." She looked for her towel on the hedge.

Following Ally, Parrish stepped through the hedge and locked eyes with her. She watched him freeze when he saw Tess, wet, naked, and wrapped in a fourteen-year-old sister.

She could feel the heat of a blush burn its way up her neck, flushing her face.

"Oh, good grief! Turn around. Don't look at me," Tess shouted. "My clothes. I need my clothes, Baby."

"Okay. Sure. I can do that." Ally blinked her tears away.

"Over there. Hurry, Ally. Please. Parrish, don't just close your eyes; turn around." Tess wrapped her arms around herself. He turned around.

"What is it? What's happened?"

He started to turn back around.

Beyond the Strandline

She made a panicked squeak and shouted, "No! Wait!" Ally brought Tess her towel and clothes in a dirty wad.

He flinched and shrugged, waiting silently while she got dressed. Ally stood at the edge of the platform hugging herself. Getting caught naked in the shower might have been funny except for the look in Ally's eyes, the fear that made her hands shake.

Keeping his back to her, he started telling her what had happened. She heard "dead" and "child" and "Goliath" and something about bloody ears, but that didn't make sense. Whatever had happened was bad, and being embarrassed about being caught buck naked didn't rate. But still.

When she pulled her jeans on, Ally started to babble.

"Ally, baby, you need to slow down and make sense." She looked past the hysterical girl to Parrish.

"I don't get it. What is she saying? You can turn around now."

He turned, and it was his turn to flush. His eyes stayed grim.

"It's bad. You should hurry, Tess. We should all hurry."

Ally had been right to scream. Screaming felt right. Hysterics felt right. Tess wanted to scream and cry and rage and hit something.

Goliath was alive. He was back.

Whoever had attacked and burned Van Arsdale had cut off his tail and both his ears. He thrashed and stamped when they tried to get a hand on the frayed rope tied around his neck. Flies swarmed the bloody ruin of his head. He snorted and blew, driven mad by pain and the smell of his own blood and the blood from the body of the dead child lashed to his back. A little blond girl, maybe eight or nine, skinny and dressed in an over-sized T-shirt and stretchy pants. They'd tied her to Goliath with strips of ratty twine.

Screaming felt right.

They buried the girl in one of the Timacuan Indian mounds, down where the old train trestle had once marched across the slow river. It was a beautiful spot. The trees arched up and over the water with leafy arms. They buried her frail body deep, under the bits of pottery and empty shells that filled the mound, hoping the rubbish would keep the erosion to a minimum in the rainy season.

The mounded shape would keep her dry when the water table started to rise during the rains. It was the best they knew how to do for the nameless, broken child.

Jess T And Kilmer complained that the river was a long way to tote the dead girl. But they agreed it didn't seem right to bury her in the big field where they buried the animals when they died, and they hadn't had to start a cemetery at the S-Line. Not yet.

Soon, Tess realized. Soon it would be time to bury her grandfather. Maybe he would like it here by the river. She'd never thought to ask him before he'd gotten so sick, and now he couldn't tell her. He'd planned everything else down to hot showers and Spanish bayonets and caustic soda for making soap, but he'd never told them where he wanted to be buried. Her head hurt thinking about the inevitable.

Gwen and her boys sang a sweet song about heaven's regard for children and lost sheep. It was a song Tess couldn't remember hearing before. Her father read from the Bible, something from Psalms.

ZeeZee wept and Ally stood like a sleepwalker, drooping weakly against her twin.

They were all there when they put the little girl with no name in the ground, Jess T and Kilmer looking almost as brittle as the dead kid. Gwen and her boys and the twins huddled together; everyone listening to her father read from the Bible in his dreamy, otherworldly voice.

Parrish and Jamie stayed back at the longhouse to watch over the man they still called Colonel. It was nice to know they were there, watching. But they wouldn't stay. She knew that. Parrish had warned her. There was no reason to think he was lying.

In the cool of the big oaks next to the river she looked at the mourners: such a small group. It took her breath away, the irony, when she saw them standing there together at the graveside of a helpless child, singing songs about lambs: a couple of old men, weepy women, and children.

What was she supposed to do to keep them safe? They'd just buried one child, beaten to death by the most dangerous animals of all—vicious, lawless men.

Beyond the Strandline

On the river bank the world smelled richly of green ferns and mysterious dark water. But even here the capricious breeze carried the acrid stink of burning.

How could they possibly stay on the S-Line and survive?

Walking back to the longhouse, Tess followed her sisters down the river path, past the saw palmetto and catbrier vine lining each side of the trail, all part of the beautiful, isolated world they lived in. They headed back to Grandfather propped up in his chair, waiting to be spoon-fed his lunch.

Tess thought she heard her sister's soft weeping as they walked. Ally tripped more than once and each time ZeeZee reached over to steady her twin, whispering . . . something only they would understand, twin secrets.

How far could they possibly get, if they did decide to run?

Parrish stretched out on Jess T's bunk. It smelled faintly of goat and Jess T, but it didn't matter. He had to get some sleep or pass out after the raid on the Marketplace and the long night in the barn, keeping watch over Tess.

He fell asleep to the sound of Jamie reading out loud from one of the Dunn boy's graphic novels. After years of enforced silence and the life-and-death discipline of the militia camps, Jamie enjoyed the sound of his own voice. No one could blame him.

In Parrish's dream, the swirls of choking pink smoke drifted around him: lambs, puppies, goldfish . . . stupid goldfish, like the one that had lived on his family's kitchen counter when he was five. The clouds puffed and shifted. He wanted to laugh at the silly shapes . . . tried to. Sure, what wasn't to laugh about, right?

He swiped at a poodle cloud that floated by, his hands suddenly slick with what looked like sticky cotton candy. Parrish tried to wipe the goo off on his shirt, but instantly smelled blood. He watched as the clouds turned to thick pink rain. Not cotton candy . . . not clouds . . . pink mist and rain. Goo dripped from his face. Kids. The mortars had reduced them to a bloody mist that hung above the ground like fog.

At his feet, a face stared up at him, just the skin of a face draped over a fishbowl. It was that Ally girl's face. Then Tess was pointing at him and screaming—her hair drenched in a pouring rain of gore.

He came awake when Jamie shook his shoulder.

"Hey, you were yelling again. Turn over. Try again."

Parrish shrugged away from his friend's hand, flopped over, and stared at a metal rivet of the Quonset hut.

CHAPTER 23

THEY'D LEAVE WHEN the old man died. Hadn't that always been the plan? The Colonel was the only thing holding Parrish and Jamie there. Right? Parrish had never believed it would last forever. He didn't believe in forever—not anymore.

The old man was quiet today, hardly more than a breathy bag of bones under his sheet. Jamie sat folded in the rocking chair next to the Colonel's cot. Parrish felt too restless to settle. He got up from Jess T's bunk, the last bed in the line. Jamie watched him as he paced.

"Tough old buzzard," Jamie offered.

It was as sincere a compliment as Jamie was ever going to give anyone. Parrish smiled. Jamie ought to know about being tough; he'd been eleven years old when they'd tossed him into the ranks of the kid militias. That's what he'd told Parrish when they'd first met. Eleven years old and as skinny as a rope—tall though, even then.

Jamie had come to Parrish as a gangly, pimply thirteen-year-old, already two years into being a child soldier. He could shoot a squirrel out of a tree at fifty feet and a man point blank in the face and still smile when he saw a butterfly on a flower petal.

Jamie was one of the few who'd managed to stay sane, stay good, even after he'd been drafted. Drafted? That was a joke; it was more like being enslaved. They'd dumped Jamie into Parrish's squad. Over their unit had been a brutal man who'd ruled them with threats of torture, starvation, and worst of all—banishment.

Being alone meant being dead—back then.

Parrish listened to Jamie rock, rested against Jess T's bunk again.

"Yeah, but the old man won't last forever. It's a miracle he's lasted this long," he paused. "We should talk about getting out of here before the hammer falls."

He was surprised when Jamie didn't say anything. The rocking chair creaked over the gray cement of the floor. Parrish straightened, staring back at his friend.

"Right?" He prompted. "We're out of here."

When Jamie avoided his eyes, Parrish felt his gut clench.

"What's up with you? We can't help these people. Do you really want to watch them all die?"

Jamie rocked faster, his arms folded tight across his chest. "You can do it? Leave them? When you know they'll be—"

"Exactly. It's nothing we haven't seen before a hundred times, a thousand times," Parrish cocked his head, narrowing his eyes, "Besides, the girl's smart. She'll figure out a way."

"The girl?" Jamie rocked harder. "Is that how you do it? Is that how you shut it off? Call her 'the girl.' She's got a name, a first and a last name. Real names. They all do. Not like us."

Where was this coming from? The longhouse fell silent. Jamie knew better than to let emotions make him weak. He knew better.

"I'm here because of the old man and that's it." Parrish gestured to the quiet figure. "I didn't stay for anyone else. Those bastards at the Marketplace are going to march into this place and burn it to the ground, after they enslave everyone connected to that idiot twin."

"That girl's name is Ally, Parrish. Her name is Ally. And her sister's name is Tess."

"Is that what this is about?" Parrish started to pace. "Girls with names?"

He thought about the dozens of girls they'd known in the militia who had passed through that brutal existence like stray dogs, anxious to please, anxious to earn a few scraps of food, anxious for anything but slaps and fists. Their faces blurred. Even the ones they'd cared about blurred—like Darby. Like his sister Darby.

"And what about this place? You know there aren't places like this out there. There's nothing for us out there. Are we really going to let those bastards march in here and take it all?" He stopped the rocking chair and leaned forward, staring at the cold, hard floor. "Sure there are places like the Marketplace, but something like this with people who wait for you to come home? You know, like they'd notice if you didn't?"

He didn't bother to tell Jamie that no one had come for Tess last night in the barn. How he'd sat up watching over her as she slept. Or how he'd kissed her and felt . . . what? He couldn't even put a name to it except maybe drowning. Tess made him feel like he might be drowning. How could he drown and still live?

He paced down the center aisle, between the rows of sleeping platforms: the twins' bed with their collection of stuffed animals, the bunk where Gwen's two boys kept their stash of sticks and rocks, and then Tess's bed. It confused him. She'd gone after her sister on the back of a worn-out mule, carrying a handgun and a tomahawk against men capable of killing children, but she didn't have pictures or drawings from her sisters.

"I don't know. Maybe we could help, Parrish?"

"Sure, we could help. But are you going to tell them about waking up screaming because you think you're being buried alive under corpses?"

He knew it was cruel, but something about finding himself standing in front of Tess's blank, sterile space made the anger inside him blaze white hot.

Jamie was on his feet, fists like rocks, mouth like a slash. "We could fight for them! Help!"

"Help them? We've tried helping people before, or don't you remember all the holes we've dug besides the one today? I've buried enough bodies. Enough. I won't bury . . ." Her face crashed into his memory, the sight of her with hay in her hair, eyes filled with worry. He lowered his eyes and his voice.

"Come on, Tallahassee. We've got nothing to hold us here. It's hopeless. They're already dead if they don't make a run for it. And they won't. I know guppies like this. I do. They should have dug more holes while they were at it down by that river, because—"

"Parrish, shut up."

"I can't help them. You can't help them. No one can," he said. "We should take the best of the weapons and move on."

"Parrish. Shut up."

Surprised by the harshness in Jamie's voice, he looked over at his friend and knew. Tess was back, behind him, listening. He turned. Her sisters stood behind her, their eyes red and swollen with tears.

CHAPTER 24

Tess couldn't feel her hands, and her head was full of straw. Parrish had pronounced them as good as dead. She'd heard him. She shook the fog away, opened and closed her hands, tried to get the blood flowing again.

She needed to eat. They all did. She should check on the firewood. Check on Grandfather, make sure Ally let Gwen check her face, make sure Jess T and Kilmer doctored Goliath. His tail stump was infected. How much more peroxide should they waste on him?

She ran through the list of things to do in her head like a chant, trying to focus on the stuff she could control and not Parrish and not Jamie and not on their plans to steal their weapons and run—Parrish and Jamie leaving them completely defenseless.

Ally and ZeeZee stood inside the doorway, the screen door gaping open.

"Shut that door. Do you want mosquitoes to eat us alive? How many times have you been told?"

Like one person, they backed away from the growl in her voice and retreated outside, letting the screen door slam shut after them: the sound as final as a slap.

Tess walked through the longhouse, ignoring Parrish, ignoring his friend. She knelt next to her grandfather's cot. Jamie was saying something, low and deep, but she couldn't understand him, didn't care to try. It was all background noise. She concentrated on the sound of her grandfather's breathing—a rusty, gravelly sound.

Was it louder today, the sound of his breathing? Better maybe. Worse? She adjusted his covers.

Jamie's voice continued to rattle in her head, a broken chain dragging across the ground. Tess needed it to stop.

She said, "Thank you for watching over him, but you should do what *he* tells you." She jerked her chin toward Parrish. "You should go. My father should be along soon to take over here. It's the one thing he can still do."

Tess pulled a sprig of Carolina jasmine out of the top pocket of her vest and put it on her grandfather's pillow. She rested her head on his pillow close to his face and let the smell of jasmine drug her with its spice. He'd always loved the smell of jasmine. She'd been lucky to find some today. She wondered if he noticed.

A hand came down on her shoulder, but she kept her eyes closed.

"Just go. I'll figure something out. We'll figure it out," she said, mostly to herself, "probably. We always have. Parrish is right. I'm smart."

She looked up into Jamie's red-faced embarrassment. At least he had the class to pretend to look concerned.

"You might want to move that," she said, nodding to Jamie's hand on her shoulder. "You're going to need two hands to cover your butt while you run away. But you aren't going to take anything you didn't carry onto this property with you."

Tess shrugged away from the pressure of his hand. He wasn't her problem. She shot to her feet and marched to stand in front of Parrish.

"Thank you," she said, pushing her hand out. He looked at her extended hand like a striking snake. "I mean it. Thank you for coming for me and Ally. We'd already be dead if it wasn't for what you did."

"Tess?" Gwen called from outside the longhouse.

Gwen called her name. It pulled at her while she waited for Parrish to make a move. He didn't take her hand.

"Our staying won't help you," he said.

"Tess, I need you." Upset, Gwen sounded upset.

"I don't have time to discuss this with you." She dropped her hand.

The screen door squeaked open and ZeeZee stuck her head in, still swiping at tears on her face.

Beyond the Strandline

"You should be going." Tess hustled passed him, through the squeaking screen door, into the sun of the clearing where her sisters waited.

"I guess we just got ourselves un-invited, and we're going, huh?" Jamie sighed. "If we're out of here, you might want to let go of 'that girl's' blanket."

Parrish looked down to see his hand fisted around the bright yellow sunflowers spread across Tess's bed. When had he come to stand next to her bed? He hadn't even noticed.

When they left the clearing outside of the longhouse, he told himself not to turn around, not to look back, because it wouldn't help. How many times had he made that mistake in the early years—looking back—only to be left with images that ate holes in his dreams? Hadn't he learned his lesson more than once?

It didn't matter.

Parrish stopped, turned, and watched as Tess pulled Ally into her arms, searched the other girl's face, and pressed the back of her hand to her sister's forehead. He saw the way Tess squared her shoulders as she spoke to Gwen, the others.

Jamie called his name.

He shook off the pull of her, the way her determination, her courage made something move in his chest, his heart. He'd only make the mess worse if he stayed. Hadn't he made the disaster at the Marketplace worse?

Hadn't she told them to go?

Following the sound of Jamie's voice, Parrish walked away from the sight of the Lane family as they prepared for the worst, sorry that he had hesitated and looked back.

CHAPTER 25

IT WAS INFLUENZA, just an ordinary flu bug, but it was a virus they no longer had any resistance to. It made the worry over what the Marketplace might be plotting against them seem like a distant rumble over the ocean.

If they all died of the flu, what difference would it make?

Gwen went down the same day as Ally. She apologized for being human and having to leave both boys in Tess's care. Gwen dragged her mattress outside closer to the outhouse, crawled under a mosquito net, pulled her blanket over her head, and isolated herself in misery.

ZeeZee started feeling bad the day after Ally started throwing up. Blake admitted to drinking from Ally's cup when his fever got high enough. He babbled about being sorry and then confessed to sneaking extra jam and eating raw bread dough when no one was looking. Then it was Blane's turn to puke his guts out. When Jess T got sick, Kilmer had his hands full taking care of his old friend.

Tess realized, in all the misery, that Father finally found something tangible and helpful to do. Something about his girls being so sick brought him back to when he'd been a father, a real one, and could make a difference. He rallied to the side of their bunk, washed bedding, carried chamber pots, tried to get the girls to keep something in their stomachs, and worried about dehydration.

Tess lost count of how many trips she'd made to the deepwater well or how many times she'd had to prime the hand pump with a bucket of river water. All she knew was that her shoulder ached like a rotten tooth from hauling buckets. The days bled together in an endless stream of vomit and diarrhea.

Beyond the Strandline

There was a rain barrel and cistern that gave them water for the sink and small chores in the kitchen. But for the flu, you needed buckets and buckets and buckets of water.

Hauling another sloshing bucket, she wondered for the hundredth time why the well had to be so far away from the actual place where they had to boil it and cool it and keep it clean and ready to use. It made no sense. It was exhausting to have to walk across the longhouse clearing and down the path, halfway to the river for water. Nutty.

Might as well be dragging water out of the river and beating their clothes on rocks at the riverbank. But it was Florida—it would be tough to find a rock big enough.

Maybe it was almost over. ZeeZee and Blake were starting to bounce back, but it was Ally . . . down to skin and bones and two glittery eyes in her sharp-boned face. The brand on her face looked like a screaming insult against her pale cheek.

Gwen was pretty much on her own, huddled on a mattress, a ball of sick misery. If it wasn't for Father and Kilmer, and well . . . she could hardly imagine what she'd have done without them.

When she stumbled over the big root of a cypress tree next to the long curve before the hollow cypress stump, she slopped half her water onto the ground. Dropping the bucket, she kicked at a cypress knee, letting loose with every bad word she knew and some she made up on the spot.

It was pointless, but it made her feel better. She was tired, and the threat from the Marketplace nibbled at the edges of her exhaustion like a sharp-toothed rat.

She hadn't forgotten the big picture. But she'd been too busy to be worried about the big picture.

The man came up from the river and straight down the creek path, and while Tess kicked at stumps in pointless frustration, he stumbled up behind her. He lunged as soon as he saw her.

Then she was face down in the dirt of the trail, blind and heaving. He was bigger, stronger, and more than willing to press her into the dirt with a knee smashed into the middle of her back.

He ground his knee hard into her spine and then bent low to whisper in her ear, "Did you get the Fortixes' calling card, little girl? Personally, I would have kept the mule and tied the kid to another kid."

The force of his leg against her backbone crushed down on the bones in her chest, making it hard to breathe. Her lungs screamed for air.

He grabbed her by the shoulders and thumped her, face first, into the ground.

"Stop squirming. I don't have the energy for this."

Her grandfather's voice echoed through the fog in her head:

"You're not going to outfight a two-hundred-pound man, Tess. You're lanky and strong, but you're a stick. The physics are all wrong. No matter what those old television shows liked to pretend, all those little girls punching out grown men is crap. You're going to have to fight sneaky and dirty, and then you're going to have maybe six seconds to get the hell out of there."

The world started to fade and blur around the edges. If she could get six seconds she'd take them. Scratching a handful of leaf grit and dirt, Tess twisted her arm as hard as she could so she could fill the heavy bastard's face with dirt. Eyes—a point of weakness and it was her only play. Go for his eyes.

It worked better than she expected. Maybe too well. He made one great coughing huff and collapsed on top of her. He was crushing her. She wriggled hard to get out from underneath the dead weight of the big man.

"Come on, it was just a little dirt, not lava." She sounded like a squeaky, airless balloon as the unconscious man's bulk pressed down on her, squeezing more air out of her.

She felt lightheaded and floaty. She couldn't get enough air in her lungs.

Scrabbling hard to her left she shoved up and out, tipping the bulk of his body off, a little, enough. It was like trying to crawl out from under a tree trunk. By the time she was free, she was wearing most of the trail.

Tess reached for the water bucket, intending to brain her attacker with it, but soon saw that it wasn't going to be necessary. That much was obvious.

He wasn't moving, not even twitching. The man's face, the part she could see behind the hedge of his untrimmed beard, was the color of meat with all the blood boiled out of it. A puddle pooled under his thigh in the dirt and leaf mold. It was hard to tell what color his pants had been under the filth. His jacket and pants were torn. If he'd come to spy on them, he'd had a bad time of it.

Her hand dropped to her side. Her pants were wet with blood. He'd bled on her, and her pants were soaked where he'd pressed against her. He was hurt, maybe bleeding out.

Had a dead man almost crushed her to death?

It was like getting close to an unconscious rattlesnake when she reached down to feel for a pulse in his filthy neck.

CHAPTER 26

Tess reached down to find out if the man in the dirt was dead; he reached up and grabbed her wrist.

"You have to help me." It wasn't a request.

His breath smelled of death and fever. He tried pulling her down to the ground next to him. Even injured he was stronger than she was. She broke his grip by twisting back against his thumb—hapkido—easy for a hundred and ten pound girl to break a big man's thumb or wrist.

She staggered back, kicking up dust, brushing at the blood he'd smeared on her arm. More blood.

"Help you? You were just talking about sending more dead kids our way. Help you? Are you half crazy?"

"I'll tell them," he said, his voice trailing off to a grumbly whisper. "I'll tell them that I couldn't find you. That you made tracks. Headed out. Couldn't find you."

Them. He was talking about blackmail, and she didn't buy it for a minute. He faded out again. What was she supposed to do with him? Maybe Mother Nature would settle the dilemma? She saw his eyes open again. They were fever bright. Was he sick too or just hurt?

"What happened to you?"

Silence greeted her question as the man slipped into unconsciousness. She watched his chest slog along, thumping in a slow, tired beat, refusing to stop.

"Great. Just great."

Beyond the Strandline

Tracking a kid killer had not been in the plan. Parrish and Jamie followed the big man's trail back to the northern edge of the S-Line, just outside the ragged boundary line of Spanish bayonets.

Parrish tried to blame Jamie for being weak, for not being able to walk away clean, but those huge boot prints in the sand had screamed louder than any of Jamie's running commentary. Since they'd walked away from Tess and her sisters, Jamie hadn't been able to let it go or shut up about it. He'd been talking oatmeal and pancakes and people who sat down to eat breakfast together since they'd left the S-Line.

Then they'd found the first boot prints at the edge of the sinkhole clearing: big, heavy, and ominous.

"What if it's that big gorilla with the whip? What if he's the one they've sent after those girls?"

Parrish knew exactly the picture Jamie had in his head. Being a sort of scout for the S-Line, Jamie had seen the comings and goings of the Marketplace muscle. He'd told Parrish before about a big brute of a man covered in hair and sweat, marching a dozen skinny kids at a time out to the latrines. He'd walked them roped together like kindergarteners from hell and kept them focused with a riding crop, the kind you used on horses, if you didn't care much about the horses. Those kids had the look, that blank hopeless expression of slaves. It was a look Parrish knew well.

Nothing to be done for those kids. They were already dead.

Jamie ran through the possibilities. He made it hard for Parrish . . . to think, to stay focused, to stay hard. Maybe, he'd wondered, they could do something for those S-Line folks by tracking down whoever had crossed into their land and stop them before anyone got hurt. Maybe even take the intruder prisoner, giving the S-Line some bargaining power, and then go. Maybe they could . . .

Crouching in the dirt, Parrish traced the boot track with his finger. "It probably is that goon. That's who I'd send to track down one skinny girl."

"Cripes Parrish, aren't you going to let yourself be a little bit torn up about what's going to happen to those . . ." He stopped, fumbling for a way to end the thought. "To that family?"

"Family? Don't you mean *girls*? I thought we'd already established that this was about girls. Isn't that your big worry here? Or interest? You've sniffed out some girls that aren't camp slams or on the receiving end of a bunch of gangbangers, and now you're thinking with your little—"

Jamie hit him.

Returning violence for violence was like breathing for them both. Parrish, his vision blaring red, head butted his friend in return. He slammed the younger man to the ground and punched him in the face.

Jamie countered by smashing his elbow across Parrish's jaw and counterbalancing against his weight. He pushed up with his legs and drove his knee up into Parrish's groin, making him roll away and gag.

Parrish had left himself wide open, too much emotion, too much rage. He was getting weak. Another reason to leave Tess and the rest of them behind; they made him weak. People like that always did. Why couldn't Jamie see it?

When Parrish could finally look up, he realized Jamie was crouching next to him with a Bowie Knife in his hand.

"Hurry up. Stab me. It would . . .probably . . . oh," he choked out, "God . . . be easier." He tried dragging more air into his lungs. "Instead of wishing . . . I was dead. I'd just be able to get it over with." He rolled to his back.

Jamie looked at the knife in his hand, seeming surprised to find it there at all. Parrish watched his friend blink his way back to sanity. It happened that way sometimes; they became single-minded creatures capable of killing friends—even friends.

"You're getting soft, old man. There was a time I'd never have gotten that close to the family jewels."

Jamie laughed, but it wasn't a happy sound. He stood up and sheathed the knife, then crouched next to Parrish in the dirt, his big hands hanging loose and easy.

"What good is it, Parrish, the things we know how to do?" he said. "What good are we? And you . . . what's the matter with you? You're no coward. I know that, but I never took you for a fool."

Parrish grunted. "Shut up, Jamie."

"Those . . . girls . . . that family is going to need our help moving the old man. Even if they do run, someone is going to die."

Parrish brought his hand up to shield his eyes against a sharp, bright shaft of sunlight that stabbed through the canopy. "If they don't run they'll die anyway," Parrish said, trying to crush the sudden memory of Tess in his arms. "She sent us away. She's the boss. We have no authority there or anywhere. She kicked us out, or did you forget?"

"You know why she did that. And the old man? He'd want us to help and you know it."

Parrish answered Jamie with silence. God, would he ever shut up?

"Come on, if this guy finds them . . ." He pointed at the tracks in the sand. "Gets to them and we could have stopped him?" Jamie fell silent, and then said, almost as an after thought, "They have oatmeal for breakfast, Parrish. Pancakes and oatmeal."

Parrish was on his back in a clear patch of sugar sand, surrounded by clumps of saw grass that rattled and rubbed in the breeze. Still early, the sun hadn't brought on the kind of heat that threatened to boil the sweat on their skin.

They should be miles from here, making tracks north, but to what? For what? He tried to remember what the goal had been, but he couldn't. Instead he remembered that he'd tried before, more than once, to keep civilians like Tess and her family alive—tried and failed.

He resisted the urge to reach into his shirt and touch the braid of her hair, the silk of it . . . It was bizarre. The kind of pointless sentiment that got you killed, got others killed.

"I'm going back, with or without you. I'm done running."

"Shut up. God. Just shut up."

Pushing to his feet he turned to Jamie's hunched, miserable figure, and kicked him square in the chest, watched as he toppled over backward. Jamie snorted his disgust.

"Okay. Enough. We'll take care of this guy and give them a little breathing room. Then we head out. Track this guy down. Send him back to the Marketplace with a note pinned to his chest. I'll let you know what and when. I'm still your squad leader."

Parrish watched hope spark in his friend's face.

"You haven't been my squad leader since the Florida-Georgia skirmish."

"Some skirmish. We lost . . . " Parrish watched hope disappear under the twin frown lines between Jamie's eyes, " too many. Forget it. Come on."

Parrish reached down to offer his friend a hand up when the force of the body slamming into his back took him down into a heap on top of Jamie. Arms reached around Parrish from behind to try to get a choke hold on his throat. Jamie grunted and shoved upward, spilling both of the men into the dirt.

There was more grunting and the wet smack of fists hitting a face.

Jamie came up from the ground, rolled, and then dragged Parrish's attacker over backward by his shirt collar.

Parrish rolled free of the wildly flailing man, someone who seemed singlemindedly determined to kill Parrish. Bad move. It was Jamie who smashed the struggling idiot in the face, knocking him back, down, and out. Jerome Fortix crumbled into a bruised mess at their feet.

Jamie's grin was fierce. It was his turn to reach out to pull Parrish to his feet. Parrish swiped at a trickle of blood from the corner of his mouth.

"Thanks," he said, grinning back.

"Oh man, what do we have here?" Jamie said.

They stared down at the unconscious attacker at their feet. Even with his eyes swelling shut and the beginnings of a royal bruise on his jaw, there was no mistaking Jerome. He didn't even twitch as the sun flooded across his face.

"It seems we've captured the crown prince of the Marketplace."

Parrish felt the beginnings of a hesitant optimism lift his mood as sweat began a slow trickle down his back.

CHAPTER 27

KILMER AND TESS tumbled the big man into the wheelbarrow; Kilmer groused every step of the way to the fishing shack.

Since when did Kilmer's job description include wheeling kid killers to a nice, clean cot, he'd wanted to know. The man was probably going to die anyway. He deserved to get rolled into the river next to a gator hole. The man was too heavy to be saved. The man was a Trojan horse and probably had other bad men riding around inside his enormous gut.

Tess let Kilmer grouse. All things considered, his complaints were pretty entertaining.

The fishing shack was empty except for the army cot, the abandoned stack of books, and a footstool. He'd left the books. Parrish and Jamie had been gone for the better part of two days. They'd left the first full day of the influenza epidemic. That's what Gwen called it, how she wrote about it in her journal. Maybe she should mention it to Father so he could write an article about it in his newsletter.

As far as Jamie and Parrish were concerned, she hoped both of them were squatting in poison oak pooping their guts out.

A groan from the wheelbarrow reminded Tess of their newest visitor, except that he was no guest. He was a spy, a scout, and she had him trapped—if he lived. Between the two of them they dragged him onto the stripped-down mattress of the cot.

While Kilmer worked on bolting a boat cleat to the floor, Gwen showed up, looking thin and shaky. Her lovely dark skin still had a dull gray cast to it. But she was walking and talking and steady enough on her feet.

"They said that you'd been attacked." She glanced at the groaning man on Parrish's cot.

She swayed, but fended off Tess's concern with a wave.

"I'm fine," Gwen said. "Well, better. You should get back to the longhouse, I think. Check on things. Get cleaned up. I can watch over this," she said, frowning at the cleat and the length of chain next to it, "prisoner? I guess?"

Gwen had brought clean towels and various potions.

"Does he need sutures?"

"Judging from the blood on my pants, I'm going to say yes."

"Not yours?"

"No. His."

"What happened to him?"

"I don't know, Gwen. We weren't very chatty when he was trying to drag me off into the woods to kill me."

The older woman frowned at Tess's prickly tone. Tess recognized the sound of leftover stress in her own voice.

"Sorry, I'm still feeling spooked. I'm just . . . tired."

It was lame, the apology, taking it out on Gwen. Frightened would have been a better word than tired, but she wasn't ready to admit to that, not yet. She pressed her fingertips to her temples. The adrenaline rush had her feeling hollow and drained and slightly nauseous. Maybe getting back to the longhouse wasn't a bad idea. She watched Gwen organize her equipment.

"No, really. Gwen, I'm sorry. Thank you for this, for coming up here for him."

The sound of chain links banging against the cleat got their attention. The dog's chain was coming in handy.

"Well now, Madame Overseer, you've got yourself your first prisoner of war." Kilmer looked like he'd been sucking on pickles. "Don't let your father find out about this. He would not be happy about you chaining people up. Not with his love-will-find-a-way thinking."

The man on the cot looked too pale to be able to kick a cat, let alone be a threat to them. The chain seemed excessive. His breathing was shallow and quick. His clothes reeked of dried blood and worse. Maybe she was being too paranoid. She took a deep breath, then felt her bruised ribs protest against her moment of compassion.

"For as long as he's here, he stays chained."

Gwen sighed and moved to the side of the unconscious man.

Kilmer finished pulling the chain through the cleat and locked it around one fat ankle with a padlock.

"Thank you, Gwen," Tess said. "It would be good if he didn't die. We're all too tired to dig another hole. And we may need him."

Eyebrows raised, she looked back at Tess, tipped her head and smiled. "Go. I'll do what I can, but his wound and Mother Nature might be the ones deciding what happens here."

She pulled a footstool over and started cutting the man's pants off.

Time to go get another bucket of water and check on the others. Tess's stomach cramped. Probably needed a drink of water and some stew and a chance to sit down for a bit.

Kilmer watched Gwen fuss from the corner of the shack.

"I'll stay and make sure this . . . guy . . . doesn't give anybody any trouble. Her potions can be pretty hard to swallow. Check on Jess T when you get back; he was doing some better, after Gwenny here doctored him up. He should be all spiffed up by now."

Tess caught Gwen's eye roll at Kilmer's nickname for her, a name she protested every chance she got. Tess felt her stomach lurch and then drop. Time to get back. She started the long walk home.

Ally seemed better, ZeeZee a lot better. Both of Gwen's boys were bouncing back like the healthy, growing guts they were and wanted something more to eat than the broth their mother had told Tess to make them drink. They tried to start a battle with Tess over broth verses stew as she hustled between ZeeZee and Jess T's sleeping platform.

"Tessie love, I'm going to make me a spot out by the outhouse and save you the worry over me," Jess T said.

"You look like something that fell out of the back of Goliath. Stay put."

129

Actually, he only looked a little bit more wrinkled up and dried out then usual. He'd lost some flesh from his leathery face, but his blue eyes still twinkled out of a nest of laugh lines. His scalp, usually covered by a battered Stetson cowboy hat, was as bald as an egg and made him look younger somehow—like a big, bald, wrinkled baby. While Kilmer was a big, lanky man with long arms and big hands, Jess T was short and wiry.

"I'm not that bad," he said. "I'm getting out of this stuffy tin can, so let me be."

"Stay where you are and use your chamber pot."

He laughed and then coughed.

"Girl, that's no chamber pot. That's a bucket from the feed room."

It was her turn to laugh.

His face turned serious. "How's the old man? Still holding on?"

"He's not sick, at least not our kind of sick. I've been taking care of him, mostly, and I'm still okay. I feel okay. So maybe we'll be the lucky ones . . ."

"Toughest old bird I've ever known, that Colonel Kennedy. Let us stay, me and Kilmer, when he could have fed us to a world full of wolves eating wolves. I'll always be glad of it."

"Yeah, but if this is some kind of dying declaration, forget it. I need you up and helping with the animals. No one can sniff out a bunch of Sambar fawns like you."

She reached out and patted his hand, trying to ignore the way her head pounded.

"If you want to bunk outside, I don't care. It might be cooler."

"Yeah, maybe later. I'm feeling pretty done in right now. Maybe later after a nap."

"Okay then. Let me know if I can help."

Tess started to feel worse than bad. The chores were suffering. The cooking was certainly suffering. Good thing all she had to do was boil bullion cubes to make broth, but the bread situation was looking shaky. It wasn't that she couldn't make homemade bread. Gwen had made sure everyone knew how to knead a proper ball of dough. Tess's bread just tended to weigh in on the heavy side, and people complained.

She left Jess T snoring while she checked on her grandfather. He would need to be changed and bathed and fed, then his bedding changed and washed. She shook off the ache in her ribs and side and let the fantasy of being able to lay down and be still for five minutes slide through her fuzzy brain.

"Good morning, Grandpa," she murmured as she laid out his razor and warm water. "You'll be happy to know I thumb wrestled a bad guy into submission. You were right, like always. No one can stand to have their thumb broken."

It was a rule that he be shaved every day, because he would have hated not being clean-shaven and looking sharp. He'd always prided himself on looking sharp, crisp, and military. How he must hate what had happened to him. Or was it that she hated him looking worse than he had to and he didn't care at all?

"Time to get ready for the day." She touched his shoulder, too aware that it was like touching bird bones covered in tissue paper.

"Grandpa?"

She started to touch him again and froze, hand hanging in midair, because she knew. There was no point in trying to wake him up. He was gone.

Sometime in the dark and loneliness, sometime when she'd been busy with buckets of water and chaining up spies, he'd left them. And she hadn't even noticed.

She straightened his blanket and pushed at the pillow. The jasmine she'd brought him had slipped to the floor, dried up and wilted. She picked it up and crushed it. She hadn't been there, hadn't been paying attention. Had anyone even checked on him today?

She felt the tears on her cheeks, but hardly knew why they were there. She kissed his forehead and pulled the sheet up over his face . . . and felt . . . relieved.

CHAPTER 28

Kilmer wanted to hitch Goliath to the hay wagon and move the Colonel in style. "Give the old man the dignity he deserved" was his take on it.

She talked him out of it. Goliath was in no mood. What was left of his tail was infected. She'd been pouring as much peroxide on the raw stub as the mule would let her, but without a tail he had no way to keep the flies off and they were driving him mad. She worried about wasting peroxide and getting her head kicked off in the bargain. Wrong to waste it if the mule was just going to up and die anyway. Wrong and stupid.

Grandfather had stockpiled cases of the stuff: peroxide, alcohol, and vinegar. But the peroxide they used for everything: cuts, scrapes, mouthwash, toothpaste, killing mold, bleaching linens. It might be enough to save Goliath, but not in time to save her grandfather the indignity of being carted off to his final resting place in a wheelbarrow.

She made good time getting to the fishing shack and giving Kilmer the news, and then Gwen. She told it in a steady, brave voice—a leader's voice. They promised to tell her father when they saw him, if they saw him. Since the girls were better, he'd started drifting off again, disappearing for longer and longer periods of time, back to his old vagueness, his old bad habits.

The man on the cot hadn't so much as twitched while Tess was there. He looked like a fallen tree trunk wrapped in torn sheets.

She collected the wheelbarrow from the side of the fishing shack and practiced looking stoic and strong and unflappable. Gwen promised to hurry back to the longhouse to help her with Grandfather's remains . . . no, not remains, to help her with her grandfather. Gwen had cried when she made the offer while Tess patted her on the back and made soothing cooing sounds.

Beyond the Strandline

Tess made it as far as the blackberry hedge before she had to stop and swallow the nausea that slammed against the back of her throat. So much for being unflappable. She gulped air and tried to breath her way through the sick feeling.

Hands braced on her knees, she bent at the waist and mumbled a plea to get her through the rest of the walk back to the longhouse. That's what life was now: one more bucket of water, getting through the next half mile, digging one more grave. Worn out, anyone would be. Tess allowed herself a minute to feel sorry for herself.

The wave of sickness gave way to tears. Her grandfather was gone. He'd been gone for months and months, but now it was real. She'd have to decide where they were going to dig a hole for the man who'd saved them all. And it was going to be Tess that got them all killed because she hadn't thought ahead and stopped Ally or knew how to outsmart the savages that lived in that ruined mall.

The tears were dripping off her chin when the man grabbed her. He had her pinned in his arms before she could yell. He'd come up on her from behind, surprised her, and dragged her off balance. She back kicked and missed. The man bear hugged her and then flipped her around to face him.

Like this morning, just like this morning, she thought, except this time it wasn't a stranger who had his hands on her. It was Parrish looking like he'd swallowed bees.

"He's here isn't he? What are you thinking? We tracked that butcher back here from what's left of Van Arsdale."

He pushed her a half a step back and held her by the shoulders, his fingers digging into her arms. His hands were hot as he pulled her close again.

"Don't you know who you've got? Where is he, anyway?"

"Let go of me. What were you thinking, sneaking up on me like that? Yeah," she gasped. "I know exactly who. He attacked me at the well. Knocked me flat. He's chained up, for your information."

"Where?" He gave her a little shake for emphasis. "I snuck up on you because I've seen the way you can throw that tomahawk of yours. I wasn't interested in getting scalped."

She shrugged his backhanded compliment away. "Your place. He's chained in the shack. It's the only place we've got to hold a prisoner."

"You put him in the fishing shack with Gwen no doubt," he said, the words strung out, hooks on a fishing line, sharp and barbed. He looked more scruffy than usual, all geared up and carrying everything he owned in his pack. His shirt was loose at the neck, ringed with dirt, and she could see the veins in his neck screaming with blood.

"He's chained up. We're not idiots. Where is Jamie?"

The bushes rattled and shook next to them as Jamie pushed through a hedge of scrub oak, dragging a bedraggled Jerome Fortix in front of him.

"What are you doing? What's he doing here?"

The corner of Parrish's mouth twitched.

"Apparently we've got another prisoner for your fishing shack jail. We found him when he rammed himself into my back. Said he and the gorilla guy got separated when a big hog came at them. Said they'd teamed up at some point. Surprisingly not real forth coming. My guess is they've been stumbling around lost."

"I don't want him. Take him back. I'm fresh out of dog chain."

"No can do," Jamie said. "Parrish says we need him."

"Then you keep him." Lightheaded, she blinked at Jamie, who quivered and shimmied in front of her. She blinked again, harder. The light cut like a razor into her eyes.

"We got the guy. We'll handle it. Ease on down soldier," Parrish said. This time Parrish made sure she looked at him, shaking her a little. Not too hard, but still. It didn't help her rolling stomach at all. She gave him her best glare.

"Get your hands off of me. I've already wrestled one goon in the mud today."

"I won't, Tess. That man is their hangman, their executioner. Are you crazy?"

"And he's pretty handy with a branding iron. I'm sure Jerome knows all about that," Jamie said. The knuckles of his hand on Jerome's shirt collar glared white with strain.

Beyond the Strandline

She struggled to focus on Parrish's face. Green eyes. His eyes were green, ringed with gold. They made her think of deer moss in the forest when the sunlight hit it. It hurt her head to look at him. He smelled like the woods and sunlight.

"Maybe, but right now he's," she said, stopping to swallow down bile, "chained to a floor, which makes him a bargaining chip. My bargaining chip."

"A what?"

"We can't leave. We can't leave the S-Line."

"Jamie, I told you it was useless. No. Worse than that, they're hopeless."

Parrish nodded to Jamie, who peeled off and headed in the direction of the fishing shack, dragging Jerome in tow.

She felt hot and tired enough to crawl under a blackberry bramble to sleep.

"You needed to go, Tess. Why didn't you go?"

"Couldn't. They were sick. All sick."

She wondered what was under all that scruffiness on his face. Tell him; tell him about ZeeZee and Jess T and the wheelbarrow for a dead grandfather.

"They got the flu."

"Tess, what makes you think you can hold onto the S-Line? You can't." He paused, noticing the abandoned wheelbarrow for the first time. "What are you doing out here pushing an empty wheelbarrow?"

He relaxed his grip. She shrugged again, enjoying the weight of his hands on her shoulders. It was like being held or even hugged—kind of. Comforting. Except he'd called her hopeless and he'd left and run away and hadn't been there for any of them, especially not her grandfather. She tried to find the energy to get angry.

"I have to. I have to get the wheelbarrow back for . . ."

But she wasn't going to tell him and have him feel pity for them, not after he'd run away.

"You left us. Why are you back here, anyway?" She sounded like a five-year-old. "You ran away. What made you come back?"

He frowned down at her. He looked uncertain for a moment.

"Jamie." He said it like it was the answer to all of life's questions. "He caught the man's trail. It was Jamie. He's the worrying sort. He wanted to track the man and now we're here. He needed to see that you all were alright."

"Jamie needed to see if we were okay, because Jamie's a prince. But not you. What does that make you?" She let her head fall forward so she wouldn't be blinded by his sparkly green eyes.

He tipped her head up with a finger under her chin. This time his frown was followed by a narrow, searching glare.

"What's the matter with you?" And then he did a silly thing. He touched her forehead with the back of his hand. The way her mom used to when Tess was little.

She felt the prick of tears again, bent over at the waist, and threw up on his boots.

CHAPTER 29

THERE WASN'T ANYTHING left in her stomach to throw up. But it wouldn't stop.

Maybe they'd be digging her grave next to the one they'd dug for her grandfather. Hadn't they buried him without her? Sure. They had to because they couldn't wait. Right? Too hot, the weather, like her forehead, her body, every bit of her. Her hair hurt. Dying wasn't the worst thing ever.

They were all going to die anyway. Better to get it over with.

"Don't cry, Tess. It'll be okay. You need to help me plan a birthday party for the girls. I've found my old crazy cake recipe, but I'll need help." Gwen's voice, soft and steady, slid into her mind the way the wet washcloth slid across her forehead. "Shhhh, sweet girl. I've got something that will help. Try to drink this."

Tess tasted mint and something sweet and elderberries and promptly threw it up. Someone held a bowl for her, but she was too weak to care who it might be.

"Jamie, when you can, take these towels outside and dump them into the big cook pot. Get the boys to watch them boil. Five minutes, remind them. Have them use the windup timer."

Why was Gwen talking to that Jamie guy? He and that idiot Parrish were cowards, runaway cowards. No one should talk to them. Hadn't they left everyone to die? They made her so angry, both of them. Even if that Parrish person did help her get Ally back.

"Ally? Are you all right? I'm not mad at you. Promise. ZeeZee tell her . . . I'm not mad."

Someone murmured low in her ear, "Hush. Hush now. They're fine. They know. Gwen, what else . . . ?" The voice trailed away.

Worried. She heard worry and something else. It was so annoying. *Leave me alone,* she thought, wanting to bat the whisperer away, but it was too much trouble to lift her hand.

Later, Gwen was back, bothering her.

"Tess, hush and drink this. The girls are better. Everyone's better. We're through the worst of it except for you."

First Gwen's voice and then the slow slide of the washcloth over her forehead.

"So you need to try and drink this."

"No, no don't make me. I'll be sick. I can't."

Desperation made her thrash weakly against Gwen's hands.

"Please, don't." The sheets were clammy and wet as she twisted away from the cup at her mouth.

"Help me. Hold her so she doesn't spill that tea."

Arms came around her, lifting her up from the damp mattress. She felt a body slide behind her shoulders, bracing her upright. She thought about trying to fight against the arms holding her, but there wasn't anything left to fight with. She gave in to the exhaustion.

The cool slide of the cloth made it almost bearable. She wanted to say thank you. Tomorrow. She would talk, tomorrow.

When the cup touched her lips again she frowned and moaned, but a voice in her ear said, "Drink it down, soldier, or there will be laps to run and latrine duty."

It was what her grandfather had always told them when they didn't want to do something. Not something Father said. Or Mother. This time she tasted honey and lemon and something metallic.

"Grandpa?" she said. "I want my grandpa here. I want him."

"Hush. Just drink now." It really was a nice voice. Strong. "Do what Gwen tells you. And stop trying to fight everyone. You're about as strong as a kitten."

A kitten? She wanted to make a fist, defend herself. Her hand felt too heavy, and her head was still full of rocks.

"I can't lift my fingers, but Goliath and the goats that need . . . something, can't remember . . . and bread. And they're coming because I messed up. And Ally's poor face . . ."

The world faded and narrowed and became the sound of that voice whispering in her ear off and on again.

"Tess, I'm sorry. I should never . . . have . . . gone. Tess, please." The whisper stopped. Someone turned the washcloth over, blissful cool replaced damp heat. "Just sleep. The rest will wait."

Rest. It was permission to rest. She took it.

Then it was Gwen's voice again, not as close, from across the room maybe, sounding serious, a little stern.

Silly Gwen to worry. That was Tess's job.

"We've got to stop the cycle of vomiting. I've given her a mild sedative but you'll have to hold her upright. If she gets sick and chokes . . . I don't know what else to do. She's already so dehydrated and without IV fluids . . ."

The arms holding her tightened just a bit. It felt nice, so nice. She let go again, drifted, and imagined the faint touch of someone's lips against her ear, someone kissing her ear. Such a little kiss.

Sighing, she slept.

The bones of her face had always cast fascinating shadows and hollows that reminded Parrish of the elegant sculptures he'd seen when they'd gone on a school field trip to the Orlando Museum of Art. Now the art was her face. She'd lost so much weight in the two days since she'd thrown up on his boots, he was afraid.

He'd seen it before, over and over. How many times? The fevers and sicknesses that were as deadly as the bullets and machetes. Kids who were strong and kicking one day, down to skin and bones the next, and without antibiotics or IVs . . .

But that wasn't going to happen to her. If he had to sit with her in his arms for the next month, he was not going to let it happen to her. Once she could keep something down, she'd be fine. He'd seen that too, the kids they'd been ready to dig holes for and throw dirt on, getting better in a matter of hours, hungry and whining for something to eat.

Jamie came in and out of the longhouse, fetching and carrying for Gwen. Every time he did he'd shoot Parrish one of his silly, crooked smiles—half sympathy, half speculation. There were questions in Jamie's eyes that he never seemed to get up the nerve to ask, which was a relief. Parrish didn't know what he'd say if Jamie did ask about his need to be by her side, to watch over her.

Somehow, Tess had become the central puzzle of his life.

Maybe it had been the sight of her pushing that wheelbarrow so she could bury her grandfather in a decent grave. Maybe.

Or maybe it was the look in her eyes when she'd called Jamie a prince and asked, "What does that make you, Parrish?" Or maybe it went all the way back to the moment when she'd hacked off her hair so that she'd be harder to drag off of a mule by her ponytail.

One thing was sure; he'd tried hard not to want this.

The longhouse had emptied out some. Kilmer was busy "guarding the spy." Kilmer's words. The spy who had managed to stay alive in spite of blood loss and a seven-inch gouge in his thigh from a boar's tusk.

Jess T had rolled to his feet as soon as he could, and with Jamie's help dragged his mattress "outside in the freshness." Jess T's words.

Gwen's boys were still hollow eyed, but they were back to being as helpful as they ever were. Gwen kept them busy with catch up work and staying out of Parrish's way.

Tess's father still fussed over the twins once in a while, but even they were able to take walks to the solar shower and do light chores. It left the longhouse empty and quiet for long blocks of time, private like. It gave Parrish time to look at her and listen to her breathe.

Whatever Gwen had given her that last time, it had stopped the worst of the vomiting, sending her finally into a hard, drugged sleep that left her quiet and still.

He tried not to let it frighten him, her stillness. He reached out and traced the curve of her cheek, fighting the terror in his head.

No one had died this time. But they did. They died all the time.

Her father had come once or twice to check on her, fumbling with her blankets or rearranging her nightstand, not saying much of anything. Ally and ZeeZee he could talk to or talk about, but not Tess. With Tess, Jon Lane slipped in and then away like a ghost, hardly looking at her. Around her he seemed like a man drowning in his own guilt. Parrish knew the look: survivor's guilt, survivor's pain.

Maybe that was it, the way her own father seemed afraid to be around her.

Or maybe it was that being there to hold her in his arms felt like the first brave thing he'd done in a very long time.

CHAPTER 30

ALONE. THEY'D LEFT her alone. Tess could feel the weight of the quilt on her chest; it was too heavy for her ribs. It was crushing her. And they'd left her alone. A smell of mint drifted on the hot, heavy darkness inside the longhouse. Gwen's mint tea for tummy aches. Tess's stomach didn't ache; it felt ripped in two.

A tear slipped from the corner of her eye, across her temple, and down into her hair. Her too short, too fuzzy, chopped-off hair. She sniffed and waited for the next tear to fall. It was late, judging from the yipping of a coyote pack somewhere beyond the river. Inside the longhouse there was a hard, frozen silence.

"Tess, don't."

His breath floated against her cheek—more mint. He'd been drinking mint tea and sitting in the dark next to her.

"Parrish?" Her voice sounded like flaking rust.

"Hmmmm? I'm here."

She tried to remember what she wanted to ask him, but her brain was leaking out of her head with her tears.

"Tea. You've been drinking mint tea."

"Uh huh, do you want some? Do you feel up to having something to drink?"

A tiny light blinked awake next to her—a candle, too small to bother anyone else, bright enough to spark a reflection in his eyes. He was there. Really there.

"Is everyone still sick?" She tried to lift her head.

"Stop. Tomorrow. Worry tomorrow. Just rest. I'll get you something to drink. You need to drink."

Tess let her muscles go limp. It wasn't hard.

"How long?"

She heard her grandmother's cup rattle against the saucer. There weren't many pieces left from the set of china, but Gwen still insisted on using the remnants.

"Three days. Here, drink." He helped her sit up enough to try a sip. His arm came around her to push her up, a solid comfort at her back.

She drank the tea and sighed, remembering. Instead of letting her go, he fussed with her blanket. His face was filled with shadows and darkness in the low light. His mouth tipped up at the corners, strong and full and gorgeous. She hadn't noticed before.

"You know what?"

"What? You sound terrible. Maybe you should be quiet now?"

"No," she said, and cleared her throat. "You're kind of pretty for a boy, except for the moss all over your face."

She felt his arm stiffen behind her.

"Be quiet. You're still delirious, obviously."

He gave her a little shoulder pat, but instead of moving his hand away he left it there, brushing the sleeve of her top.

"No, if I were delirious I'd tell you that I wished you had a terminal case of diarrhea."

"You need to sleep."

She could hear the laughter in his voice.

"Tell me," she said, hesitating, not wanting to sound needy and silly, "I mean . . .You're here. I didn't think you would be."

Expectant and lonely, quiet swirled through the longhouse. She reached for his hand. Dizziness washed over her when he slipped his fingers through hers, bringing their palms together.

"Parrish?" Her voice cracked.

"I'm here. I'm staying." He said it so softly that she had to turn her head to hear him. He brushed her hair back from her face.

It was enough. She sank into his arms, into a drugged feeling of content. Tomorrow, she'd worry tomorrow since he would be here.

Almost asleep, she thought she heard him say something else:
"I can't seem to find a way to leave you."

Dust swirled in lazy marshmallow clouds in the storage shed. It filmed every can, box, and barrel. Tess sighed when she saw how out of control their long-term storage had gotten.

"Maybe they'll forget about us," ZeeZee said, sounding as chirpy as a finch from deep inside the gloomy shed.

Tess glanced at Parrish and was surprised to see him smile at her sister's wishful thinking. It was the first time since she'd been able to sit up and eat some soup that he'd come around. She suspected he was worried she'd overdo.

"Maybe," he said, as he dragged another crate down from one of the highest storage shelves. Tess opened another dust-caked box to discover Epsom salts—more Epsom salts. She started to laugh. Parrish studied her with a puzzled smile.

"Well, it seems Grandpa was determined that we'd never get constipated or die from having a splinter."

She held up the bag to show ZeeZee, who'd popped out from behind a pile of folded Levi's to find out what Tess was laughing at, a can of dehydrated corn in her hands.

"That's what you took with you to the Marketplace, I remember . . ."

ZeeZee's cheerful voice faded away when she saw Ally standing in the sunlight of the open door of the shed. She stood there stoically, her hand on a stack of mystery cans with strange notations like PFin-Can#29 in Grandfather's scrawling handwriting.

Ally shook her head, reassuring her twin.

"It's okay, Zeez. It was real, and it happened, and I'm not going to fall to pieces about it anymore."

Both girls still had dark circles under their eyes and a thin, transparent look to them since they'd recovered from the flu. But mostly they were back to their fairy-haired selves, except that Ally kept her hair down now, letting it curve over the worst of the mark on her face. ZeeZee still treated her twin like an ornament made of spun glass. It would take time, regardless of Ally's brave words.

Hopefully, they'd have enough time.

Tess looked over at Parrish who worked with his sleeves rolled to his elbows, hair tied back, and a frown line between his eyes that told her he was focused on his goal: finding more ammunition and weapons.

"Well at least I got a tin of lip balm out of that trade—homemade. Honey. Yummy."

Ally ducked her head, but not before Tess saw the shadow of a quick smile. Something in her chest broke free, seeing that smile.

"This can't be all of the ammunition," Parrish said, brushing the worst of the dust off his cargo pants. Tess noticed there were frayed holes in both knees. Did he know how to patch them? Sure, of course, he did. He'd been on his own a long time. She felt a pang of guilt, knowing that he'd been distracted lately—filling in around the ranch, worrying about their situation.

"There's ammo for the gun you left at the mall and shells for the shotgun. Some ammo for the hunting rifles. That's it. I found the re-loader, but without the raw materials to fill the shells. I know there's got to be a cache. Buried maybe. He would have thought of that. Known how to do it right, so the weapons and ammo would be protected."

"Grandpa must have thought we'd never need them. He never told me."

Parrish looked skeptical. "He knew. He just ran out of time."

"Maybe Dad would know, Tess?" Ally said. It was the most chatty she'd been in a long time. Parrish had been right to put her sisters to work this way.

"Any clue what's in those?" He looked at Tess and pointed to a shelf full of cans that were missing their labels.

"Could be anything. We'll have to open them up." She thought about it for a minute. "There might have been a notebook with the abbreviations he used. I want to say that I've seen a notebook. I'll look for it," Tess said.

"Why don't you girls open a couple of these mystery cans while I help Tess out?"

The girls couldn't help but spark to the idea of uncovering some hidden treasure tucked away in the stash of food storage. Waving a can opener, they went to work on their first can and started peeling back the lid.

Tess and Parrish left the girls with their assignment.

"Over here. He kept a lot of records and notes in this footlocker by the door. Maybe in here."

The footlocker was padlocked, reminding Tess that while her grandfather had been a careful prepper, he'd always been a little paranoid about his preparations. Probably why she didn't know where he'd stockpiled the weapons.

Can't tell what you don't know, Tess.

It made her feel better to be able to still hear his voice in her head.

"Hang on. I know where the key is." She hustled by the twins who were laughing at opening a can full of Q-tips wrapped in plastic.

"Get those to Gwen. I'll bet she'll be glad to know we still have some."

They started in on another can while Tess rattled a bundle of keys off of a nail.

"We've tried not to use the long-term storage if we could help it. In case of, well, an emergency. That's pretty funny when you think about it. Anyway, fresh is best, but I'm worried this stuff is going to start going bad, if it hasn't already."

Kneeling, she fumbled the key into the padlock. Parrish knelt beside her and helped her pry back the lid. Papers, documents, birth certificates, some photographs, and she pounced. The record book.

"We haven't kept up with the inventory the way he would have. See this column: how many cans stockpiled. Then this column: how much or how many we've used."

He pulled the book from her hand. She tried to ignore the way his fingers slid over hers. Silly. She was being so silly. But every time he touched her—by accident, in passing, when she'd been so sick—something inside her tilted and sang, a thrill of expectation. Ridiculous. He'd barely spoken to her lately.

She felt that thrill because he'd decided to stay, to help, and she was able to feel the noose around her neck loosen, just a bit. That's all it was. Silly, stupid girl, she was getting as bad as her sisters. She needed Jamie and

Beyond the Strandline

Parrish—that's all. There was no fantasy of Amazon girl power now. The S-Line needed everyone they could beg, borrow, or kidnap.

She'd let herself get lost in thinking teenaged girl stuff for a moment and hadn't noticed that he'd gotten quiet too. He held a photograph in his hand, turned it so she could see.

Ally and ZeeZee laughing on the porch of the old ranch house, in dress-up clothes from their grandmother's closet: feathers and hats and high heels. Tess was sitting on the top step in her pink overalls, a book in her lap, prickly because Mother had asked her to look up from her reading.

Behind the back shelves, the twins giggled over something they'd discovered. The photograph reminded her that laughing and giggling had been easy once, automatic.

Looking up from the picture she discovered his eyes on her, eyebrows arched, a soft smile on his face. She pulled the picture out of his hand.

"What? We were snappy dressers." She studied her sisters' faces in the snapshot. They were so little. "Happy. Do you remember happy?"

"You think I don't remember," he said. "I remember. I just try not to."

She wanted to ask him about his memories, about the good times, the fun, the people, about why he would want to block that out. Mostly she wanted to ask him why, why he was here, and why he'd decided to stay.

It was his turn to study the picture. "Why weren't you dressed up?"

"Oh, much too old and mature for any of that nonsense. I wanted to, but I was trying to be so grown-up. I thought the twins were silly, but now I realize that I was the real pain. That's what I remember. What a putz I could be back . . . before."

Sighing, he said, "Sure I remember. I ran track and liked this cheerleader, Brittany something. The cheerleaders used to wear their uniforms on game days, and I'd follow her to class, too afraid to ask her out. That made me a goof. You might have been a pain, but I was a goof. Yeah, I remember." He looked past her now into some distant memory.

Tess reached out and touched the sleeve of his shirt.

"Maybe we'll figure it out, how to be happy like that again? Could happen, right?"

She watched his smile turn to a crooked smirk.

"My mom took this picture of us. I think she was disappointed in me for not joining in," she said, shrugging. And there it was again, the ambush of endless, aching loss—and she understood why he'd want to hide it all away.

It must have shown in her face, the pain of it, because he reached out and put his fingertips on her cheek. He leaned closer.

"Tess, I remember."

Then he used both hands to cradle her face, and inside her the thrill became a song. He studied her face in that careful, steady way of his, his eyes falling to her lips.

She wanted to say that she believed him, trusted him, needed him, and that she was grateful. But no matter how many words she used it would never be enough to say what she felt, what was eating her up inside.

Instead she leaned the short distance between them and pressed her mouth to his. Impulse and gratitude and the singing in her veins made her do it. She half expected him to push her away.

There must have been something singing in him too, because his hands moved over her face, his fingers pushing through the tangle of her curls to the back of her head. He pulled her closer.

CHAPTER 31

Kneeling in the dirt and dust and jumble inside the shed, he slanted his mouth to match her beautiful, generous, too soft mouth. She kept her lips closed and pressed hard against his. He could tell that this was something new, something foreign to her. Her innocence ran through him like an unexpected jolt of electricity.

Stop her. Stop this. Make her understand. The words sprang into his head, an explosion of warning. He should never have started this, should never have let her start this. Never.

He lightly pushed her away. He watched his rejection hurt her, embarrass her.

"You are like a dream to me," he said, whispering and wishing he was anywhere but here in the dirt and dust with her. Wasn't this what he'd tried to avoid? "A dream I wish I could stop having."

He watched the confusion skitter across her face, and then the wall came down between them. Her backbone stiffened.

Good, he thought and then tried to convince himself that he meant it.

In a heartbeat, she'd turned as prickly as that girl in the photograph wearing pink overalls with a book in her lap. How could he tell her that she'd been in his dreams, haunting him, tormenting him . . . and that he wanted . . . what?

He frowned.

"Some dream," she snapped.

"I didn't say it was a good one." He knew she would take it wrong. How could she not? "Tess, I don't want you to think that . . . well, I'm not boyfriend material."

Confusion turned to anger, flashing in her eyes like gray rain clouds; she dropped her head as a flush stained her still too-thin face.

"Tess, I'm sorry. It isn't that I don't . . . want . . . something more, but I can't want it."

She flinched when he lifted his hand to reach for her again.

"Tess, you can't understand . . ." he started. "You don't know." He let his hand drop.

She cut him off. "Don't tell me that. Don't tell me what I can or can't understand." She dropped her eyes. "Leave it alone. I shouldn't . . . I just wanted you to know . . . Oh, forget it. I'm making it worse. Just drop it."

He wanted to say that she dazzled him. That he thought about her constantly. That when he'd run, he'd been running from her and when he'd come back, he'd come back to her, for her, to be near her and not just for stolen kisses in a barn.

Maybe, if things had been different for him before he'd met her, maybe if he were different.

Something crashed against the metal shelves where the twins worked. More giggling echoed and bounced against the heavy insulated walls.

"Okay. We'll forget it," he said and then cleared his throat, changed the subject. "Having our hands on Jerome is a stroke of luck. You may not think so now, but—"

"Be quiet. Ally still doesn't know that he's here at the S-Line. That we have him," she hissed out.

"What? You need to tell her before she finds out by accident, and it feels like we tricked her," he said, echoing her whisper. They sat in silence, glaring at each other.

It took a minute for the unmistakable sounds of someone throwing up to register through their anger.

Tess was on her feet before the gagging sound had a chance to stop.

"Oh no. Not again."

She disappeared in the dark behind the rows of shelves. He could hear the worry in her voice and ZeeZee's sudden cry.

Beyond the Strandline

He waited, listening to the back and forth and finally Ally's muttered reassurance, and then he went to Tess and her sisters.

Tess still held Ally's hair back from the girl's ashen face.

"I don't know what happened. We were having fun opening the cans and then we opened this one. It's just spice—lemon pepper. It smells good to me," ZeeZee said.

Wiping the back of her hand across her mouth, Ally took a deep, shuddering breath and dry heaved.

"Close up the can, ZeeZee. It's the smell. It's bothering your sister," he said.

ZeeZee pulled a loose plastic lid from the ground and snapped it over the can.

"I don't know what's wrong with me. Is it the flu again?"

All three of them turned their worried eyes to him. He shook his head and watched realization flood into Tess's gray eyes, followed by fear.

Parrish reached down and took the Number 10 can of spice out of ZeeZee's hand and pushed it back onto the shelf.

Squatting next to Ally, he brushed her hair back, away from the brand. Her skin had gone from gray to a faint green. The brand blazed like a wretched signpost.

"Ally, is this the only time something you smelled made you sick?"

ZeeZee looked confused when Ally started to cry.

He watched Tess's face crumble as fear and pain for Ally settled into the stiff set of her shoulders.

"You can't know. It's too soon," Tess said. But her voice was bleak. It came out clipped—half question, half demand. "How can you know?"

"Tess, it's not the first time I've seen someone with morning sickness."

Parrish reached out and put his hand on Ally's head, brushed a strand back from her face.

She looked up at him.

"Ally, I think it's time you told us everything that happened to you at the Marketplace."

CHAPTER 32

OUTSIDE THE STORAGE shed, Parrish waited for Ally to speak while the twins situated themselves side by side on the lip of an old tire. Tess plopped down on the grass in front of them, legs crossed. She pulled bits of Saint Augustine grass free, peeling the blades apart before throwing them over her shoulder.

The story spilled out of Ally like pus from a boil. To her credit, she didn't waste time wishing it could all be different and chewing on the "if onlys." It was what it was, and she told it that way.

She described how wild and itchy and resentful of the rules and restrictions of the S-Line she'd been, admitting she couldn't remember which rules she'd objected to the most. She had been a naïve, rebellious teenager and had gone to see the Marketplace to show her family and everyone else that she could.

What she'd been was a normal fourteen-year-old kid.

No one from the ranch had shown her the way through the hedge of bayonets. It had been a girl called Newt, who'd been with a girl named Blink, two of the Doe Kids from the camp. On one of Ally's tantrum hikes she'd come upon the two girls, swimming naked in the river, a couple of skinny-dipping intruders.

It had been like seeing dinosaur babies in the woods. But then Newt and Blink had smiled at her, and they'd become kids; younger and wilder than her, but just kids. Once you got past the nest of snarls they called hair and the patchwork of scraps they wore for clothes, Newt and Blink were just two girls. They'd shown her the way along the river and out through the slough.

After that, most of her tantrums had been faked. Excuses to meet up with the Doe girls at the old train trestle, skinny-dip, and hear about life beyond the S-Line. Even ZeeZee hadn't known about their meeting place or Ally's plan to go to the Marketplace until she'd left. It had taken her months to get up the nerve, and then she'd gone.

Parrish realized that it made sense now. Why the Doe Kids had rescued Ally, risking the wrath of the Fortixes. Kids making friends; that had been all there was to it. And it had gotten one of those kids killed, so far. They'd be lucky if it stopped at only one.

"The Fort . . ." She hesitated, brushing at her scarred cheek with her fingertips, and then said, "Those people at the Marketplace are always bothering the camp, but the Doe Kids keep watch and fade away into the woods like squirrels. They never catch them. Well, mostly they don't."

A shadow passed across her face and they all thought about a little grave down by the river.

"Right? They almost never catch them," Tess prompted.

"Yes, and they didn't catch me," she said, for the first time sounding confident. "They didn't have to. I just walked right into their arms. They told me not to go, the Doe Kids did, but I kept right on walking into . . ."

She wrapped her arms across her chest, clutching at herself.

No one said anything for a while, and the bird noises in the bushes got louder and closer. Little skittering movements followed by tentative chirps and whistles filling the void of awkward silence.

"He remembers you, Tess. That Jerome Fortix. He remembered all of us. From before. From Sunday school. Grandma's class. Still, he was surprised to see me. And then they all started asking me questions: Where did I come from? Where was I living? Where were you? How many men were with us?"

She looked up at the sky and then stood up. ZeeZee made a move to stand too, but Ally shook her head.

"I knew right off it was no game and that there wasn't a fountain, and there wasn't going to be one. I didn't tell them anything, Tess. I wouldn't."

Parrish watched Tess's face, gauging if he should step in yet or not. But she kept her eyes on her hands and the mindless work of ripping and tearing going on in her lap.

"And then his mother was telling me that she was a midwife and needed to examine me. That pig, Jerome, told her that he wanted me, to keep me, like some kind of pet or something, and if I didn't shut up and agree, they'd sell me on the coast to pirates. That's what he said, 'pirates.'" She snorted. "Can you believe that?"

The shadow of a Red-tailed hawk marked her face for a moment, then passed.

The tears started then. First Ally, and then ZeeZee. Parrish saw the moment ZeeZee understood that Ally's world would never be the same; ZeeZee shivered in the heat and sun and then folded her arms tight against her body as she cried, the way Ally had hugged herself. It made them seem so alike that gesture.

"But I wouldn't tell." Ally stopped and gulped air. "I mean the F can stand for a lot of things, right?"

Tess looked up at her sister, dry-eyed.

"Yeah, it can."

"So I didn't tell and that's when . . . when . . . he . . . Tess, he thinks we're married. They all stood around and watched when they burned my face and then his father mumbled a bunch of nonsense."

Parrish felt an old familiar despair. Living in a world where everyone made up their own rules, well . . . there was no sense to it, no rhyme, no reason. He'd seen it drive people crazy.

"They stuffed a rag in my mouth so I wouldn't yell. They said we were married. They let him . . . do things to me. They said it was okay. They told me it was okay, but it wasn't."

Tess pushed to her feet then and gathered the softly weeping girls into her arms. "Ally, F can stand for a lot of things." Holding them tighter, she whispered, "I know, Sweetie. I should have told you, stopped you, done something—"

But Ally wouldn't let her finish. "No, even if you had I wouldn't have believed you, and I was so determined . . ."

She couldn't finish.

It was ZeeZee who finished the sentence, a new hint of steel in her voice.

"And now there's going to be a baby. And we're going to love your baby and protect it and keep it."

Tess hugged them tighter. They buried their wet cheeks into her chest.

Parrish watched the fierceness of Tess's love sweep across her face.

Ally looked at Parrish with weary, grown-up eyes. Still thin from the flu and now morning sickness, with her long fall of corn-silk hair, she made him think of Christmas ornaments: angels and stars and silver tinsel.

"Thank you for helping Tess," Ally said to him.

"Ally, try to remember everything that you can. It's important that you think about everything you did say, that Jerome might have said. We need to know," Parrish replied.

He tried to be understanding and, what was the word? Empathetic? Yeah, time for empathy. But they needed to understand there wasn't time for much of that, not with Jerome and the big man chained to the floor in a shack next to the river.

"Jeez, Parrish, let it be for now." Tess turned her stormy gray eyes on him.

Ally stepped back and brushed Tess's arm.

"No, Tess, he's right. He needs to know. We all need to know where we stand." She turned toward him, standing straighter, not as tall as her older sister but straight, shoulders squared. "Nothing. I told him nothing and it made him angry but not so angry that he wanted me gone. He'd decided to keep me. There were girls there when I first got there that disappeared, just gone. So if you hadn't come for me the F would still stand for Fortix."

"Okay, but Tess and Parrish did come for you and you're back. They got you back." ZeeZee looked at each of them in turn, a dare in her eyes. "And I know what the F stands for, okay? It stands for *family*. Ours. And that's the end of it."

CHAPTER 33

TESS TOOK FLOWERS to her grandfather's grave; it was just some lantana she'd found near the barn after she'd finished the morning milking. Lantana was nothing but weeds, but she'd always loved the tiny clusters of multicolored blooms, small enough to go into her dollhouse in tiny vases. They didn't smell pretty, but they were bright and cheerful; the butterflies loved them.

Kneeling, she took her time arranging the bouquet.

She mixed them with maidenhair fern that grew near the deep well, planted there by her grandmother twenty years before. The mix of flowers and fern made her think of them both. Her grandmother was buried in the civilized cemetery in Oviedo, now a looted ruin, and her grandfather was buried here, in a place only the family would recognize as his.

The smell of lantana clung to her hand, sharp and bitter, a reminder that there was poison in some plants—even ones with pretty flowers. And people, there was poison in some people.

Now the poison was at the S-Line and the man they'd always counted on to keep them out of it, Colonel Kennedy, was dead and buried, all while Tess had thrashed and burned with the flu, another kind of poison.

She couldn't say when she realized that Parrish was there, watching her. It was unnerving the way he moved through the woods, never making a sound, like the animals he hunted. She didn't bother turning around to make sure. She knew.

"You shouldn't be out here alone now. You know that," he said.

That's what he had to say? He was going to be a nag after what she'd found out about Ally and Jerome and the rest of it? And now Jerome was here unbeknownst to Ally; locked up in the fishing shack with the other one, the spy. What was she supposed to do with them? She needed to think.

"Right. The buddy system. Check. I'll get right on that." She watched the slow drift of water and the skitter of a water bug marring the surface of the Little Big Econ River.

"I'm sorry, Tess."

She shrugged, trying to stay indifferent to the flutter in her stomach, the way her hands had that annoying tendency to tremble at the sound of his voice.

"Sorry? About what? The buddy system is smart."

"No, not that. Sorry for your grandfather, because we couldn't wait for you to get well. Your father, he made a nice speech of it. That's what Jamie said. I stayed with you."

She felt him close the distance between them to come and stand behind her next to the grave.

She smiled, reaching to adjust the lantana on the mound covering her grandfather. She looked at the smaller mound next to it, where they'd buried the little girl. She should remember to ask Ally if she knew the kid's name, and then she'd bring flowers for her too.

"Yeah, my father is all about words, but words aren't going to be enough are they?"

When she turned, she was shocked to see him clean-shaven. His cheekbones were high sculpted lines in his lean face. His mouth was fuller than she'd realized and his jaw harder. She could see why the twins were always going on about the mysterious Richmond Parrish.

"What happened to you?"

He reached up and touched his bare face. He smiled a charming lop-sided grin. "The girls found a Number 10 can of safety razors. It's been awhile."

"Too bad they didn't happen to open a can of shoulder-fired grenade launchers while they were at it."

He chuckled. "None of those," he said, holding out his hand. "Can I talk to you about something?"

She reached up and let him pull her to her feet. He gestured to the curve of one of the live oak limbs that dipped next to the trail in an elegant looping curve.

"Come on. Sit."

Frowning, she shook her head. "I need to get back. I shouldn't." Two could play at the "keeping my distance" game.

"Please."

She sat, feet in the leaf mold. He sat next to her, close, slipping into the curve of the branch; it was hard to keep a "friendly" distance from each other on the makeshift bench. They had to sit hip to hip.

"This thing with Ally . . ." he said, letting the sentence trail off.

Tess kicked at the litter of fallen leaves under their feet. She gave it to him like a report: "Gwen mentioned trying to abort the baby, but in her opinion, that would be worse than letting my fourteen-year-old sister come to term. If Gwen made a mistake, if her uterus ruptured, if she got an infection—there were so many bad endings. Besides I don't know that Ally would agree to it; really I don't know that I'd let her agree to it. But for her to have this baby, naturally . . . God. There's no leaving now. I can't see dragging my pregnant sister across what's left of this state, this country, hoping for what? ZeeZee's already planning where the baby's bed should be in the longhouse. They still don't understand, not really, even now. How can they?"

"Okay. Then we have to figure out another way." He pulled a book out of his jacket, handed it to her.

"Gee, you shouldn't have." She turned the hardcover book over, saw that the cover had started to come loose from its binding. "*Hostages in the Middle Ages* by Adam J. Kosto. Friend of yours?"

"No. I found it in a college library, UCF. On my way here."

She turned it over again, ran her fingers along the line of medieval figures on the cover. She started to laugh: the Middle Ages? Is that what they were being reduced to? "Is this an assignment?"

"Kind of. We can't win a full-out war with the Marketplace. I counted two-dozen military-aged men when I was there. Tess, we need to be smart.

We already have one half of the equation. We need to provide the other half and then call for a treaty."

"Why? We have Jerome. Don't we have all the power?"

"Do we? They'll come for him when they figure it out. I would. Does Ally know yet that he's here?"

"No, and I don't know how to tell her."

The branch bounced and swayed under the weight of their bodies, as good as a porch swing. He opened the book, flipped to a specific page, and pointed out what he wanted her to read.

"In medieval Europe hostages were given, not taken," she read. She looked into his frowning eyes. "Really? Who do you suggest we give them?"

His smile was sad. He lifted his brows and waited.

"We could give them Kilmer, but I'm afraid they'd give him back in a week."

That made him laugh. "I think you know who it should be. They'd want the one they think was responsible for Marco's death."

"Who? You? Why not me?" She jumped up from the tree limb and rounded on him. "But what if they decide you're better off as a dead man?"

Parrish propped his rifle against the tree. It was such a part of him, that she hadn't noticed him carrying it. He lifted his hands in surrender.

"They won't. That's the beauty of the system." He pointed to the book in her hands. "You keep Jerome, and they keep me. Otherwise there'll be more dead kids." His voice went hard. "Tess, I can't . . . I won't bury more kids if there's another way."

"But you came back. I thought you wanted to be here . . . with . . . with . . ." She dropped her eyes, suddenly afraid, "Us. We need you to show us what to do, how to get ready for this.

"I know what to do, Tess. I know how to get them ready. But they look to you for answers, for leadership. You need to be their leader. I can't do it."

"So you'll abandon us again?" She said it as mildly as she knew how, but saw the muscles of his jaw go rigid with anger regardless.

He jumped to his feet. The oak branch bounced, hit the ground, and vibrated to a stop. She watched him and waited for the branch to be still.

"Sure. You bet. If I stayed, I'd turn your sisters into killers, because it's what I do: turn babies into baby killers. And I'm good. You know how I know? Because I'm still here and I don't mean at the S-Line. I mean alive, and a lot of the others aren't."

His face had gone to granite—his cheekbones cut glass under his skin, the muscles of his neck straining, his eyes fierce, green fire. He wasn't looking at her or anything in front of him.

This wasn't a button to push. This was an open wound.

As quietly as she could, she tried to make him understand. "I don't want you to be here if you're going to hate us in the end."

He looked at her then as if she were standing too far away to hear, as if he had to cock his head to catch her words. Then his hands were on her arms and he was yanking her to him, flush against him. She could smell the soap he'd used to shave with, see the nick he'd cut at the corner of his mouth, and those eyes that sparked and smoldered, a green landscape burning down the world.

"In the end, we're all probably going to be as dead as that kid over there in the dirt. The difference is that there isn't going to be anybody to scrape a hole out for us to go into if we can't make peace. Hate you? If only I could."

She let him hold her, his hands slid to her wrists, his eyes blazing into hers.

"Okay." He acted like a man being eaten alive. But why? She tried to think of some way to let him off the hook. "Don't. Don't help us. Don't go to the Marketplace for us. How can we help but drag you down with us? Or make you—"

She didn't finish. She couldn't. His mouth was an angry assault on hers, demanding, maybe even pleading.

"No," she said, her hands against his chest. She pushed at his strength. "You can't make me forget what I want to say. I'm mad at you for even suggesting . . ."

His mouth hovered over hers. "I don't want you to forget. I want you to understand. I want you to be afraid of me."

She wanted to ask why, wanted to remember how terrible it felt when he inevitably pushed her away. She tried. Failed. She couldn't have named the moment her fingers curled into the cotton of his shirt.

Beyond the Strandline

Her world collapsed into the circle of his arms, the press of his body against hers, his mouth tearing the breath from her body. It was lightning, without thunder.

When his hands slid down her back to caress her and pull her tighter against him, she welcomed it, wanted it. The intensity in his touch bordered on desperation. His lips fell to her neck as she let her head fall back, her eyes closed.

She needed this. How could she not know how badly she needed this—needed him?

Shocked at herself, she realized she would have let him do anything in that moment if he asked it: And felt it then, a small, dark frisson of doubt and fear of the power he had over her.

It undid him. Her complete and total acceptance of his urgency, his wanting of her, his need that bordered on anger came close to breaking him. Before in the storage unit, that had been a silly kid's game, the barn a moment of tenderness, but this . . .

This was a wildfire, and it was going to burn them both down to the ground if he didn't do something about it.

Somewhere in the sensible part of himself, the logical part that drew up plans and made suggestions, that knew how war and strategy worked, in that part of him, he heard a roar of warning. They had to stop this. He had to.

He forced his hands to her shoulders, and moved her back. Pressing his forehead to hers, he let himself breathe while he listened to her gasping, needy pants.

"What are you doing?" she said. "Are you trying to drive me crazy? You tell me that you're leaving and then you . . . Do you know what I did that time . . . after we kissed in the shed? I stole my sisters' mirror, which is pretty sad, because I never look," she gulped, "at myself, but that isn't the point." She shook her head. "I looked at myself and tried to understand what was wrong with me to make you push me away. And then this?"

Trying to drive *her* crazy? He wanted to laugh. He tried to imagine what Colonel Kennedy would have said about some idiot ROTC cadet putting the full body press on his granddaughter.

She took a step back and looked at him with serious eyes.

"Tess, if I could march into the Marketplace and trade myself for your safety, I would start walking right now. I won't hurt you. You shouldn't care about me. I'm just here. Available. If I weren't here, you would—"

Her words slammed over his. "Be alone. Hurt me? You kiss me like that, and then you talk about leaving *again,* and that's not supposed to hurt?"

He tried to turn and walk away. He tried to tell himself she was better off without him and all those dead kids that lived inside his head. But even now it was so hard to leave her alone with her anger.

He studied the heat in her cheeks, her clenched fists.

"Tess," he began. He watched her chin jut out farther, if that was possible. "Am I supposed to stay and you wind up like Ally, pregnant, and then what? You've never seen anyone die in childbirth, have you?"

That shocked her, he could tell and probably not just because of Ally.

"Have you?" he repeated.

She shook her head.

"Well, I have!" The sound of screaming erupted across his memory, and then the silence. The silence had been so much worse, but how could he tell her that? How could he describe what he tried so hard to keep buried away? "If I go to the Marketplace, you'll be safe. You'll all be safe."

She bit her lip and frowned, waiting for him to explain. Desperate, he changed the subject.

"Tess, why did you have to borrow your sister's mirror? Don't you have a mirror?"

"No. I borrowed theirs because I wanted to know," she said, suddenly looking unsure, "if I looked as different as I felt after you kissed me." Suddenly defiant, she shouted, "Do you want to know what I saw?"

He backed away from her, afraid of what she would say.

"My mother. I saw my mother, a woman that my father turned over to killers to save me. And you know what else?"

He shook his head.

"I looked confused and hurt but happy."

"How many times can I say, I'm sorry?" he said. Turning, he walked away from her—again.

Reaching up she touched her swollen mouth, the spice and poison of lantana still thick on her fingers, and watched him go.

CHAPTER 34

Tess hefted Parrish's book, judged its weight. Maybe she could use it to wedge open the feed room door when she was sweeping it out. Weapons. What they needed were weapons—not books. They needed guns and Jerome in chains and more guns and no more talk of Parrish going anywhere.

She tucked the book into her vest, and headed down to the fishing shack. The wind teased at her hair, lifting one curl and then another, coming in odd fits and starts. One minute the leaves would dance and rattle around her as she walked to the river, and the next minute the trees were as still as a painting. Tropical storm weather. More rain, probably a lot.

The hinges of the screen door squealed, announcing her arrival, drawing the attention of her father and Jerome who sat slumped against the cot where the man who'd attacked her still lay unconscious.

Instead of Gwen or Jamie, it was her father sitting in the opposite corner of the shack on the one and only stool—far enough away from the chained men to tell her that even he wasn't stupid enough to put himself in their reach. Maybe there was some sense left in his head after all. Maybe.

He came close to smiling when he saw her, but quickly snapped a serious expression onto his face instead.

"Surprised to find you here. Where's Jamie?" Tess asked.

"Jamie stepped down to the river to check on some fishing project or other he's been working on. Gwen's swamped catching up with the baking and what not, since the Big Blue Flu Epidemic—that's what I'll be calling it in my latest edition of *Common Ground*."

He seemed clear eyed and calm, sitting on the stool, leaning back against the wall with its green, flaking paint.

"Mr. Fortix here has been describing what's been happening beyond the borders of our little home here at the S-Line, back at the Oviedo Marketplace and other spots. But Mr. Arnold here hasn't been doing very well," her father explained.

The big man rattled when he breathed. Arnold. So he had a name.

She ignored Jerome when he jumped to his feet. Someone had slid the rings from a horse's snaffle bit around his wrists and then threaded the dog chain through the rings. He held his wrists out to her, pouting.

"Come on. You've got me chained to a dead man. It's creepy."

Jerome Fortix rattled the metal at her. He was a pale copy of his father's dark good looks—or what *had been* his father's good looks—past tense. And now she had a name to put with the big flat face on the bed: Mr. Arnold the Spy.

"Don't talk to me. I have nothing to say to you." She adjusted the strap of her tomahawk bag, watched Jerome's brown eyes follow the gesture as she ran her hand over the handle of the tomahawk.

"Tess! Mr. Fortix is our guest! And it's been so long since we've had one."

"Right. Our guest. And what has our guest been saying?"

"Oh, that the Marketplace has been something of an experiment in trade and consumerism, and that they've had some success there. I'm actually happy to hear about some of it. I'm not convinced that the monopoly of the Fortix family over the enterprise is a particularly healthy thing, but it's a point of discussion for another time."

Her father, sitting in his frayed golf shirt, looked like a sleepy baby.

"And what did Mr. Fortix have to say about the little girl they hung by the neck until she was dead at the entrance of their fine fair-trade establishment?"

"Hey!" Jerome said. "That's not on me. What makes you think that kid was innocent? You don't know anything about the Beach Tribes on the coast. You people have no idea who's out there, and what they want. Don't think you understand us or what we do." He reminded her of a toddler pitching a fit, his face flushed and sweaty.

Behind her, the sound of soup splashing and tin bowls hitting the wooden floor mixed with Ally's muffled scream.

"What's he doing here? Tess, why is he here?"

She watched her sister scuttle back toward the screen door as if she'd walked into a house full of corpses.

"Ally, stop. It's okay. He can't . . ."

"Alpha! I found you! I'm so glad to see you." Jerome's voice rose with excitement and anger. He sounded like a squeaky mouse. "Please, tell them to let me go. Sweetheart. Please."

"Shut up. You shut up." Tess had pulled the tomahawk free and marched over to Jerome in a second. She angled the handle of the tomahawk across Jerome's throat, replaced it with her forearm, but made sure to let him see the double-edged blade. "Shut. Up."

She glanced over at her father. "Keep him quiet or I will make it very difficult for him to have anymore lovely conversations with you, or anyone."

Her father stood up. He held his hands out, palms up, and said, "It's important to hear what people aren't saying, Tess. The unspoken traumas that bring them to do terrible things. And then they can't forget. We all—"

"Unspoken traumas! God, Dad." Tess suddenly saw her sister wiping the back of her hand across her mouth, because the smell of lemon pepper in the stew had made her throw up.

He slumped back on his stool.

Ally turned and bolted out of the fishing shack. Tess went after her, but Jamie had beaten her to it.

When he saw Tess, Jamie turned a mellow shade of red, but he didn't let go of the trembling girl in his arms. Ally turned bruised eyes to Tess.

"I wanted to help Gwen out. I brought dinner. Does everyone know that he's here? That he's found us? ZeeZee? Does she know?"

Tess reached out to stroke her sister's hair. She flinched.

"I was going to tell you. Jamie and Parrish found him wandering around the ranch. He and that Arnold guy. We're keeping him. He's . . . he's a bargaining chip."

"They sent him. They sent him and he found me." The trembling would have knocked her to the ground, if Jamie hadn't been holding her, steadying her.

Jamie caught Tess's eye and the pain in his face made her gasp. *He likes her.* The thought came like a gift: *Jamie liked Ally.*

Beyond the Strandline

Her stomach dropped. How could they keep Jerome at the S-Line, keep him out of Ally's way, not to mention Jamie's? Keep the creep from driving her sister mad?

Jamie held Ally as if she were something precious, something too fragile to be real.

And her father sat inside that shack mumbling about "unspoken traumas" and the "family of man." It was all she could do to keep from dragging him out of there by his shirtfront.

"Jamie, I'll walk her back. Can you stay?"

He nodded and then whispered something to Ally, before pushing her gently away. Like the day on the trail coming back from the Marketplace, Ally took off. She did not look back or wait for Tess.

"And send my father out. Keep him out of there." She didn't wait to hear if Jamie understood or not. "I have to go after Ally. I don't want her by herself."

"Go. I'll take over here."

She tried to keep Ally in sight, but her sister wasn't having any of it.

"Ally, wait." She watched her disappear into the gloom of the big oak canopy.

Her father caught up to her on the path that branched one way to the deepwater well, and the other to the longhouse.

"Please. Tessie," he called.

Her name came out in a breathy cough. Sitting and writing didn't help much with endurance, apparently. He had that stubborn look that told her he was about to launch into a fatherly lecture on tolerance. She couldn't do it. Not today.

The breeze kicked up a tiny dust devil at her feet, coating her hiking boots in dirt.

"Tess, I—"

"Don't go back to the fishing shack. That boy is not your friend. He's not a companion or a fellow truth seeker or a common grounder."

She watched his eyes cloud with confusion.

"You need to know that the Marketplace is not a wonderful experiment of economic rebirth. It's a pit where they buy and sell children. Where they brand women who prostitute themselves in exchange for protection."

He sputtered and waved his hands limply through the air. "But, surely there's someone there who sees the benefits of seeking the common . . ."

"Don't say it. Please. Do. Not."

"Tess, I just want—"

"I know what you want. I do."

He blinked at her with his fairy-blue eyes, Ally's eyes.

"It's time to hear what I want. I want my mother. I want my grandfather. I want all those Sunday school lessons to mean something. Grandma said we could pray and God would listen and miracles would happen and angels would appear and three fish would turn into Moby Dick."

The cicadas started a thrumming serenade from the long grass next to the trail as heat crackled and shimmered through the air.

"And I'll tell you what I want most of all. I want to figure out a way to go back to the beginning when no one knew we were here, because I would. I'd go back! I'd go back and tie Ally to her bunk bed so that I wouldn't have to make a choice about who to kill, because it feels like that, like someone's going to die, because if anyone here goes to the Marketplace they'll be as good as . . ." She almost said dead, but in that moment she found she couldn't do it. "Gone. They'll be as good as gone. Parrish says he's going. We keep Jerome, and Parrish goes to the Marketplace—hostage exchange. You'll be so pleased. He read about it in a book. But he'll still be gone, and I don't think I can bear that. I'd rather give them you, if I thought it would work."

A quick, light breeze dried the sweat on the back of her neck. It made her feel oddly shivery. The cicada's stopped their song, frightened into silence as she left him on the path, speechless, for a change.

Tess caught up with Ally not far from where her father stood. Parrish had come up from the well to bring the hostages water, and was standing there beside the branded twin when Tess reached them.

"Ally, you say the word and he's gone. I mean it. I'll kill him myself."

Parrish watched as Tess grabbed for her sister's hand. He'd come to bring water but had stumbled onto a whole lot more. No one was walking away, not this time. Parrish set the bucket of water down, crossed his arms, and watched her try to get through to the younger girl.

Beyond the Strandline

"He fell out of the sky and then stumbled into Parrish and Jamie's arms." Tess waved a dismissive hand toward the fishing shack. "Jerome's a monster. I won't let him upset you anymore."

Ally turned toward Tess but looked at Parrish.

"Do you hear this?"

Parrish adjusted the rifle strap across his chest and noted Jon Lane making his sad little exit, back toward the river. The woods closed in around the escaping man, the canopy looping across the path like drapery.

Parrish gave Ally a short nod.

"I hear it," he said. "I hear what she's saying."

"Yeah, but does Tess?"

"What are you two talking about? I saw how upset you were back there. I should have told you, warned you." Tess kicked hard at a tuft of grass at her feet, ran her hands through the short chopped ends of her hair.

"Stop it. Stop blaming yourself," Ally said.

Parrish watched Tess's eyes go from soft gray to flint.

"Do you understand what Parrish is suggesting? That we keep that monster here at the S-Line, in exchange for someone from here. There's a book. A whole book. Right, Parrish?" Tess turned her stony eyes on him.

He hesitated long enough to let some of the emotion wind down. "I've dug a lot of graves," he said. "I'm not backing down on this."

"Tess," Ally began, "are you really suggesting that you're going to kill a human being, even if it is *that* one? Will you bury him too?" Ally toyed with the top button of her shirt, slipping it in and out of the buttonhole. Parrish watched her. The words were right, the sentiment civilized, but there was something odd in the way Ally stared off into space when she spoke, her eyes on some distant scene she wasn't inviting anyone else to share. "Really, Tess? Kill Jerome because he can't go back. And what would that make you? What would that make me, if I let you?"

Suddenly, the big brindled mutt from the Marketplace smashed into Tess, knocking her to her knees. Ally screamed and scrambled toward her sister. Parrish had his rifle off his shoulder and aimed before the dog could finish licking the shock off Tess's face.

Parrish moved to peel the dog off of Tess, but she waved him away. She put her hand over her face and lay still in the dirt of the trail.

She giggled. Giggled! And then laughed.

"It doesn't stop, does it?" she choked out. The dog went into spasms of joy at the sound of her voice. Looking at the dog, she said, "I thought you were dead. Why aren't you dead, you moron? Maybe we can trade you for something."

The dog's tail whipped back and forth.

"Oh, go lick yourself."

Hysterical laughter clawed its way out of her throat. The dog sat next to her and cocked his head at the sound. When she rolled to her side and curled into herself, the laughter threatened to become raging tears.

"Don't Tess," Parrish said, taking a step toward her.

Ally stopped him with a shake of her head.

"Tess?" Ally bent down to comfort her sister, had just started to put her hand on her shoulder when she looked up, her face going instantly white and still.

Parrish turned to follow her worried gaze and saw them.

They were hard to see at first because of the way they kept to the shadows along the trail. They reminded him of reluctant deer. There were a dozen or so, dressed in rags and bits of clothing that were meant for adults. They stood like wild animals poised to flee at the first sign of trouble. Watching the dog, they waited.

"Tess. Get up!"

Her tears had started to calm, fading to hiccups.

"Tess, we've got company."

She looked up, one hand reaching out for the dog's huge head.

"How many?"

"A baker's dozen. Thirteen or so."

She pushed to her feet slowly.

"Doe Kids, or what's left of them. Do you think they're here to make good on the deal with Goliath?" She laughed at her own joke and something in Parrish's chest flopped at the sound.

"They look hungry," Ally said. "I hope Gwen's got a lot of stew in the pot."

Beyond the Strandline

The dog walked to Parrish, licked his hand, and then bounded back to the tree line to stand next to an older boy. Parrish knew him, the kid they'd left Goliath with, the boss kid. He vaguely remembered that he called himself Stone.

"What do you think they want other than food, clothes, and more than leaves over their heads?" Tess swiped at her runny nose, shot him a crooked smile, and walked straight to the boy in rags who waited at the edge of the woods.

CHAPTER 35

Parrish knew Kilmer wasn't happy about the sudden influx of mouths to feed before the old man started to speak.

"What are we supposed to do with those ones?" Kilmer said, his jaw muscles clenched in lumpy knots.

Gwen clucked at him, shook her head.

"Hush. 'Those ones,' as you call them, could be me and my boys if we weren't here. Help me with this." She swung a pot of rabbit stew at Kilmer until he caught the handle. "Over there at the picnic table. They'll come to the table to eat when they smell the food. I'll get some bowls."

So far, the Doe Kids had stood and watched quietly, following the steaming pot with hungry eyes.

The oldest boy walked to Parrish, one leader to another. He kept his bony shoulders set, standing as tall as his fourteen or fifteen years allowed. He carried a machete sharpened to a razor's edge. The kid had priorities.

"I'm Stone."

"I remember you from before. We left the mule and dog with you."

The kid stared at him with a frightening mix of despair and pride.

He was wearing a man's shirt that someone had hacked off at his hips, and a man's belt that wrapped around his waist twice. On his feet he wore a pair of women's UGG boots. It was a brand name that floated to the surface of Parrish's memory like a bubble; his sisters had thought it was a big deal once, wearing boots like that. He saw them, Darby and Brittany and Ella, posing for the camera. Parrish shrugged off the vision.

Stone was the best dressed of the group. There were thirteen of them altogether, and from the looks of things they'd been living under palm fronds for a while, probably since Goliath and the dead kid. The youngest looked about five or six and the oldest fifteen but, with malnutrition factored in, it was hard to tell.

"We're here for the mule. We want it back."

Parrish knew better than to throw the kid's desperation back into his face. He could hear Gwen coaxing the others to sit, to eat, and watched them break for the food one by one. Most of them scooped the stew out of the bowls with their hands.

"Understood. But the mule's not up to speed just yet. He didn't show up in the best of shape, you know?"

For the first time, the boy looked uncertain. They both knew Parrish wasn't talking about the mule.

"They buried her by the river." Parrish nodded to Tess and the others. "They did a good job of it."

The tension faded from the kid's shoulders. He gave Parrish a quick, sharp nod. Satisfied.

"Go. Eat. The mule situation can wait."

Stone turned to stare at Kilmer as he dished out Gwen's stew, hesitating. He waited for the others to sit, to eat. Kid had priorities.

"Go. It's good. You're safe here."

Parrish watched as Tess said something to Gwen and then looked over at him. He forced himself not to turn away from the look in her face: need and expectation and . . . what? They needed him. She needed him. He felt his stomach clench. His hand tightened around the rifle in his hand.

Gwen filled Parrish in on the food situation; they needed fresh meat and they needed it fast. Milk and eggs weren't going to be enough if they were going to allow all the Doe Kids to stay. Rabbit was fine for now, but they were between litters—too hot for baby bunnies. The bucks wouldn't be fertile until the fall. What they needed was venison.

Kilmer watched the Doe Kids with sharp eyes. They couldn't be trusted. They were half-wild and twice crazy, in his opinion. Didn't take a mind reader to figure out what was in Kilmer's head. Jess T stayed silent, same as always.

Gwen wanted them to stay. That was just as easy to figure out. Parrish could tell by the way she drifted in and out of their group, trying not to hover, wanting to reach out, trying not to spook them.

When she'd asked Parrish about going hunting, she'd barely looked at him; she was too busy keeping an eye on the children like a nervous hen.

Blake and Blane stood next to Jamie, all three of them wearing identical frowns of disapproval. Tess seemed neutral in the silent debate going on among the group, while Ally and ZeeZee sat alone on the ground, giving up their seats at the picnic tables.

Parrish was staying out of it and doubted the Doe Kids could even be convinced to stay. They were wild and broken; he couldn't see them crawling into the structure and confinement of a Quonset hut on the S-Line and liking it.

That wasn't on his plate, if they stayed or went, but bringing home something more than a brace of catfish was. And Gwen wanted venison, one of the big sambar deer or a couple of axis. Native to India, the axis were smaller than the sambar, but filled the stew pot just as well.

He felt his own bubble of tension pop. Hunting was something he understood, something that would require all of his focus and attention. He welcomed the assignment.

Patting his pockets, he took stock of his ammunition. The rifle in his hand felt like part of him. Jamie kept them both supplied with enough ammo from scrounging and—not to put too fine a point on it—stealing, because being a drag on S-Line supplies and ammunition had never been part of the deal. The Colonel had understood the need to raid.

"I'm going with you." Tess was at his shoulder before he realized. He watched her rummage through her own vest pockets.

"Nope, I hunt alone."

"Not even Jamie goes with the great Richmond Parrish to hunt? Really?"

"Not even. If I go after a sambar, it's an all-nighter. Gwen's worried about wiping out the rabbit stock trying to feed this bunch. We've more than doubled in less time than it takes to walk to the outhouse."

He watched one child, boy or girl, hard to tell, tip the bowl of stew up to their mouth and drain it. The kid wore what looked like a plastic tablecloth with a hole cut in it around the neck. The kid's hair was a rat's nest. Most of the Doe Kids took a bowl of stew and retreated to the comfort of a tree trunk or squatted at the edge of the clearing.

"I know we've grown," she said. "And we need to talk about it. Change up some stuff. I'm coming with you. Seems like a good time to be using the buddy system. Don't you think?"

She looked at him with a smirking grin and those big eyes of hers that made him think of clouds before the storm and the excitement of wind whipping through the tops of trees along the river.

He mentally shook himself. See? Already distracting him. That's what she was—a distraction. But he didn't have time to argue with her. He needed to be out at the blackberry stand before sunset, hopefully before the rain blasted through. Overhead the clouds skittered and rolled in bands from east to west, not quite forming thunderclouds. The wind rose and fell, capricious and teasing.

"Yeah, okay. I don't want to argue. I don't have time. Bring your skinning knife and a backpack for the meat. We've got a hike ahead of us, and it has to be tonight, while we still have some moon. Before the rain."

She made a sound, a sigh, and looked so relieved he almost smiled. It was easy enough, letting her come with him, but he wasn't planning on admitting it.

"I have to get my backpack. I'll meet you at the deepwater well," she said, backing away, looking eager and a little bit suspicious.

"I'll be there, Tess. Stop looking like I'm about to cut and run. But hurry it up."

He caught Jamie watching them, realized he'd overheard. Jamie looked at him with raised eyebrows, open-mouthed shock, and a hand to his forehead, faking a faint. It was enough of a hint at the razzing he was about to get.

Parrish walked over, stopped, and barked, "Shut it, Soldier."

Jamie shrugged it off and Blake and Blane snorted.

"You too!" Parrish shot the boys his fiercest glare. "And listen, I need you both to do something for me while I go out to get everyone dinner."

Parrish outlined a couple of ideas for border security that had the boys' eyes shining.

"And if you know what's good for you, you won't let your mom know too much of what you're up to. You," he said, pointing at the still smug Jamie, "make sure they get it right."

He watched Jamie glance over at Gwen, and saw something in his friend's face shift and soften. He looked like somebody's puppy. It was Parrish's turn to raise his eyebrows; Jamie didn't want to upset the boys' mom. What was that about? Then he watched confusion and frustration and longing grow in his friend's face as he searched the group around him. Parrish realized his friend was looking for Ally Lane.

"Have you seen Ally?" He began.

"Probably needed the latrine. Hey, get on it, you boys. You heard me. Alcohol, glass bottles, rags. Kilmer and Jess T will help your mom."

Parrish looked Jamie full in the eye.

"You can help her, you can help both of them," Parrish said, glancing to Gwen and then back to Jamie, "by setting up a perimeter to keep anyone else from the Marketplace off of us."

Jamie's smile was grim. "Yeah, there's that. And you. Don't lose anything out there, okay?"

"Like?"

"Your mind."

"Under control."

Jamie was smart enough to keep another, bigger grin under wraps.

"Just get on that little project," Parrish paused, glancing back at Gwen. "And listen, I'm wondering about stockpiles the old man might have hidden, buried guns, ammunition caches. Any thoughts on that, you need to let me know. If we can't work this out . . ."

Jamie nodded, slung his rifle on his shoulder, and shooed Blake and Blane in search of glass containers suitable for making Molotov cocktails.

Sweltering. It was sweltering and breathless inside the ramshackle shack where they'd chained him up. Jerome yanked at the bolt in the floor. They'd managed to find the one solid piece of wood in the entire crappy place. The bolt was solid.

Jerome kicked at the cot where Arnold lay. Maybe between the two of them they'd be able to yank the chain free. That plan didn't look too promising, though. Arnold was still breathing, but that was about it. He'd sunk farther and farther into a rasping, heavy state of unconsciousness. The black woman had done her best, probably, but what else could she do?

Chained to a dead man, that's what it felt like. Jerome yanked harder at the bolt. He leaned back against the wall and closed his eyes. Someone should be coming soon: food, water, to empty the bucket they had given him. Geez, they had him crapping in a bucket. Perfect.

He cursed the heat and slammed backward into the wall, closed his eyes, tried to ignore the sweat rolling down his face. Night couldn't come soon enough.

Something—a breath, a gasp—had him snapping his eyes open.

She was there, her fist curled around the short hilt of a skinning knife.

"Alpha. What?"

"Don't call me that. Don't call me anything. In fact, you are not going to speak. Don't speak."

Her hand didn't tremble or shake. She held the knife as steady as a rock—a big, sharp, killing rock.

"What are you going to do with that?"

She took two big steps closer and jabbed the knife at him.

"Shut up. You don't get to ask me questions. You. Will. Shut. Up!"

She came close enough for him to see the sweat on her forehead, the strain around her eyes, but not close enough to fall inside the circle of his restraints. The rage in her eyes baffled him. Hadn't he come here to see her? Check on her? Explain himself? He raised his hands, palms up.

"Okay, you're the boss."

He waited and watched her eyes turn glassy with tears.

"I want you gone, from here, from our lives, from my life. I told my sister some garbage about not falling to your level." She stopped and inhaled, closing her eyes. "And I meant it, for Tess. I won't let her do something that would make her bleed for the rest of her life. I won't." Her eyes snapped open. The tears were gone.

"Absolutely. You toss me those keys, and I'm gone." He saw her glance at the key ring on its bent nail next to the door. "And then you can come with me."

Shock rocked her back; she stumbled sideways two steps into Arnold's cot. His breathing turned sharper and harder—louder—a rusty saw blade against concrete.

She tipped her head at Jerome, bewilderment settled like a mask over her pretty, soft features.

"Why would I go with you? Ever?"

"Can I talk now?" he said and jingled the chain at her.

"Talk? What could you possibly want to say to me?"

Typical woman. Couldn't make up her mind. "I'm not sure why you're so pissed at me. I tracked down Arnold for you. Then we followed your trail until Arnold got lost and then a big boar took him out. What an idiot. I needed to talk to you. See you. That's why we came, I came to find you. Isn't that what you women like? That romantic bull crap? A man that will go to the ends of the earth for them?"

"Romantic? What are you talking about? You branded me. I didn't want you. I begged you to let me go. You picked me out like a horse at an auction."

He thought about the first time he'd seen her: so blond and clean, so blue eyed and softly curvy under her boy clothes. All the other girls, the ones his father found, they were always dirty and skinny, not like girls at all. They were like scarecrows. Of course he'd picked her out. She was a prize, the best one.

"Why wouldn't I want you? You were so clean. I liked your eyes."

"You made me marry you because I take baths?" She stared at him as if he were something she'd found growing under a stump.

Arnold started to pant. Jerome kicked at the frame of the cot, annoyed by the distraction.

"Stop," she said, and moved to the opposite side of the cot to look down at the big, unconscious man. Reaching down, she put her free hand on his chest.

"Forget him. Let me go. He's done." He tried rattling his chain at her. Break through that foggy look in her eyes, and get her to understand his impossible situation.

"He's dying." She straightened up and backed to the screen door. "I need to get someone. I should leave you here. Let you think about everyone that's dead because of your family."

"Don't go. Let me out of here. If he dies I'm stuck here, chained here." He could feel the creep factor crawling over his skin. "Seriously, get me out of here or kill me. Isn't that what you came here for?"

It sounded good, real dramatic, when he talked about her killing him. He liked the way it came out.

She looked at the skinning knife in her hand like she was surprised to still find it there. "No . . . Maybe." She looked confused, shook her head. "If you go, you'd have to promise not to come back."

Arnold gasped and spluttered, red foam appearing at the corner of his mouth.

Jerome leaped to his feet.

"Alpha, help me. I helped you."

She looked at him, incredulous. "Helped me? You think you helped me?"

It was his turn to be puzzled. "Sure! I saved you."

The big man on the bed began to thrash and moan, then muttered someone's name. It sounded like Lucy or Lucky.

She turned those blue eyes of hers from Arnold back to him. Even now, chained, he could remember the thrill of her, belonging to him, being his.

"Yeah, yeah, they would have sold you if I hadn't stopped them, said that I wanted you for myself. Don't you get it? You were safe with me. What are you doing here in the middle of . . . what is this? Nowhere."

Behind her, the screen door screeched open and then slammed shut. It was that redheaded stork guy, the one they called Jamie. Jerome felt his stomach clench, trying not to let the hate boil over. He needed this guy to let down his guard. He slumped and watched Jamie pull the girl, the girl that belonged to him, through the door and out into the falling darkness.

"Alpha! Ally! Get me out of here. I forgive you for running away. I mean it!"

Outside, Jamie yanked the skinning knife out of Ally's hand.

"Does Tess know that you have this? Are you kidding me? What did you think you were going to do with this? Are you crazy?" He stuffed the knife into his belt. He was talking so fast he couldn't get the words out quick enough. "Ally, what would we do if he'd gotten the knife and turned it on you?"

At some point in the tirade he'd grabbed her by the arms and pulled her close enough to make her have to tip her head back to look up at him. Inside the fishing shack Jerome howled.

"I just wanted him to go away. *Make* him go away. I left the ranch and now Tess is talking crazy. Hostages. War. She offered to kill Jerome for me. And that girl, that little Doe girl," her voice fell to a whisper. "I got that little girl killed. I thought—"

He pulled her into his chest, felt her hands fist in the back of his shirt. What flowed through him felt fierce and pure and strong. He knew. He knew what she was feeling. And he knew what he would be willing to do to protect her from it.

"Ally, it's done. And now we deal with it. That's all there is." She trembled in his arms. "Together. We deal with this together."

She started to cry. He didn't try to stop her.

CHAPTER 36

PARRISH DIDN'T TELL her where they were headed, and Tess didn't ask. She knew enough to stay quiet and keep up. She didn't bother to tell him that she hadn't been able to find her skinning knife and had to bring her fillet knife instead. He didn't seem interested in conversation anyway. He didn't mention the rifle she had or ask if she knew how to use it, which suited Tess just fine. She wasn't in the mood to be insulted.

He moved along the deep well trail and then out to the river, headed east, deeper and deeper into the tangle of jungle that used to be a protected state forest. Now it was wilderness, a labyrinth of heavy vines and stringy mulberry. He led them into the heaviest of it.

The sambar deer her grandfather had imported from China and allowed to "go wild" preferred the wettest parts of the refuge. They also liked the night, but they were worth the effort. The big animals would provide enough venison to keep the stew pots full for a while. They needed that—the fresh meat and the security of full bellies. It was hard to feel ready for trouble on empty stomachs.

When the jungle became a wall, Parrish veered left along the river's edge. Judging by the sweat soaking her shirt and the burn in her legs, they'd been walking for a good hour when he crossed over a deadfall that cut across the river. He scrambled over the heavy, fallen tree trunk like a cat.

Tess wasn't sure whether to be pleased or hurt when he never looked back to check on her. The trunk was thick with moss under her feet and trailed slime where it touched the water. The end of the fallen tree on the far side of the river ended in another impenetrable wall of greenery. She couldn't imagine how he was going to get them through it. At the end of the downed trunk he turned east again, dipped under a huge thatch of palmetto, and disappeared.

"Hey!" she shouted, and then stopped to breathe in air so crisp and clean it made her light-headed: no cook fires here, no grubby Doe Kids. "Hey, not fair . . ."

She pushed through after him and then stumbled to a stop, staring.

The river forked beyond the deadfall bridge, one branch of the river twisting back on itself into a softly curving sliver of white sand beach. The pool was fringed with water hyacinths. The main river flowed passed, dark and dank, while this other branch flowed out from a clear-to-the-bottom pool. Bream and minnows flashed in the water, their silver bodies disappearing into the purple flowers that rimmed the crystal clear water.

A hedge of wild blackberries rimmed the fifteen-foot-wide strip of pure, white sand. The blackberries were a favorite food for the sambar.

"Oh man. This is beautiful. Why's the water so clear?"

"Quiet."

Tess snorted. "The deer won't be out until tonight. Nocturnal."

She lowered her voice anyway, too aware of the way sound traveled over the water and through the woods. It was hard enough to be in the right place at the right time when it came to hunting.

The pool of water was slick, motionless glass. The purple lilies bloomed and bobbed on the water's surface.

She watched Parrish scout the riverbank, waited until he walked back, and then stood next to her, close enough that she could feel the heat coming off of him. He smelled like sun and salt and man. It rocked her enough that she had to take a half step back.

"There's a game trail through the brambles on the far side to the edge of the water. They're using this pool pretty regular. It's clear of gators. They tend to hang out in the darker water, mid river."

"Why's it like this? So perfect? The water?"

"A fresh water spring," he said, nodding his head to the far side of the pool. "One of three on this side. I'm surprised you didn't know about this place," Parrish said and shook his head at her. "They'll come tonight."

Sweat rolled down her cheek. The water looked better every minute. "Not if we smell like we do now."

He looked down at her, reached out, and pushed a damp strand of her hair back behind her ear.

Don't. She almost said it.

"We're going up, and we're going to be quiet. They won't be able to smell us." He walked to the water's edge, bent down, and splashed water on his face, head, and neck. She watched the ripples radiate out from where he touched the water. He looked back over his shoulder at her, lifted his eyebrows, his eyes glowing green, lines crinkling the corners: an invitation.

She joined him, kneeling. The sand was cool, inviting, even through the heavy denim of her jeans.

Swinging her weapon's bag onto her back, she reached down to cup the water in her hand. Suddenly, a blast of fresh spring water hit her in the face like a slap. She blinked at him through wet lashes and gasped. He pretended not to know what he'd done.

"Was that you almost having some fun?"

He looked at her then and smiled. It transformed his face, that smile, and made her forget about the water dripping off the end of her nose. Shaking his dripping hair, he stood up and pulled her to her feet. The secret spring started to fill with afternoon shadows.

"We go up," he said, pointing to the deer stand in the oak behind her. "If you have to pee you should go now, unless you want to make the climb more than once."

"And the fun is gone." She nodded and laughed a little. "Be right back."

By the time she climbed to the top of the deer stand, he had stretched out flat on his stomach, the rifle resting next to him. It was a good stand: homemade, big enough for two people to rest side by side, one of those mysterious projects he'd always seemed to be working on. It wasn't just a couple of boards nailed across some branches; he'd dragged a sheet of plywood through the woods, nailing it to a sturdy platform of two-by-fours. Plenty of space to stretch out, lay flat, be comfortable while you waited for the nightlife to arrive.

The sun slanted into the invisible west as the afternoon drained away. The leaves rattled when the breeze teased the tops of the trees. They probably had half an hour until twilight and then another two before the waning moon came up enough to make a difference.

"Did you have help with this?" It was a whisper. She doubted he even heard her.

He grunted. His eyes stayed closed. He was using his backpack as a pillow. She found it easy to see that he'd spent a lot of time out here—alone.

"Sure, okay, quiet. I'll be quiet. But Parrish, you need to talk to me at some point. I know you've got Jamie and Gwen's boys working on Molotov cocktails."

She sat with her knees tucked up to her chin and kept her eyes on the patches of sky overhead. Anything was better than looking down. They were twenty feet above the clear water.

"I can't imagine the boys actually heaving homemade bombs and making them work." She sighed, realizing she didn't expect him to answer. She was on her own, thinking out loud mostly. "I mean those two can hardly be counted on to wipe themselves. Maybe the Doe Kids could, they'll be a bit tougher."

He didn't move. She thought he'd fallen asleep. Taking her chance, she looked at him. His hair was still wet. It was as dark as chocolate where the water had touched it. Without the hedge of his beard, the bones of his face were more pronounced, the sharp curve of his cheek an elegant line. It was a beautiful face—strong and fine, all at the same time. His lips were full when he wasn't grimacing or frowning at something she'd done or said.

The sun had burned him brown and etched the beginning of lines at the corners of his eyes. They made him seem smarter somehow.

Tess realized she liked looking at him. She liked looking at him very much. It helped to have him to look at, to be able to focus on Richmond Parrish's strong, clean profile and contemplate what went on behind those dark-lashed eyes, anything other than what might be coming next down Highway 426 from the Marketplace.

Shadows slanted through the leaves. Splotches of darkness grew as the night closed in. She let herself uncurl and relax. She lay back, closed her eyes, and appreciated a quiet moment in the treetops.

"I can," he said.

Not asleep then. It was her turn to grunt a response.

"Hmm?"

"Blake and Blane, I can imagine it. Those two blowing up stuff, people. Throwing bombs."

She turned her head and saw that Parrish was looking at her. His eyes were warm with an inner light, a fever of color.

"Today they're children, boys, but I can do it. I can train them, teach them, and I can make them into killers."

Tess held her breath knowing that he was talking about his life before, before Blake and Blane, before the S-Line. The dark part of his life that he kept locked away. Her heart started to thump painfully under her ribs.

"I know how. It's what I did. We took them out of their homes, their camps, their schools. We put guns and blades in their hands and we showed them how to butcher other human beings." He flipped to his back, stared up at the sky.

The Junior Militias. He was talking about those gangs of child soldiers that the government had set loose on the country and each other out of sheer desperation.

"Parrish, it wasn't a choice." She tried to sound certain, convinced.

"Wasn't it?" He sounded half-asleep, almost dreamy. "I could have walked away, but they brought us in, beat us, kept us stoned, drugged. It made what we were doing easier. At first, I thought . . ."

His voice changed then. It sounded as if he were talking about someone else, someone he didn't like very well.

"And in the end, I didn't think at all. In the beginning, I told myself that I could protect them, that if I cared about the boys and the girls I could . . ."

He sighed. She stayed very still, afraid to spook him with questions or curiosity.

"He was someone's brother, a kid named Orlando, and his sister; we swept them into our unit, near here. Her name I can't remember. I've tried. But all I can see is what was left of her face when our commander, Hines, handed her brother the .357 and forced him to pull the trigger."

She gasped and pulled away from him, just a little, before she could stop herself. Before she could think what it would mean to him.

Looking at him now was like looking into a bottomless pool of dark water, the light in his eyes was disappearing in the darkness as the sun drifted away. What could she say? What could anyone say?

Crickets started a late-day song down in the leaf mold, busy living their tiny lives.

"We'd brought in a lot of them that week; young, they were always getting younger and younger. The bigger, older, stronger ones were being eaten alive in the bigger units, dying by the hundreds, thousands. If they were big enough to hold an AR-15 we swept them in: ten, nine, some younger. By the end, we didn't care if they could hold a gun. Some of them couldn't lift the barrels. No one cared.

"I didn't care by then either. Couldn't. I was like that stuff on the outside of the corn. That dead stuff."

"Husk," she whispered. "It's called the husk."

"Yeah, that was me: The Great Empty Husk. It wasn't the first time I'd seen a kid forced to kill another kid, or even his own parents or a teacher, but there was something about this time, maybe because the boy hadn't cried or screamed or blubbered."

"But how could they? What could force you to do that?"

"There was a little brother, maybe three years old. We . . . they used the little ones against the older ones. You'd do anything for your sisters, right? People you care about. Caring, it's a problem. They were burning the kid, the little brother with a heated piece of rebar, while the sister watched."

She didn't answer him. He already knew the answer to the sister question; Tess would do anything for her sisters. Already had.

"Orlando, her brother . . . shot her. First he shot the sister, and then he shot the little brother dead," he said, matter of fact, his voice dropping to a dull monotone.

Beyond the Strandline

A last slash of sunlight knifed into her eyes. She squeezed them shut. A mockingbird played at being an eagle, its clever voice chattering out a fake raptor warning.

"Orlando, after he shot the little brother, he turned the gun on himself. He knew what he was doing, handling that gun. Someone had taught him, given him the skill."

A sudden gust of wind thrashed the leaves around them. Leaves and bits of tree spun away in a whirlwind.

"I left that night." He fell silent.

"Parrish, I'm so sorry," she said, rolling toward him. Tess sat up so she could touch him, offer something, anything.

She froze. He lay on his back with his hand to his forehead, while the unmistakable sight of a tear tracked its way down the side of his face. He kept the back of his fist against his forehead, never allowing himself to look at her.

"Don't be sorry for me."

"Why?" She touched him then, her hand registering the steel of tensed muscles. Her stomach cramped. Dread swept through her. " Why not?"

"The little brother, he had these huge brown eyes, curly hair, you know, like Blane and Blake. Cute. He was wearing a T-shirt; it had one of those fast food logos on it—pizza maybe. There was a birthmark on his leg—one of those red marks. Stork bites. That's what they're called. He was just a baby."

There was something hard and cutting in his voice she didn't recognize.

"Gwen's boys, they remind me of him. Orlando, he was a good shot. He'd been trained, prepared. Someone had shown him how."

"Parrish," she said, squeezing his arm, trying to get him to look at her.

"Don't you want to know how I know noticed the birthmark? You're not very good at interrogation, are you?"

She almost shook her head, almost. *Don't tell me. I can't hear this.*

"He was a good shot. Bam. Bam. Bam. Three shots, three kills. Done. And there was blood and brains on my face because I'd been holding the little one down while they burned him. So, like I said, I can see Gwen's boys learning to do pretty much anything. I saw it all the time."

CHAPTER 37

THE MOON HAD barely crested the tree line when Parrish took the shot. The sambar buck took little more than half a minute to sniff the air before he'd walked to the edge of the pool and dropped his head to drink—confident, too confident. He'd grown lax about the dangers, gotten careless. He'd smelled nothing, suspected nothing.

Parrish took advantage of the oddly gusting wind that blew their scent away. The shot entered the buck's body near his left shoulder, exploded his heart. He took four steps and fell.

Next to him, Tess scrambled down to the dead deer without speaking to Parrish or looking at him. He followed, a hard lump in his chest. The deer meat would keep them going.

But if Tess froze him out, what would keep *him* going? Now or ever? She hadn't tried to touch him or say anything to him since he'd told her what he'd never told anyone. Had never *been able* to tell anyone.

He pulled his skinning knife out of his belt and joined her as she opened the body of the buck. Hot blood rushed over her hands. It was good that they were so close to the water. They'd be able to wash up quickly and easily.

"We can carry some back in our backpacks," she suggested, all business. "What do you think about hanging the rest and coming back for it? It's still pretty hot. We won't be able to leave it for long, but we could send Jamie and maybe Kilmer back for the rest. There's probably a couple hundred pounds of meat here. We'll have to hurry."

She sounded matter of fact. He watched her work swiftly and skillfully using a long fillet knife. The moon created small patches of light, not ideal for field dressing, but it beat trying to clean the big animal in the pitch dark.

"Do you want a fire, or is this light good enough for now?"

"Good enough."

He helped her pull the guts out of the big animal's body. She stared at the empty carcass.

"Let's take it all. I can do it," she suggested. "Leave the head. Sling the body on a pole. Get it home, or at least closer to home than this. The meat won't last long in this weather."

He looked over at her. She was a wild child in the silver light of the moon and stars, blood to her elbows. There was a dark smear of blood on her cheek. It looked black in the half-light. She was Diana, the huntress.

"Sure, we can try. Do you have paracord?" He usually backpacked the meat out when he was by himself—lots of trips, sometimes.

"Yeah, but you don't need it, just slit its hamstrings."

Nodding, he turned to find a strong enough sapling for the carcass, surprised to feel her hand on his elbow.

"Parrish, it was a great shot."

He shrugged away from her hand, reminding himself that it was better not to care. Not if she couldn't stomach the person he'd had to be all those years.

"It's what I do."

"I know," she said. "And you should know that I'm stronger than I look."

CHAPTER 38

TESS *WAS* STRONGER than she looked. She'd show him. She'd help him carry the gutted deer back to Gwen and the others. There were too many to keep fed, if she was being honest, but were they really going to turn those children away, knowing what they'd face—had already faced—because of her and Ally and Parrish?

She would show him. She would show them all.

He'd hacked off the sambar's head to lighten the load on her end, strung the deer's slit tendons onto the pole, and hefted the bulk of the deer's weight on his end. She'd almost complained about getting the lighter end, out of pride, but now as they struggled along the darkened trail, she was grateful. The pole dug into her shoulder, rubbing a spot raw.

The sapling across her shoulder bent under the deadweight of the big animal. The smell of blood filled her nose and fresh blood dried on her face, making her face itch as it crusted over. Sweat stung her eyes, soaked her shirt. Parrish carried his end of the sapling without saying anything when she stumbled on a root or pushed at a branch with her hand. He had to be able to hear how hard she was breathing, but he didn't say anything.

Parrish was so quiet as she struggled to help carry the carcass back to the others that it was hard to know how he felt about her stumbling, bumbling help.

When she went to her knees after catching the lump of a cypress knee with the toe of her boot and the deer's severed neck dragged in the dirt, he'd dropped his end of the weight and suggested they take a few minutes.

"Don't be proud. It won't kill us to rest."

"Sorry—"

He cut her off.

"It's heavy, that's all. We'll take a break. Why be sorry?"

She rubbed at the indent in her shoulder and concentrated on trying to get her breathing under control.

He stood with his back to her, hands hanging limp at his side, the rifle slung across his back. The moon was gone, dipping into the crisscross of tree limbs. But she could still see him by starlight; the set of his shoulders, the weight he carried even when he wasn't carrying anything. Silence drifted between them. Finally, she had to know.

"Why did you tell me?"

He didn't turn around when he answered her.

"I don't know. I've never told anyone else. I've always thought that I never would."

Their voices were soft on the cool night air, hardly louder than the whisper of the breeze in the leaves around them.

"Does Jamie know?"

"No. They're all dead that were there, I think." He stopped, took a breath. "No. He doesn't know. He was on patrol when it happened."

He fell silent, turned to face her for the first time since the tree stand, since they'd gutted the deer.

She watched him shrug.

"I told you because you need to know that there are no heroes coming to your rescue. There's just me and Jamie, and he's always been the better man or maybe the luckier man—I don't know. But I'm not what you think."

"What I think," she said, "is that I'm not sure how anyone could still be standing after living through what you've been through. We—my sisters, me—we've been on some kind of island in the middle of all this, and I feel stupid with it. We're like helpless, protected children."

She reached out to touch him, but he wasn't in front of her anymore. He smashed back into her.

The big cat had come down on him from the overhang of the branch, cloaked in the gloom and shadows, drawn by the smell of blood, silent with its hunger and need—like everyone and everything else. The panther's body catapulted him into her, slamming her back into the trunk of a cypress tree. She stumbled in the dark over the deer's body at her feet and went down.

The cat shrieked at her enemies, determined to warn them off of the fresh blood and meat. There were cubs to feed and starvation to keep at bay.

Tess rolled away from the thrashing claws. She heard Parrish grunt under the weight of the big cat. Her tomahawk was in her hand before she'd finished rolling to her feet. The darkness was a heavy black wall on this section of the trail. It was hard for her to see where the animal ended and the man began.

She heard herself yelling nonsense at the wrestling forms in front of her: "Be still! Quit moving!" The sound of cursing, followed by the heavy thud of a fist hitting the cat's jaw or head helped her hone in on the bulk of the animal's body. She threw herself onto the cat, feeling for its neck.

Underneath her the body of the panther twisted back toward her to combat this new threat from above. With the blade in her right hand, she swung the tomahawk into the face of the thrashing, snarling beast. The blade bit into flesh and muscle as hot blood splashed across her hands and arms. The tomahawk hit bone. She could feel the vibration of it up into her teeth.

The cursing stopped as the animal twitched underneath her, blood pumping out of it in spurts.

"Oh my God, Parrish, don't die. You can't be dead!"

She felt for him beneath the dying panther.

"Parrish!" She screamed it now, only to be answered by silence.

She rolled to her feet, trying to heave the panther's dead weight off of the body underneath.

"No. No. No."

A wet, sick spluttering met her denials, and then a sweet fit of coughing. He shoved while she pulled. The cat rolled off to the side.

He grabbed at her in the dark. His hands were slick, but they were strong and alive, his fingers biting into her arms.

"Geez, woman, have I told you how good I think you are with that thing?"

He pulled her into his arms and kissed her hair. "I'm glad you insisted on coming along."

Beyond the Strandline

It was her turn to push him away. "I'm glad you're not dead. I'd have never been able to drag you home by myself."

While Gwen worked on his shoulder, he couldn't help noticing how tired Tess looked. There were still smears of blood on her face. Her cheeks were still hollow from before, when she'd been so sick.

Tess had wrapped his shoulder up tight with a pretty decent bandage she'd made from a bandana. Everyone on the S-Line carried one. It was standard equipment. She'd helped him drag the deer carcass to camp, dumped him in Gwen's hands, and then headed toward the barn.

She'd seemed quiet to him since they'd gotten back, but, after all, they were running on fumes again. It had been a long night. It left him hollowed out when he thought of what he'd confessed to her. Couldn't explain why he'd done it—not even to himself, except that she had to know, sooner or later. She's *just tired*, he told himself. That's why she'd gotten so quiet.

Parrish wanted to ask about Blake and Blane, and by default Jamie, but he thought he should wait until after their mom finished stitching up his shoulder where the big cat had raked it open. It was just a flap of skin, pretty superficial, but he didn't want to take the chance of annoying her while she shoved a needle into him. She worked with a single-minded determination that told him she was trying not to think about the other stuff: Blake and Blane, feeding thirteen new mouths, the end of their home, the end of the S-Line, the end of safety.

She muttered something under her breath as she jabbed the curved needle through his shoulder.

He knew better, but he asked anyway.

"What? What did you say?"

She looked surprised when he spoke, as if the chair he was sitting on had decided to hold a conversation.

"I said, 'Mountain lions. What a great idea.' Let's re-introduce mountain lions back into Florida and bring back Florida panthers so hikers would have the full experience when they wandered through the swamps. Another one of those ideas that might have made sense once upon a time." Frown lines deepened as she concentrated.

The strange thinking of governmental agencies, he thought. It was as good as anything to fixate on. He almost smiled.

"Fish and Game could have hardly known that the world was going to get so mountain lion friendly and so soon," he said.

"No, I'm sure that's true. Well-meaning idiots."

She finished stitching, pulling the last suture tight, knotting it.

"It was going to be video games and toll roads forever, wasn't it?" she said.

He wasn't sure what he was supposed to say to that. He could hardly remember sitting in front of a plasma screen and endlessly shooting at pretend alien invaders. If he had the chance, would he go back to it, to the endless battles against cartoons?

"Gwen?"

She answered him by pouring rubbing alcohol over his shoulder; he jetted to his feet, crushing back a vicious curse.

"Sorry, I should have warned you."

She didn't sound sorry. He figured he'd better have it out with her now, rather than later.

"Where's Jamie?" he asked.

"How should I know? He's got my boys following him around like a rock star with free tickets to a concert."

"Gwen, we don't have a lot of options in all this. He'll take care of them. If there's anyone I'd trust my boys to, it's Jamie Tallahassee."

"See! That's what I'm talking about. That's not his name. You know it's not. What kind of people don't tell other people their names? Their right names, the names their mommas gave them?" She took a breath. "What have you got him doing with my boys anyway, Richmond Parrish?"

Sarcasm dripped off of the last part of her statement like good, thick syrup.

Parrish tested his arm, trying to rotate it against the tight sutures. Torn tissue soaked in alcohol screamed in protest.

"He's got them preparing to fight for their home—for you. It's that or we fail."

He started to say that she should try being proud of them, but closed his mouth when the sound of something exploding carried across the quiet morning and into the clearing in front of the longhouse. They were small bangs, all things considered.

"What was that? You tell me right now!"

Gwen Dunn looked at Parrish, holding her suture needle in front of his face like a tiny dagger.

CHAPTER 39

BLAKE'S EYES WERE a little glazed, while Blane's sparkled with the battle lust of a nine-year-old boy that had gotten to heave Molotov cocktails at a couple of bad guys.

Parrish could see that Jamie was doing his best to ignore Gwen as she ran her hands up and down the boys arms, looking for injuries, burns, anything she could bandage or cocoon. He concentrated on giving Parrish his report. Gwen was just going to have to learn to live with the new normal of their lives. Guerrilla warfare. Waged by children. For Jamie and Parrish it was business as usual, unless they managed a peace treaty.

"Parrish, only two men, that we saw. I thought . . . I don't know . . . I expected more. Solid weapons though. They're camped at the edge of 426 near the hard curve and the old rail line. Must have found the place where we were dragging through the underbrush with all this coming and going. They might have found the mule's tracks. Who knows?"

Jamie swiped at the dirt on his face. He kept his voice low.

"Any sign that they're coming at us from down the river?"

"Not that I can see."

"The old man knew what he was doing when he decided to bury this place up against a swamp. Parrish, there's too much perimeter and too few soldiers."

"Coming at us from the old front gate doesn't really play. There aren't any trails or roads in. There's just the river, and where Tess hacked her way out, but that's hardly quick going. We'd hear them. We'd know. And they'd have to come at us almost single file. It's the river pretty much or nothing. So what kind of send up did you give them?"

Eyeing Gwen, Jamie tried to look guilty underneath his glee, but had the presence of mind to signal to the boys to keep their mouths shut with a quick shake of his head.

"We doubled around and set off a couple of smoke bombs, just to let them know that they might not have all the facts."

"What do you think?" Parrish asked.

Gwen slammed her way out of the screen door, trailing bandages for the washtub and a bad attitude. Parrish thought how much he'd like to rip that squeaking, whining screen door right off its hinges.

Jamie shooed the two boys after their mother.

"Go, help your mother. There's a lot of fresh venison that needs to be boiled up."

The boys saluted Jamie before bolting to their next assignment.

The screen door slammed again.

"I think those Marketplace guys wouldn't give a crap if we'd thrown hand grenades into their campfire. I think they think they've got our number. They may not know we've picked up a dozen more skinny kids to worry about, and I doubt if they care. The first blast shook them a bit, but they didn't seem too worried. And that might be their downfall."

He pointed to Parrish's shoulder.

"What happened to you? That girl figure you out and slap you with that tomahawk of hers?"

"No, but a panther looking for a deer steak almost did. It's wild and woolly enough around here without unwelcome visitors, and that might be to our advantage too."

"I'll tell you what'd be to our advantage: finding a stockpile of AR-15s and the ammo to fill them."

"Yeah."

"Parrish, you should know. There's something else."

He could feel the weight of bad news settle on his neck. The cramp of muscles beneath the bandage on his arm ached like a rotten tooth.

"What?"

"They sent a note. We found it on the fence, down from the road. They're waiting for an answer. That's why they're not on us already. They've got plenty of time, plenty of time to march in here and kill us all. They want the kid back. Prince Jerome." Disdain dripped from his voice.

"Good. We can use that."

Ally and ZeeZee had strung the deer up in the tree by the fire pit and gone to work on it with knives. They waited for the kettle of water to roll before they tossed in hunks of back strap and roast.

Tess and Gwen's boys joined in as soon as they were back from their chores. The biggest boy, Stone, helped them. They all knew that the faster they got it into the pot, the safer eating it would be. If life had been running on normal, they'd have fired up the smoke house and done the job right.

They worked quietly, each wrapped in their own thoughts, their own worries. The twins had pitched in to help without being asked, but Tess had been too preoccupied to notice.

When had that happened? Butchering was a job they usually avoided like poison. Too messy. Too bloody. They weren't little girls anymore.

She glanced at Ally and noticed how white her face had gotten as the blood smeared higher and higher up her arms. It couldn't be easy. Tess's heart tipped sideways. Jamie sat at the picnic table, gun parts strewn across a plastic tablecloth like the tumbled parts of an oily puzzle. Tess watched him slide a quick, longing glance at Ally. Tess hoped he got his gun back together in one piece.

"Hey, ZeeZee, how about some more water so we can wash this stuff off of us? I'd rather not drain the rain barrel dry," Tess suggested.

She dipped her head, saying nothing—not arguing, or complaining. She picked up an empty bucket and headed out to the pump.

"Wait up, ZeeZee," Jamie called out. "Buddy system. I'll walk you." He touched the pistol at his belt. "I'll finish this when I get back." He pointed at the gun parts.

Ally barely registered ZeeZee leaving, but she cut a quick look at Jamie, a faint question on her pretty face.

Beyond the Strandline

Gwen came over and poured a Number 10 can of dehydrated potatoes into the boiling pot. Venison stew. Maybe you couldn't live on bread alone, but you sure could live on bread and stew. Gwen stirred the kettle, her mouth clamped shut.

"It's good to have Jamie and Parrish back, don't you think?" Ally said.

"Jamie," Gwen snorted. "That big kid? He took my boys out on what amounts to a practice panty raid against murderers." Gwen stared into the kettle, the Number 10 can forgotten in her hand. She snorted again.

"And the boys are back. They're fine," Tess said.

Tess sat at the picnic table next to the kettle and started cleaning her tomahawk. Time to change the subject. "Hey, where are all those Doe Kids anyway? Have you been able to talk to any of them? Find out if they *can* talk?"

"Kilmer and Jess T took them off to the river to see about washing the lice out of their hair. We should start a pot boiling with water for them to wash those rags they're wearing. The girls brought out extra clothes for them, most of them. That Stone kid," Gwen said, nodding toward the boy still working with Ally on the carcass, "won't take anything, and barely admits that he's wearing clothes. I'm thinking of sending him to make a gut pile out past the last fence. I know you had to field dress the deer to get him back here, but there's still the bones and hide to deal with, and I don't have time, not today."

Blane carried a hunk of roast to the kettle with two hands just as a naked boy jetted into the clearing and smashed into him, pushing him to his knees. The roast rolled in the dirt. Kilmer hobbled into the clearing, then over to Blane, yanking him to his feet. Blane picked up the dirt-encrusted meat, flopping it on the table. Blake started trying to pick sticks and gravel off the filthy meat.

"Sorry, Tess, Gwen. They aren't taking so well to getting de-loused."

"Why is that one naked?" Gwen pointed.

"When we got to the river, the lot of them shed the rags they're calling clothes, and jumped in for a quick dip. It's a skinny-dipping stampede down there. Jess T wanted to start throwing a lasso around them and dragging them out like spring calves."

The boy scrambled to the top of the picnic table.

"Hey, watch the gun stuff, pal," Tess barked.

The dog, damp from the river, skidded to a stop at the base of the picnic table and started barking at the kid.

Parrish walked out from the woods rolling his shoulder, testing the bandage for security. He stepped over to Tess and looked up at the boy. He pointed at the ground and said, "Down, Wart."

With a quick shake of his scraggly hair, the boy hopped to the ground and then darted away from Kilmer, heading for a knot of underbrush. Kilmer looked like he might collapse. His face resembled a boiled beet.

The dog chased the boy out of the bushes. Parrish tried to grab the slippery kid as he darted past. Refusing to be dragged into the chase, Stone ignored the craziness.

"Tell him to put his clothes on," Tess demanded, looking at Stone.

He shrugged, "He'll put clothes on when he's cold."

"Now!" she ordered. She must have shown just the right amount of authority. After shrugging again, Stone turned and went after the naked kid.

Parrish cursed and cradled his wounded shoulder. The boy raced across the sand of the clearing just as Tess's father wandered into view with Jerome Fortix in tow. Jamie left ZeeZee with her sloshing bucket of water at the bend in the trail when he saw Jerome and her father.

"What's he doing here?" Ally choked out.

Jamie was at her side, had an arm around her shoulders before Jerome could shout back. Jerome stabbed a finger at Ally.

"She tried to take a knife to me! It's not safe back at that hut you're holding me prisoner in. And what about Arnold? He's awake and he's hungry."

"For a dead guy, he looks pretty good," her father offered. "That Mr. Arnold seems to be doing much better."

"Pretty good? He looks like a zombie. Get that black woman back there to do her job."

Jamie walked over to Jerome and punched him in the mouth, knocking him to the ground. Tess watched her father reach down to help Jerome up.

Ally went crazy, pushing her father aside so she could kick the cringing figure on the ground. She spit at the fallen prince as Jamie pulled her away.

"Ally, don't," ZeeZee yelled, dropping her pail of water. "Ally, he's not worth it!"

"Not worth it? He knows about us. He's here and he knows about us. And now he has to stay because he knows we're here."

"Ally, please. This is the kind of violence we have to stop," Father said. "Let it begin with us."

"Dad, what are you doing?" Tess demanded. Then she turned her anger toward Ally, "And what was he saying about a knife? A knife? Who had a knife?" Tess jumped up. "What does he mean, Ally?"

Her father started yipping something about "giving peace a chance."

The din in the clearing started to sound like a flock of sandhill cranes during mating season. Stone appeared, leading the escaped boy firmly by his ear. The kid was yelling his head off.

"Shut up, everyone," Gwen yelled, banging her stirring stick against the stew pot. "Somebody get more water. That filthy meat is not going in my stew."

"You can probably hear this caterwauling all the way to the river," Kilmer said. He picked up ZeeZee's bucket of water and swung it onto the tabletop. "If they didn't know about us before, they do now."

Probably right about that, Tess thought. They were being loud enough to be heard all the way to the coast, but in all the chaos and yowling, one comment had registered—something about Ally and a knife and Jerome.

CHAPTER 40

Gwen took charge; she sent Tess's father back to the fishing hut with stew, Jerome, and an assignment: Feed Arnold. Check his leg. Get Jerome out of Ally's sight and away from Jamie's fists.

Stone made the naked kid put on his clothes, wash his hair.

Ally went after more water. The errand seemed to calm her. Jamie offered to help, but she told him to stay and help Parrish look for clean clothes to change into. The boys washed dirt off the roast; ZeeZee stirred stew.

And now the clearing smelled like food, venison stew: good, thick, venison stew. Steam rolled away from the boiling kettle in a wave, creating a siren's call. Without a sound, the Doe Kids started to drift back from the river into the clearing, their eyes fixed on the kettle of stew like puppies waiting for a chew toy. With wet hair and staring eyes they watched and waited. Jess T had had more luck with most of them than Kilmer had with the kid Parrish called Wart. They stood and waited patiently, watching Gwen's every move.

Food—the universal language.

Gwen shooed them toward the picnic table, but instead of sitting down they ringed the clearing, watchful, still uneasy after the din and chaos earlier.

Ally came into the clearing trying not to slop clean water over the edges of the bucket she carried. ZeeZee went to her and together they finished carrying it to the table. Water still sloshed. They giggled. It was a sound so familiar, so normal, that it took Tess's breath away. It frightened her.

Nerves crawled under Tess's skin. It felt like an omen or a warning, the laughter. It was all so precious and so fragile. She turned to the longhouse and slammed her way inside. She needed answers. Jamie and Parrish were rummaging for clothes out of a footlocker that belonged to her grandfather.

"What happened? What happened with Jerome and Ally?" Tess demanded.

Parrish sat on the footlocker, while Jamie held a clean shirt out for him; she watched as he struggled to push his bandaged shoulder into a sleeve. He was pale but clear eyed. Good. No fever. Yet. When he winced trying to button the front of his shirt, she choked out a sigh and pushed past Jamie to help Parrish with the fastening.

"You could at least help him button the idiotic thing."

Jamie backed away, mumbling, then reached into his pocket and pulled out Tess's skinning knife. He didn't explain.

"Thanks. I've been looking for this. Are you going to help me with what happened at the fishing shack? Or am I going to have to pick and nag and torture you?"

"What's to explain? I made a mistake."

"You did? Didn't Jerome say Ally had the knife? What mistake did *you* make?"

Jamie shoved his hands in his pockets and hunched inside his oversized work shirt. He looked young—like a kid that had just gotten caught breaking curfew.

"The mistake is that I didn't kill that bastard when I had the chance, when I found him wandering around crying. *Crying* for cripes sake. What a . . . worm."

Parrish hung his head and tried rolling his shoulder again. He stayed quiet.

"We need him." Tess hated saying it, hated the way the idea of using him as a bargaining chip felt in her head.

"Need him?"

Parrish looked up at his friend. "We're going to negotiate. He's our ticket out of this. He stays."

"Stays! Do you know what that's going to do to Ally? What it's already doing to her? That he's here? I walked in and found her holding a knife on him," he said. "She's never going to be the same. Sure, I get that." A frown clouded his face. "Okay. But murder? Murder, it eats you. It eats your guts."

Parrish stood up and reached out. Jamie jerked away and, without looking at Tess, slammed his way out of the longhouse.

"He'll figure it out. He's solid. They'll follow if you lead," Parrish said. "By the way, your eyes look like radishes."

"Thanks. I guess that means that they're red, or does that mean that they're white? Radishes are both."

He sheepishly looked down at his half-buttoned shirt. Jamie's little outburst had interrupted Tess's fastening job. She stepped closer to him to finish what she'd started, and tried hard to concentrate on buttoning his shirt and not on the tan, smooth skin underneath it.

He stared down at her fingers on his shirtfront.

She worked quietly, buttoning the last two buttons of one of her grandfather's old work shirts. It was loose and roomy on Parrish. Sooner or later everything in storage made an appearance—even a dead man's clothes were fair game. The shirt smelled faintly of her grandfather's old cologne, Obsession.

Before she finished, her hands shook a little bit.

He caught her trembling hands in his own, and squeezed them. She gave herself a mental shake. It was a good technique, she had to admit. He was probably good with skittish mules too. Maybe he wasn't trying to push her completely away with what he'd told her on the deer stand. Maybe he was trying to reach out to her somehow. As confident and detached as he'd tried to seem after that awkward conversation, she could still see some uncertainty in his eyes, his hands trembling only slightly less than her own. As much as he tried to push her away, Tess only felt more drawn to Parrish as they stood there alone in the longhouse. She stared at their joined hands and looked up at him, at his head still bowed. She saw that his eyelashes were too long for a boy. She should have been a little bit jealous. But it wasn't jealousy that fluttered in her stomach when he touched her.

His lips firmed, thinned. She saw that the fleeting moment of vulnerability and emotion had passed. Stepping away from her, he went to his pack and pulled out a sheet of paper.

Construction paper? She hadn't seen construction paper in a long time. He handed it to her.

Beyond the Strandline

Someone had scrawled a note on the pink paper in thick black strokes.

Ms. Lane,

Give us our son and brother and the girl Alpha, or prepare to lose everything. Two days.

"Do not engage an enemy more powerful than you." Sun Tzu

Wendy Fortix of the Marketplace

Tess saw the words, the heavy, thick lines. Wendy Fortix had written them with crayon, maybe, or a grease pencil. The threat dripped across the paper in black, ominous words.

It was so much like those other words uttered to a man, his wife, and their three daughters as they'd tried to cross a bridge. The memory was like a molten streak of fire inside her head.

Give us the woman or . . .

"Jamie found it when he went out with the boys. The Fortix men had stuck it on the fence post at the edge of the ranch. They're waiting. This is good. It gives us time. We should use that."

"What's this mean? This 'Sun Tzu'?"

"*The Art of War*, it's a very old book. Someone fancies themselves a warrior," he said. He shook his head and smirked. "The rest of the quote is: 'And if it is unavoidable and you do have to engage, then make sure you engage it on your terms, not on your enemy's terms.' It's good advice."

He took the pink paper out of her hands.

"We have what she wants, Tess. We have Jerome. This proves it."

"Yeah, and you want to walk in and surrender yourself to a group of people who thought tying the body of a dead kid to a mule was a good idea. What makes you want to trust them? How can you possibly trust them?"

The panther's blood on her vest smelled raw and sickly sweet. Or was it Parrish's blood? It made her head hurt. So much blood already.

"Parrish, what are you thinking? This can't work."

She watched a muscle in his jaw twitch.

"I'm not going over this again with you. You can't know that it won't work. We'll see. Get some sleep." He turned his back to her and started toward the door.

She followed him and grabbed at the back of his shirt. She heard him suck air through his teeth. She'd forgotten the stitches in his shoulder.

He tried to shrug her off, refused to look at her.

"Tess, lie down. Rest."

"Don't treat me like a child."

"Then stop acting like a child."

"Why aren't you more worried? Did you already strike up this deal with the Marketplace? During the time you left? Don't think that I've forgotten that simple fact: You left us!" She yanked at the shirt, demanding that he turn around, face her. She didn't care that he hurt. "Don't think I'll *ever* forget that."

He spun around so fast that he caught her open mouthed and flat footed. He was in her face.

"But I came back. I didn't have to. I never have before, believe me, and I didn't want to tell you about the note because I knew what you would do. You'd suck up the threat of it like water and probably march into their camp and get yourself killed. I'll take those two days. All of it. We need them. To rest. To eat. To think. We need this. You need this."

He grabbed her by the shoulders.

"No. On second thought, there's nothing to think about." He wasn't quiet now. "I can do this. I will do this. I'm going."

"No. You're not." She tried to pull away but his fingers dug into her skin. He shook his head.

Tess struggled against his grip. "Stop touching me! You're always touching me and then telling me that it's wrong. I'm so sick of you getting close to me and then throwing me aside when *you* don't think you can handle it anymore."

"This isn't about you and me. It's about staying out of a civil war. Can't you understand that?"

His blind determination scared her, his certainty that he could single handedly stop their enemies by sacrificing himself was infuriating. His moments of tenderness and then hostility broke her. Without thinking, she raised her hand and slapped him. The sound cracked against the metal walls of the longhouse like a bell.

"No! I can't let you. I won't sacrifice you to save the rest of us. I'd rather see the entire place burned to the ground and live in an open field and watch Ally have that baby in a ditch. I'd rather kill her myself." She felt her hands go numb and heat creep into her face. "My father did it. He *gave* my mother away. Those savages demanded and threatened, and I watched them drag my mother away. They tore the hair out of her head. My father killed my mother to save us."

Now it was his turn to look shocked.

"My mother." She gagged on the word. "They took my mother."

A small sound caught Tess's attention, broke into the red blanket of her panic and terror. Someone gasped.

Ally stood inside the screen door, her face white under the brand on her face. Father stood behind her, the light hallowed out around his white hair, his eyes wide and his mouth slack.

"Tessie," her father began.

Ally rounded on him.

"Shut up. You need to shut up now. Okay?"

When he flinched, she reached out and patted his shoulder. "Please. Let me talk now. You need to let me."

Ally walked to Tess, pulled the pink paper out of her hands. When she'd finished reading the note, she calmly folded the paper into smaller and smaller rectangles. When it was small enough to tuck into a shirt pocket, she looked at Parrish.

"Well, it's one option isn't it?"

"I can't listen to this." Tess kicked the screen door open. With a final screech and whine it sailed off its hinges, out into the clearing. She stomped across it, Doe Kids scattering like chickens in front of her.

CHAPTER 41

PARRISH FOLLOWED HER. She didn't stop walking until the trail turned into a path and then the path became not much more than a hint of someone passing through the quick grass. She only hesitated once, probably long enough to register the way the grass lay down, smashed by footsteps; Stone hauling hide and bones away from the longhouse.

The sky was an impossible blue, the air strangely still and expectant.

He followed her to a place they called the Last Fence, the eastern border of the S-Line. It was the last section of ten-foot-high galvanized fence that had once surrounded the ranch, tall enough to satisfy the laws regulating the raising of exotic animals—the laws that seemed so pointless now, ridiculous even.

A half a dozen vultures balanced on the remaining steel posts, while a dozen more fought over the deer's hide. The skin and bones would have been heavy hauling. He was impressed that Stone had gone the distance, with a backpack stuffed full. Sure, they could have buried it closer to home, but that just encouraged scavengers into camp. Better to haul it out here. Keep the rabble at bay, make a gut pile.

He saw her watching the vultures pick and squabble over the bloody leftovers. If they left anything at all, the coyotes and pigs would converge on the remnants tonight. Didn't look like there was going to be much to choose from, not with this mob fighting over it. Scraps.

"You probably need this."

She turned. Parrish held his canteen out to her with his good arm, noted that she barely looked surprised. She took the canteen, shook her head, and sipped water.

"You did it again. Slipped up behind me."

"Come on. You knew I was following you."

She shrugged. "Yeah, I did."

"You know we don't have all day for your temper tantrum. You should hurry it up."

She looked up at him in disbelief, open-mouthed.

"If that's what you came out here to tell me you should have saved yourself the effort. You can't keep doing this to me. It might not mean anything to you when you kiss me . . . when you make me care." She stopped, shook her head at him. "Oh, never mind and go away. I'm trying hard to hate you."

"Good. Probably your best bet." He tried to make it sound like a joke. Thought he might have gotten close to hitting the right note, even though he knew the truth was there underneath all the turmoil between them.

He accepted it, had known it was coming. Regardless of the way they felt about each other, it was always going to come to this—her needing to hate him rather than being hurt. Him pushing her until she either revolted or cracked. Better now than later.

He concentrated on getting air back into his lungs, to slow the hammering in his chest. It was hard to breathe: partly from running after her, partly because of the way his shoulder ached like a rotten tooth, and partly because of the way she was looking at him.

Bringing the water had been a good idea. He swiped at his face. She'd headed out without thinking, without even bringing her tomahawk—never a good idea to be unarmed and unprepared. Not in this world.

The sky started to weep. Rain fell from a sun-bright sky like tears from above—a sun shower. Another sure sign they were in for a storm. He closed his eyes and let the sprinkle cool his hot face.

Surprised, he felt her push the canteen against his arm to get his attention, watched as she turned her face up to the quick, light rain. Good enough, then. He drank.

He saw her watching him clear eyed and calm. He was stalling. He knew that. Her calm bothered him more than tears and tantrums, more than slaps across the face. He watched two vultures play tug-of-war with the deer's tail. He plopped down in the dirt to enjoy the rain.

"Charming. Quite a getaway spot you've got here by the gut pile."

She ignored the comment. "Yeah," she said. Then pointed to his cheek. "Sorry, for that."

She watched him rub his knuckles over the bruise that was spreading across his face where she'd slapped him. She sat down next to him, but just far enough away to show that she was nowhere near forgiving or trusting him again. He'd kissed her and then ignored her far too many times for that.

"Tess, listen to me." He scooted closer to her, but not too close to spook her. "When the bad comes for the people you care about, it changes everything—forever. Others say that you should be able to get over stuff like that, forget about it," he said, dropping his voice. "But you can't. You don't, and you won't get over it. You live with it, and if you're very lucky, the nightmares stop after a while. Don't be sorry. I'm going to take it as a sign that you might miss me."

Her face collapsed. Angry tears made her eyes bright.

"Is that some kind of joke? It's cruel to joke about this."

He sighed. The pine hammock and its inhabitants creaked and croaked the way they always had, all the little creatures going about their business, busy with the idea of being alive.

Parrish tried not to let her tears dissuade him from what he wanted to say to her. "Hear them? The birds? The lizards? I was like that not too long ago, going about my business, day to day, just living." He looked at her and continued, "But then, then I realized that somewhere in the last couple of weeks, just living stopped being enough. And maybe I felt a little greedy because just living wasn't going to work for me anymore, not if I couldn't keep you safe." He ran a hand over the back of his neck, flinched when the movement pulled at the stitches in his shoulder. "I want to kill the men who put the fear in your face, but this is war, and there's no place for stolen kisses and sentiment on the battlefield. We need to push our feelings aside until we figure out how to save our home."

She looked up, visibly pulling herself together.

"You're right," she said, waving her hand softly at nothing. "We have to think about the S-Line. Home. My home. Our home."

Beyond the Strandline

Her eyes were still glazed, her voice a little bit dreamy. Rain dripped.

"You know what it means, right? What S-Line means?" She caught his eye, searched his face.

She'd thrown him—again.

"It's a ranch brand, the S with a line," he said. "I mean, I guess."

"Sure. That too. But it's short for something: Strandline."

He shook his head; he hadn't known. He'd assumed that it was the name of a simple cattle brand.

"What's it mean then? Strandline?"

She stood up, sending the vultures into the sky in a mad puff of feathers. Rain plopped into the dirt around them, pocking the ground, and then stopped as suddenly as it had started.

"On the beach, it's that line along the edge of the sand when the tide washes out. It's all the stuff that's left after high tide, the seaweed and shells—that ribbon on the sand."

"Yeah, okay, the garbage and crap washed up from the ocean."

"Sure, but it's also the good stuff, you know, the treasures, the most beautiful shells and the sand dollars. That's what my grandfather wanted us to see: After the tide goes out there are treasures left behind after the high water. We're the strandline. We're what's left. Don't you get it? My grandfather bought this place before I was born, got it ready, prepped it for us, so we wouldn't be pecked to death by vultures or worse. My grandfather knew. He knew. And we've ruined it."

Her eyes darkened as she glanced over to the scrabbling birds. He wasn't sure if she even knew that she was crying. He pulled at the woolly leaves growing in the dirt next to him. He took her hand and threaded his fingers through hers, pulling her to her feet as he stood up.

She held up a finger and waggled it at him. "Don't. I can't take your games. I always lose."

He folded her gently into his arms. "Hush. I tried to tell you that I'm a bad bet, and you don't seem too concerned about that. Even though we can't be much more until this is over, let's at least be something. I can't take the games either."

"But you'll cheat."

"Only most of the time. It's a bad habit." He held her easily in the circle of his arms. When she tried to pull away again, he said, "Let me while I can. Tell me about the Strandline."

She tipped her head at him but quit trying to pull away.

"My grandfather knew," she said. "The way my mother knew that day on the bridge. She told my father not to stop the car, but he didn't listen, and we lost her, and he didn't do anything to stop it. I didn't listen either, and I almost lost Ally . . . and now you. I'm going to lose you, and I can't. There has to be another way to fix this. Something we haven't thought of . . . some other way. "

She searched his face as if she'd never see it before. Her eyes sparkled like rain in sunshine. He reached out and wiped the rain and tears off her face with the leaves of lamb's ear, knowing how soft they would feel, wanting to show her . . . what . . . that there was still softness in the world?

"You know what we call that stuff, right?" She looked at the wad of fuzzy green in his hand.

He tossed the leaves away and waited. "What?"

"Cowboy toilet paper. You just wiped my face with toilet paper."

He felt a smile grow, felt his heart contract.

"Beats a sharp stick in the eye."

"Or a slap."

"Tess?" He cupped her cheek, felt her press back against his hand, heard her sigh.

"Before, I tried to tell myself that this thing between you and me was just because I was your only choice, that you were lonely, that you were desperate. But I knew better, from the beginning I knew better. And it scared me. You scared me. Caring so much scared me."

Standing in the soft shadow of the overhang, damp from the rain and close to tears, he thought she was the most beautiful thing he'd ever seen.

"I can't promise I won't try to pull away again. I'm broken . . . just a broken shell on the beach, Tess."

That got a smile. It was sad, but it was a smile nonetheless.

"Yeah, but it's not fair for me to slug a damaged 'shell,' even though I'm just as broken as you are. We'll figure this out. We will. You don't run, and I won't punch you. Okay? Deal?"

It was his turn to smile.

Vultures hopped and fought while she waited for his answer. He gave her a quick nod.

"Deal. Come on. Let's go home. Let me take you home."

CHAPTER 42

Wendy Fortix loved the smells: of honey, of essential oils, of beeswax, anything fragrant she could find. Her workshop was like an island of pleasant odors in the middle of a sea of stink. That's the way she liked to think about her workshop, once a janitor's closet, where she mixed and measured and cooked her concoctions. Some days she came to her closet just to breathe.

The world stank of blood, dung, sweat, and fear now. It all stank. When the lights had gone out, so did the perfume of the old world: the air fresheners, the perfumes, the soaps, all those beautiful soaps full of oil and scent.

Hadn't she made it her mission to bring back some of the delights of that civilized and pleasant place? Of course it was. Didn't she send her men out to beg, borrow, or steal what she needed to bring a bit of beauty to the women and girls of the Marketplace? Absolutely.

At her workbench, she turned a long mold full of aloe vera soap over and watched it slide free. She patted the pale yellow bar, and admired the faint hint of mint. In another couple of days she'd slice it into bath bars and tuck it away with the rest. Last count, there were eight hundred bars of soap: handmade, confiscated, stolen . . . no, not stolen . . . "collected."

Marco understands. No . . . not present tense . . . had understood. Past tense. Hadn't he always looked for propane for her little camp stove? Hadn't he made sure her workshop had a chimney for ventilation and a skylight? Hadn't he always brought her as many bars of soap as he could find? Sure, he had. Past tense.

Checking her camp stove, Wendy watched coconut oil and beeswax melt into each other. She breathed it all in, letting the smells calm her. She had lots of beeswax, but all of the other ingredients were gone or almost gone. Someone would have to go in search of the important stuff soon. Marco . . . no, not Marco.

There was a scratch at the door, not a knock. They knew better than to knock. At least *that* hadn't changed.

She opened the door.

A round pumpkin of a man waited for her invitation to speak—Dory Newton. He smelled. Wendy stepped back, reached for a bottle of peppermint oil. Unscrewing the cap, she tipped oil onto her finger and dabbed it under her nostrils. Such an ugly, smelly little man, but clever with the generator. Marco had found him useful, had depended on him. She sighed.

"Nothing. We've heard nothing from Jerome or Arnold. They're just gone, disappeared," he said. He kept his eyes on the ground. "There's been no response to the note we left."

"No!"

He shuffled back a step.

"Not disappeared. I know that girl. That girl's family. I remember them from before. The grandmother, Georgina Kennedy, and I went to church together."

What she didn't tell him was that she'd only seen her from the back row of the church. The raggedy Fortix family, riddled with bad luck and need, always poor, always pitiful, sat at the back, staring at the affluence in front of them. She stared, month after month, at the back of Georgina Kennedy's golden head seated next to her husband, the dashing colonel. They were supposed to be dead—gone. The ranch burned. The S-Line dissolved into wilderness and ruin.

Breathing through her teeth, she said, "No. They haven't disappeared. They're there. They have Jerome and Arnold out in that stinking swamp. The S-Line has until sunset tomorrow and then we'll . . . see to setting this right. Go. Inform the others. Get them ready."

Turning her back, she dismissed him completely. With a dropper she carefully counted out twenty-five drops of vanilla and wondered if Georgina's husband had thought to stock up on coconut oil.

CHAPTER 43

When they finally got back to the longhouse, Tess collapsed—facedown, still wearing her boots. Ally and ZeeZee had managed to pull off her hiking boots, her filthy vest. But they'd given up after that.

Gwen had pushed Parrish into her boy's bunk. He hadn't wanted to admit that his shoulder throbbed and that his head felt like an overripe tomato. Better to just sleep it off, but not before Gwen got a hold of him.

Clucking like a worried hen, she changed the bandage on his shoulder, poured more alcohol over his stitches, poked at the wound, and managed to make him feel a lot worse.

"We'll check it in the morning. How's your head?"

Before he could jerk away from her, Gwen had her hand against his forehead and a thumb on the pulse in his wrist. She handed him some aspirin.

"Hopefully they've still got some kick in them. The girls found them in the storage shed, dry packed. You've got some fever, but that's not completely unexpected. No more wandering around for you until we make sure this doesn't get worse."

The rebellion must have shown on his face because Gwen gave him a bare-toothed grimace designed to intimidate small boys and frighten people into flossing regularly. "If you want to die, and you will if you don't take care of this, then by all means, don't listen to me."

He glanced over at Tess's bunk where she slept like a dead person. Exhausted. And they still had to figure out how to come out of this thing with the Marketplace in one piece.

"Okay, you bet. You're right. Absolutely."

Gwen didn't look convinced.

"Fine," she said, patting his leg. "I don't believe you for a second, but we're going to pretend that I do. Sleep. Tomorrow is another day, Scarlett." She laughed at his confusion.

"Great line from a great book," she explained. "Maybe we'll get a chance to talk about it soon. Sleep."

"What book?"

"Gone With the Wind."

He wasn't sure if she was kidding or not. It seemed a bad title to be joking about right now, because it could be gone, all of it . . . whether with the wind or something else.

The next morning, there was mist and fog from the longhouse to the river. It rolled along in fat, damp clouds along the trails of the S-Line. Tess liked when the fog rolled in. It made all the hard edges blur, softened the world, and turned everything into a fantasy. When the twins were little they'd play hide-and-seek in it, half the time giving themselves away by giggling.

Tess walked fast, determined to be off the S-Line before anyone could stop her. She snuck out of the longhouse before anyone else had gotten up.

Parrish had been hot to the touch and breathing heavy when she'd left, probably fighting an infection. Gwen would know what to do about it. Hopefully. Tess made herself believe it.

The Doe Kids had found their way into nooks and crannies under the overhang of the longhouse: under and on top of the picnic table, tucked into blankets and sleeping bags like baby marsupials. Hopefully Kilmer and Jess T would think to build a shelter for the new kids, something more permanent than having them cuddle up against the metal of the Quonset hut, but she couldn't think about that right now.

She hadn't trusted herself to go by the twins' bunk, afraid she'd wake them up and tip them off that she'd decided to leave.

She needed to get to the Marketplace and deal with the consequences of all their actions.

The fog felt right, hiding her from everyone like a curtain created for secrets and secret missions.

CHAPTER 44

When she reached the fishing shack, the fog played tricks on her. A tree next to the porch appeared to have grown arms and legs and a shock of red hair.

"Jamie! Oh my God, Jamie." Tess's heart hammered so hard she'd thought she'd be sick with it when she saw him tied to a tree outside the fishing shack. White and slack jawed, he looked dead. He'd been a bony lump in the drifting fog.

She had her tomahawk out and was working on cutting through the heavy rope looped on his wrists before she heard the snore. He was snoring. He wasn't dead. He was asleep.

She cut his hands free and then watched him stretch and yawn.

"Holy crap! I thought you were dead." She jumped to her feet and lunged toward the fishing shack. "Jerome." Saying his name felt like doom and failure.

"Hey, Tess, don't. It's okay. He's still here," he said, rubbing a lump on the side of his head the size of a tennis ball. "They didn't take him. Boy, I'm glad you wandered by. Why did you?" He rubbed his wrists. "Bringing something to eat?" He sounded hopeful.

"Checking up on you." She felt the weight of the tomahawk in her hand. She wasn't ready to tell him that she'd been passing by on her way to the Marketplace.

"Jerome is . . . here? What? Why would they leave Jerome? Wait a minute! Who's they?"

"Looks like your hostage exchange idea has caught on," Jamie said, rubbing his writsts. "We should get moving. They were here pretty early. And I've got a few things to say to that sister of yours."

Tess shook her head. Inside the shack, she heard Jerome rattling his chains.

"Hey!" Jerome yelled. "What's with all the craziness around here? I'm hungry."

"My sister?" She stared at Jamie, the truth dawning on her the way the fog had drifted away. "What are you . . . are you telling me Ally did this to you?"

"No. Not that sister." He started. "And ZeeZee had some help." Jerome clanked and whined. Jamie walked up the steps and slammed his fist against the frame of the screen door. "Shut up in there. You'll live."

"Who are you talking about?" She watched him gather up his rifle where, presumably, his attackers had left it on the porch. "Ally and ZeeZee hit you on the head? They managed to get the jump on you? I find that hard to bel— "

Jamie managed to look disgusted and chagrined all at the same time. "No, Tess. I didn't let two girls crack me over the head. Just one."

"One? But you said *they*?"

"It was ZeeZee and that kid . . . the one they call Pebble or Rock or Stone or whatever. He sicked that dog of his on me, too. They took Arnold. I think your sister thinks she's going to be the S-Line's great sacrificial lamb," Jamie said, his eyes going cool and flat. "But I don't think that boy has any idea of sacrificing anyone except maybe the people who hurt his kids and the dead girl. You know when they tied that kid to that mule, the little girl. Turns out, it was his sister."

Her heart ached. Another sister. Stone's sister. "The little girl we buried."

"Tess." Jamie shoved a magazine into his AR-15. "We should hurry."

There was an elephant sitting on his shoulder, with a blow dryer—a big, hot elephant. He remembered blow dryers. Hadn't his sisters been constantly drying or curling something? Sure, he remembered. But they weren't around anymore—not for a long time. Tess. Tess was around and there was something important he needed to remember about that, if he could just get the elephant off his shoulder.

Parrish instantly regretted opening his eyes. The light inside the longhouse might as well have been molten lava. It *hurt*. Before he thought, he jerked his arm up to block the blaze of light. The elephant became a big cat's claw. And that *was* real, the panther on the hunting trip.

"Hey, be still, let me look," Gwen said. "Parrish, you've got a fever. We need to soak your shoulder because I don't have any more antibiotics. Parrish, are you listening to me? We need to take care of this."

Somewhere a pan rattled. Somebody was making oatmeal, maybe pancakes. It made him want to laugh; if he felt better he might be tempted to have a stack of pancakes. He pushed himself up.

Ally was there next to Gwen, helping with the nursing duties.

"Where is Tess, Gwen?" Ally asked.

"She was out and about early. You know how she is in the morning. Early."

"Is ZeeZee with her then? Out early too?" Ally said, then handed Gwen a cloth soaked and steaming.

Not pancakes then. Boiling water.

"Thanks." Gwen wouldn't meet his eyes as she pulled the dressing off of his shoulder. He sucked air in through his teeth when she slapped the hot cloth onto his skin. "ZeeZee left before the sun was up, helping me out. I sent her for garlic."

"Shouldn't she be back by now?"

"No. Not necessarily."

She looked at his shoulder as if she could see the infection creeping around inside the wound, hoping to find a way to squash the germs one by one.

"Parrish, you need to let me clean this again. Ally, bring me that peroxide."

It felt wrong, and it wasn't just his head or the scalding pain that ate at his shoulder. Something else, something was off. He glanced over at Tess's bunk—clean, neat, tidy. It was the way she always left it when she was out and about. Perfect. Maybe too perfect. She'd been so tired yesterday, exhausted really.

The book. The book he'd given her, the one she'd dismissed and tossed on her nightstand. His book about the Middle Ages, because that's where their world had ended up after the grid collapse. Straight back to a time where warlords built castle keeps and still defended their territory to the death.

The book was gone, and he couldn't think of a single rational reason why she would take it, except for one. She was going to the Marketplace in a hostage exchange.

Beyond the Strandline

Anger burned behind his eyes the way the fever burned over his skin. He'd let his shoulder make him dull and slow, and she'd slipped away. He pushed Gwen away when she tried to wrap his arm in steaming cloths.

"Just put the bandage back on. Tess's not coming back," he said and watched Gwen's eyes grow round with worry and Ally's fingers whiten as she wrung the cloth in her hand too tight. "You stay put. I mean it." He pointed at Ally. I'll bring her back."

"And Parrish, I think that ZeeZee should be back by now," Ally added, worry clouding her face.

"Yeah. I know," he said as he swung his legs over the edge of the bunk.

The ground rumbled. Tess could feel it under her feet, in her arms. There was something so familiar about it. But not an earthquake, not in Central Florida. She felt stupid for not being able to put her finger on it.

"Tess," Jamie hissed into her ear. "Your sister? She have access to a swamp buggy?"

"What are you talking about?"

There was still a thin film of rainwater in the ditch where Tess and Jamie watched the road leading into Oviedo. Jamie had suggested they wait and watch before going after ZeeZee and Stone. Maybe it was a survival sense you developed when you had to fight for your life every day.

Tess exhaled, not realizing she'd been holding her breath in the first place. It was a swamp buggy, the kind that hunters had used in the backwoods—old enough to be pre-computer circuits or chips and still functioning. Its massive balloon tires were taller than Jamie. A modified army truck with a flat platform that, once upon a time, would have been lifted with hydraulics for hunting. The truck poured black smoke from a rusted tailpipe. It was as if a rumbling, belching monster had appeared in the peace and stillness of the hardwood hammock.

They dropped down when the buggy lumbered by, crushing saplings and bumping over enormous potholes.

Tess pressed her face into the edge of the ditch. There was dirt in her mouth. A dribble of dirt fell into Jamie's hair as the swamp buggy passed.

"Who?" She mouthed to him.

He shrugged and shook his head.

The machine groaned and squealed when it hit a hard curve and had to make a turn.

She watched Jamie chance another glance.

"Eight armed in the back, and a couple more in the cab. I'm going to say ten all together."

"Where are they from? Why didn't we know about them?"

"All good questions. Tess, did you notice anything strange about that group?"

He waited for an answer without looking at her.

When she didn't answer, he said, "No? They weren't men. I'm pretty sure they were all women—armed and dangerous women. Great! Amazons! Their faces were covered, a puzzle we'll have to worry about later. Right now, we need to decide what we're going to do about the swamp buggy Amazonian brigade that's between us and your dopey sister, a kid named Stone, an annoying mutt, and their wounded, leg-dragging prisoner."

CHAPTER 45

ARNOLD WAS SLOWING them down.

ZeeZee thought bringing him along would be a goodwill gesture, and that he'd be glad to go back—free to be back with his people at the Marketplace. Instead, he'd moaned and dragged and complained every step of the way. The bandage on his leg looked dry and clean enough, though.

Stone acted like he didn't notice when they'd reached Van Arsdale, the Doe Kids' camp, or what was left of it. It was hard to know what it might have looked like before. Everything was gone, blackened and burned right down to the dirt, except where the lumps were—knobby, melted lumps. It was hard to know what they had been.

Stone reached out and touched one. It pinged when he flicked it with his finger. Something made of metal.

"Car bones. We made tents out of them, our homes."

Arnold slumped to the ground next to one of the burned-out car chassis, panting for effect.

"I need a minute. I hope you thought about clean water. I don't need the trots from drinking out of a filthy mud puddle."

ZeeZee watched Stone walk over to the big man on the ground and spit. The glob pooled in the ashes next to Arnold. The man jerked back, smacking his head on the car frame behind him. He rubbed at the back of his head.

"Hey, kid, you are one nasty creature. You know that? What did you think would happen when you stuck your nose into Marketplace business? What did you think you were messing with?"

Whatever Stone started to say back to Arnold got drowned out in a crazy, rumbling whine coming at them from the highway. ZeeZee didn't have words for the sound. She slammed her hands over her ears and froze. Stone dragged her backward away from the crossroad. When she stumbled, he grabbed her shirt and pulled her into a hump of scorched scrub palmetto that rimmed the destroyed camp.

Arnold rolled to his knee; his bad leg straight out to the side. Blood had begun to seep through the bandage. He tried to stand up, but fell clumsily. The monster on the road roared and squealed closer. He tried crawling away from it.

"Help him," ZeeZee whispered.

Stone looked like he wanted to spit again. He got to his knees, took a step, and then collapsed onto his butt and crab crawled back into the fronds of the palmetto.

"What is it?"

Stone put his finger to her lips, hushing her. The dog belly crawled after Stone, obviously too worried to bark. Smart dog.

A thatch of mulberry saplings growing in a pothole bowed and snapped as a massive green vehicle rolled forward. Its axles squeaked and moaned. The sound gave the beast a kind of screeching voice, protesting every inch of the journey it was on. Stone pulled ZeeZee farther down into the dirt, and clamped his hand over her mouth.

She hadn't even realized that she'd started screaming until he had squeezed the breath out of her. She could hear Arnold yowling as he kept trying to reach them, dragging his bad leg. The truck stopped in a puff of exhaust as the armed women poured out of the back and off the sides of the screeching vehicle. They swarmed over Arnold. He cowered under their screams and fists.

Stone made no move to help him; he was too busy dragging ZeeZee farther into the gloom of the surrounding tangle of the Black Hammock.

CHAPTER 46

THE GROUND WAS covered with tracks—small and feminine. Arnold had not died easily. The women had been merciless, cruel, and brutally efficient. And they'd been fast. Tess and Jamie stood frozen with shock when they found the body, still bleeding and warm.

"Cut him down," Tess ordered. She sucked a breath in through her teeth when she saw that it was Arnold and only Arnold—no Stone or ZeeZee. She'd been holding her breath and hadn't realized it.

They'd tied him to one of the ruined car frames and cut him in a dozen places, probably for information, maybe just because he'd been in the wrong place at the wrong time. Cutting his throat had finished the job.

Whatever the motivation, the results were the same. He was dead, and the flies were celebrating. The smell of death hung over him like a thick, wet, bloody blanket.

"Cut him down," Tess repeated, trying to ignore the taste of bile in the back of her throat. Wrong place, wrong time. Maybe. And maybe it was their fault that this had happened to him.

"No." Jamie kicked at the car chassis. "I'm not cutting him down."

"What do you mean *no*?"

"The less people know that there are other folks running around messing with their little projects," Jamie said, looking at Arnold's body with distaste, "the better. Besides, I have a very bad feeling about this. Forget him. No, better than that, don't forget. Think about what he did to you, or wanted to. Think about that little girl in the dirt down by the river. That will keep you in the right frame of mind."

The fist squeezing Tess's heart convulsed. It got harder to focus for a minute. Jamie looked at her. His frown deepened.

"If you're going to vomit, then do it. But we need to move."

"I'm not," she snapped and swallowed her panic and waved him off. "But ZeeZee and Stone. They're not here. Where are they?"

"Not here and that's good, but let's get them back before this group gets to them or the Marketplace. Come on. Besides," He said, settling his pack with a shrug of his bony shoulders, "there's something I need to show you near here, but we need to move now."

Tess couldn't believe what she was seeing. Jamie stood at the gate of a rag-tag enclosure, corralling five stunning white horses. They swished their tails at flies and dozed in the late morning heat.

"Where did you get them?"

He'd built up a pretty decent enclosure using fallen logs, saplings, and blackberry brambles, ten feet tall and impenetrable. It made her think of something a person might build in Africa to keep lions out. He pushed open an old metal gate hanging from a single post. It squeaked. The sound made her think of the swamp buggy.

"I didn't get them—I found them. They were running wild out here, down to skin and bones," he said, reaching for a rope halter that had been hanging on the gate. "Someone's babies." The beautiful horses crowded around Jamie like puppies, looking for scratches and pats on the nose. "I kept them hidden because . . ." He shrugged.

"Because they were eating horses back in the day." She thought about Goliath's close call. "Still might. Who knows about them? Does Parrish?"

"Naw. He hates horses. Probably be okay with eating one. Help me," he pulled two bridles out of a toolbox on the ground. The leather was mildewed, needed cleaning. She rubbed the green mold from the reins with her thumbs.

A memory fizzed up in Tess's mind: a man riding a beautiful white horse along the side of Van Arsdale. Tess had been with her mom, and they'd been on their way to the Marketplace Mall. Mother had pulled off the road as they watched the man ride his horse across the highway and down the dirt road on the opposite side. The horse was a creature out of a fantasy: glorious neck arching, tail flowing, hooves as delicate as china cups. At the last minute, the rider had turned in the saddle, smiled, and waved at them before disappearing around a corner.

The big metal building! That's what the big metal building had been. The one that the Doe Kids had kept Goliath in. It was a barn for those white horses—Lipizzaners.

She wondered what had happened to the man who had loved these horses. She shook off the thought, as she pushed the bit into the horse's mouth.

Jamie kept the saddles in a pump room in the middle of a neighboring cow pasture. He'd looked at her with a goofy grin when he pulled the saddles out of the tall, narrow shed and handed her one.

"Welcome to my humble home," he said. She didn't know what to say to that. He lived in a shed a bit bigger than their outhouse, but not by much. The tin roof was mostly rust. They saddled the horses in silence.

"Let's hurry and get your sister before whatever's going to happen hits the fan with that bunch of Amazons in the swamp buggy and the idiots at the Marketplace. Riding makes us a little bit faster. With luck we'll get in and out quick because of these beasts."

After walking back to the horses and choosing one, he threw his leg over the saddle, found his seat, and stroked the silk of the horse's neck.

Tess gave her horse a pat and remembered the day when a handsome man waved to her from the back of a beautiful white horse.

They headed down Van Arsdale Street, leaving Arnold to the flies and crows, past the burn scars that radiated out from the camp like ripples in a pond. Hoping quietly that ZeeZee and Stone had thought to run in the opposite direction from the groaning, creaking swamp buggy.

Outside the Marketplace, they tied the horses close enough to be able to get to them in a hurry. They seemed content to nibble Spanish moss and sleep in the shade of the scrub oak where they were tied.

While the horses dozed, Tess and Jamie watched the mall from a small rise of mounded dirt. From their spot they could see the hanging lamppost, the little girl's body still displayed as a warning, the old mall sign, and the east parking lot.

At the lamppost the Amazons slowed their approach, hesitated. A few pointed at the dead girl. They rumbled on, not bothering to cut the body down. When the swamp buggy, bristling with weapons and women, rolled over a rickety hay wagon in the parking lot, flattening it, Marketplace dogs erupted. Kids scattered. A few armed-guard types, a sad lot of old men and boys, rushed out of the building and then quickly retreated back into the shadows of the gaping entrance when they saw what had caused the dogs to panic.

Jamie watched it all through a telescoping monocular. It looked like something a French pirate would use in a bad movie, a real brass antique, too nice to be a movie prop. He'd pulled it from his backpack as soon as he'd flopped down on his stomach in the dirt.

Tess raised her eyebrows at him when he lowered it.

"Want to try?" He handed it to her.

Tess put the glass to her eye and was surprised at how close it made her feel. Women hustled their children out of the beds and cabs of the mad collection of ruined vehicles. Their fear as they rushed into the building felt almost physical. So many women now, but where were the men?

She handed the spyglass back to Jamie. "Not exactly standard equipment."

"What? I was almost an Eagle Scout," he said. "Be prepared, I always say. And the museum where I got it wasn't using it anymore. What did you see? What are those Amazon queens up to?" He went back to spying.

A momentary explosion of sunlight from behind skittering storm clouds hurt her eyes. Shielding her face, she watched as the women and children of the Marketplace in the parking lot, abandoned by their men, dragged each other out of the line of fire. The ragged, panicked retreat ended, and a strange, tense hush fell over the place.

The noisy, obnoxious swamp buggy rolled forward. Tess studied the Amazon women. Jamie's name for them seemed to fit pretty well. They wore a uniform of sorts—cargo pants, hunting vests, assorted scarves covering their hair and faces. More importantly, their weapons looked new, clean, and efficient. Tess scanned the parking lot.

"They look like a paramilitary group of some kind. No ZeeZee or the Stone kid anywhere," he said.

Beyond the Strandline

"This feels pointless. Maybe we're whistling in the dark, and they headed back to the S-Line when they saw that crazy contraption and all those guns. Maybe. God, wouldn't that be a break." She pushed flatter into the dirt, digging in.

"If we're lucky that's exactly what happened." Jamie collapsed the spyglass and slipped it into a pocket.

Suddenly, Tess felt a hand grab at her ankle, someone behind her in the underbrush. Kicking like a mule, she stuffed her fist in her mouth to keep from screaming. Jamie rolled to his back, his Bowie knife appearing in his hand as if by magic. Tess picked up a chunk of tree branch and swung at the hand still pulling at her leg.

Out of the rustle of underbrush, Parrish stood up and then fell forward, straight onto Tess in a dead faint. Two bright red spots burned high on his cheekbones in his dead white face. Under the scruff of his beard, he looked waxen.

Jamie stabbed his knife into the ground, grabbed Parrish by the arm, and pulled him off of Tess.

"Shit, Parrish!" Jamie sounded more relieved than angry. "What a moron."

Shocked by Parrish's stillness, Tess felt for the pulse in his neck and then reached for water.

"Hey. Hey. Come on. What were you thinking?" The wound on his shoulder had started to seep. She could see the pink and yellow tinge of pus and blood through his shirt. "Geez, what was Gwen thinking letting you out?" She poured water on his face.

"She didn't let me do anything," he spluttered. "Just . . . did it. I just did it."

When he tried to push her away, she pushed back, scooting to the bottom of the dirt mound, out of the line of sight of the Amazons. She helped him tip his head back. He drank some water instead of fighting her. He pushed her hand away again.

"Forget it, Parrish. Stay down or you're going to give us away."

"No. This is a good spot. We'll be fine for as long as it lasts," he said. He looked at Tess with fever-lit eyes and then gave in, resting his head in her lap. "Besides I brought you something."

"Tess," Jamie said. "Behind you. Look."

ZeeZee and Stone peaked out of the hedge of scraggly scrub oak. They looked dirty and hot, but in one piece. ZeeZee smiled, a look that was one part chagrin, one part relief. Stone tried looking militant and tough, which would have worked if it wasn't for a smear of dirt on the end of his nose and the goofy dog sitting next to him, tongue lolling.

"Get down! Get back," Tess hissed and pointed to the woods. "Good grief, why don't we all just stand up, yell *charge,* wave some red capes, and issue a declaration of war? What were you two thinking? Never mind. Just get down."

Tess watched ZeeZee grab Stone's hand, pull him back into the dark and quiet of the tree line, and heard her sister's soft murmur. Leaves rustled when they passed. "And don't think I'm not going to hear all about the half-cocked plan you had taking Arnold out here. Thanks to you he's dead now. So much for any prisoner exchanges or goodwill gestures!"

Parrish kept his eyes shut and smiled when Tess hissed her warning to the teenagers.

"I'm here to take you home," Parrish said. "Them too."

"I'd like to see you try. Are you trying to kill yourself? I could swing a cat and knock you out. Between you and those two."

Ignoring the commotion behind them, Jamie went back to his stomach, watching the parking lot. He had the spyglass out again.

Tess felt Parrish's head. His skin burned against the back of her hand.

"We're getting out of here. We have horses. Come on, you're riding home." Tess started scooting back out of the line of sight of anyone who might be watching.

"Horses? I hate horses," Parrish said. "They buck."

"What? Don't care. We. Are. Leaving." She pulled at the sleeve of his shirt. Jamie cleared his throat.

"What?" Tess said.

"I don't think so. I don't think we're leaving. Not yet."

"What are you talking about? Plainly the girl guerrilla band, those Amazons of yours, have changed the dynamic around here. I'd rather not be here when it comes crashing down." She heard someone shout from inside the Marketplace, more shouts from the parking lot.

"They're not my Amazons." He shoved the glass at her as she scrambled back up the pile of dirt. "Look for yourself."

The worry on Jamie's face made her hurry. Bracing herself on a downed tree trunk that further blocked them from view, she started to scan the bad actors in front of her. In the arching, main entrance of the mall there was some kind of back and forth scuffle. There were raised voices, people pushing and pulling, and then a lone figure stepped out from inside the building into a brief splash of sunlight.

"Oh God."

Jamie dropped his head onto his crossed arms. "Yeah."

Something in Jamie's voice brought Parrish out of his slump. He rolled to his stomach, pushed up between Tess and Jamie, and looked for himself.

"Tess, what's your father doing down there?"

CHAPTER 47

TESS KNEW EXACTLY what he was doing. She watched the classic sweep of her father's arms as he threw them wide, as if to embrace the whole wide population of the Marketplace and everyone in the swamp buggy. He was just in the warm up phase of his *Humanity of Humans* speech, and he was going to get himself killed—in front of them. It wasn't a short speech.

Behind them, ZeeZee gasped. Tess rounded on her sister.

"Zeez, go. Go home. I can't worry about you too. Have Stone take you back. Now. Go. We'll figure this out, but you're not helping." Tess watched her sister, hurt and worry in every muscle of her body, melt backward into the rustling palm fronds. Stone was nowhere to be seen. Stone didn't worry her, if anyone could take care of ZeeZee, he could. He knew this place down to his bones. He'd get her home.

"Go home," Tess ordered. But they'd already disappeared. She pushed them out of her mind.

"How did your father even get here?" Parrish said. He sounded puzzled more than shocked. "That man can barely find his way to the latrine."

It wasn't fair—the criticism—and she knew it. Jamie and Parrish only knew her father as the broken man he'd become, but she remembered the trip from West Virginia after Mother: the roadblocks, the burning cities, the starving people, the fear, and the endless back roads. Father had saved them, scrounged food for them. He'd gotten them to the Strandline—the way Mother had wanted him to.

"Why wouldn't he be able to get here? It's where he met my mom." She swallowed hard. "He sold her an ice cream cone, rocky road ice cream. We were all somebody else once." She watched her father talk and talk. Watched the way the women trained their weapons on him. How long would their patience last? If only she believed they had a sense of humor or tolerance or humanity. She didn't. A huge black cloud raced over their heads, plunging the parking lot in shadows and gloom. A bright, angry breeze whipped dirt around.

An eternity crawled by as the three of them watched helplessly. Father looked happier and happier to have an audience, and she knew exactly where he was in his speech about brotherly love and common ground and peace in our time . . . with half an ear, she heard Jamie and Parrish curse softly as the tension grew.

"Well, he's here," Jamie concluded. "However he did it. Now what?"

"This can't end well." Parrish rasped, "Tess, we can't help him."

"We can't let this happen. I can't let this happen." She watched her father throw his arms open, raise his face to the sky. She shifted forward, drawn to her father's insane courage. Jamie grabbed her arm.

"We should make tracks," Jamie said. "Before—"

One of the women in the bed of the swamp buggy shoved her rifle into her shoulder, her body language suddenly fierce.

It wasn't conscious. Tess was up and over the crest of the hill before she could think or plan or second-guess. The sound of Parrish hissing her name dissolved into the sound of a dog's bark and someone from inside the Marketplace yelling—kids' voices.

As Tess reached the edge of the pavement she heard, "Dad. Daddy. Come back in, Daddy."

It was ZeeZee and that stupid dog and Stone. They'd circled around while everyone was distracted. Sure. Stone would have known how to do it, how to hopscotch his way through the vehicles. Like her father, he knew this place.

Tess froze and watched as their little orchestrated drama played out. The dog hopped and danced like a possessed rabbit around Tess's father. He kept right on talking, absently patting the dog's head when it bounded close enough.

The woman in the swamp buggy lowered her gun, shrugged when the others glanced at her. Apparently, reassessing the situation, she raised the gun again.

Tess covered her mouth and fell back as Stone joined ZeeZee. They grabbed and yanked on Father's arm. Finally he stopped talking long enough to take note of ZeeZee and Stone. The dog trailed behind as they pulled him back into the dark interior of the Marketplace. Where were the others? The Marketplace guards?

"ZeeZee, Stone, my father. They're trapped," Tess whispered.

Tossing the spyglass back to Jamie, Parrish grabbed Tess around the waist while the women watched Jon Lane disappear.

"Are you crazy?" He said and pulled her back and down between he and Jamie.

"My family . . . they're my family."

"Sure. But those people aren't."

Jamie shoved the spyglass at her and pointed to the corner of the building on the far left. A second group of scarf-wrapped soldiers trickled from an overgrown hedge of azaleas bordering the west parking lot. It was a flanking maneuver against whoever they expected to be defending the Marketplace. Letting her father ramble on had fit seamlessly into their plan.

"Remember me saying 'when it hits the fan'?"

She nodded, felt horror grip her, tried to picture where Stone might hide her sister, her father.

"Well, it's about to," Jamie said.

He pointed to the far right side of the parking lot where another squad moved in. The women in the swamp buggy were the diversion, just smoke and mirrors from the real threat.

Tess was on her feet again. "My family is in there."

Parrish grabbed for her hand. Too late. The swamp buggy driver had seen her. She slapped the side of the cab with a gloved hand and pointed to their hiding place.

"*Now* we are going," Parrish insisted.

Jamie slid back into the woods as the guns swung toward them.

Inside the Marketplace, gunfire and screams ping ponged over each other. Parrish and Tess stood frozen in the spot where the driver had seen them. They watched as two squads of women rushed into the building from opposite sides, the women in the swamp buggy taking the front entrance. The driver stayed behind, using the open door of the cab as cover, keeping them in her sights through her scope. Tess and Parrish fell flat to the ground. They watched as she put her head back and howled, swinging the deer rifle up to the sky, she popped off a few pointless rounds. In a sudden lull of sound from inside the building, they were able to hear the noise the girl was making. Not howling. Laughter, she was laughing.

Retreating to her workroom, Wendy listened to the gunshots. They were methodical and disciplined—almost boring in their predictability. Pop. Pop. Pop. There were less and less screams. The pounding on her workroom door stopped.

Wendy Fortix waited calmly, listening with half an ear to the sounds of invasion below.

They were very organized, the women who had come for Marco or because of Marco. Who knew? It wouldn't matter even if she had the answer.

Had to admire their level of organization. They'd known exactly what to do: distract, invade, crush, and destroy. Perfect really, and all that pretending to be willing to listen to Jon Lane's ridiculous speech as a small part of the drama; really, quite brilliant. They'd listened while their squads had come at the Marketplace . . . from everywhere.

When Lane had shown up to talk peace treaty and hostage exchange between the Marketplace and the S-Line, hadn't she been reasonable, even intrigued? And then when he'd offered to confront the invaders, it had been so easy to let him. Sure . . . why not? Hadn't he made it possible for her to retire from the whole nasty business? Let a man take the lead, the way Marco would have if he hadn't gotten himself killed.

Besides, if they'd killed Jon Lane it would have served his nitwit daughters right. Hostage exchange! Thinking about Jerome being the captive of her husband's murderers made the rage boil in her head.

How had Jerome gotten himself in a hostage situation in the first place? And with those girls who'd wandered into her home and destroyed everything. First that stupid blond girl and then her sister. They'd ruined everything—her home, her family, her personal safety. Until Marco had taken over the Marketplace there hadn't been any safety anywhere, and now it was gone. All the men had faded away after Marco died. One by one they'd defected, slipping away in the nights and days afterward. It took a strong, ruthless man to hold strong men in times like these. The only men left had been the ones too weak or too dumb to run, but the gunshots below were taking care of those slackers.

All because Marco was dead. He'd have known what to do with this gang of vengeful bitches. He would have seen it coming, this attack.

Opening her last bottle of lavender oil, she let the odor calm and soothe the tremors that kept threatening to crawl into her hands, her face, her body. The Marketplace had gone silent. Wendy cocked her head and reached for her backpack. Time to look less like a queen and more like a drone. She ran her hand over the name on the jumpsuit she wore: *Benny*.

"Okay, Benny the Mechanic from Sears," she said to no one. "Time to find a new hidey hole."

Calmly, Wendy Fortix kicked the crumbling drywall to dust that hid the escape tunnel in the back of what had once been a storage closet of the Oviedo Marketplace Mall.

CHAPTER 48

THE DRIVER OF the swamp buggy hadn't fired any more warning shots as Tess and Parrish crawled back into the cover of the woods behind them. His grip on Tess's wrist was a ring of steel. He wasn't giving her any options, not this time. He had seen too many firefights, seen too many lost causes. The Amazons had played it perfectly, rolling into the parking lot in their loud, obnoxious swamp buggy, catching the Marketplace asleep.

"Stop." She didn't scream at him. Her voice came more as a grating hiss against the backdrop of the gunfire coming from the Marketplace. "Stop!"

Finally, she simply collapsed to her knees, daring him to drag her. He couldn't. He cursed the fever that made him sick to his stomach, sick enough to puke.

"You're lucky I'm sick," he spit. "Or I'd drag you all the way back to the Strandline on your butt."

"I'm not going," she panted when he tugged her off balance. She broke his grip then, fast and easy, the way she'd been taught. She pushed up from the ground. "I'm not leaving them. They're mine. They're my family."

He knelt in the pine needles next to her, reached out, and helped her sit up. He flopped onto his butt and dropped his head between his knees.

"I have to get them. Parrish, what's happening in there?"

"You wouldn't consider that Stone might have a handle on this situation, would you?"

"Stone . . . he's a kid," she said, swiping the back of her hand across her mouth. "A mule-eating kid."

There was dirt on her cheek. Sweat left trails through the grime on her face. Sweat and dirt and blood. He couldn't lose her either. Not Tess.

Parrish shot to his feet at the sound of thrashing and crashing in the underbrush behind them. Jamie popped through a scrub oak, fell, and rolled to his back. Parrish aimed into the still vibrating branches, covering Jamie's retreat.

"Stand down. It's just me. They're not interested in us—yet. I get the feeling they just didn't want us interrupting them."

Jamie sat up, his rifle cradled in his lap. Reaching down, Parrish helped his friend to his feet. Tess sat in the dirt, chin to her chest, trying to slow her heartbeat.

"They're only shooting men, probably eighteen and over. And they know what they're doing. That's as clean a military action as I've seen in a long time," he paused, checked the safety on his rifle and jerked his shoulders. "Since . . . well, you know." Jamie glanced at Parrish.

"Did you see them?" Tess's voice sounded muffled. She kept her head down, pressed to the leg of her jeans. "My father and . . ."

He shook his head. He'd seen dead men but none that he recognized.

CHAPTER 49

WENDY FORTIX HAD run it through her head a thousand times. First, dress and grab the bag. Second, bash through the wall and crawl through the old ductwork. Finally, exit down the drainpipe. But then the drainpipe had been turned into funnels for the rain barrels, so she'd made them cut a tree and lash it to the side of the wall, just inside the blind corner.

She'd gone soft. Hadn't kept in shape. Marco had made it easy to imagine never having to run again. The Marketplace had done that too, but then those girls . . . just two weak, grasping children.

She hesitated at the edge of the concrete ledge, swung out, and started to shimmy down the tree trunk while slivers of wood burned their way into her hands. Every splinter was a reminder, a punishment. The air stank of gunpowder and blood and fear and memories of having to drink filthy water out of ditches.

"You're not walking back into that place without having a way to walk back out. I won't let you." Parrish refused to look at her or make eye contact. "Wait, Tess, I'm telling you to be patient. Feel that." He held his hand up.

"What? What are you talking about?"

"The wind. It's dropped again, because the storm has sucked all the humidity out of the air, all the energy. A storm is coming, and if you wait we'll be able to use that. Not yet."

"You going to stop me? That's rich coming from a guy who's using an oak tree to hold himself upright?"

"I won't. But I have friends in close places who will."

From a branch over their heads where he'd wedged himself in the fork of a tree to keep watch, Jamie glanced down at Parrish and then at Tess. She watched Jamie trying to decide how to play the angles. He opened his mouth to say something. She cut him off.

"Don't bother, Chief. Just keep your spyglass in action." Tess stood with her back against the trunk of Jamie's overlook. The noises inside the Marketplace had stopped: no gunfire, no screaming, no one came out, no one went in. Jamie could only see a single woman guarding the swamp buggy.

"I'll wait, but only until tonight. I have to know. I have to."

Parrish pulled her back after she'd drifted forward toward the last place she'd seen ZeeZee . . . and her father.

"Tess, don't."

She jerked free, afraid to look at him, afraid she'd lose her nerve and agree to abandon her father and her sister. Afraid she'd be talked into believing that Stone would have the moxie to get her family out of the Marketplace and home.

"At least let's put together some kind of story, some way for Jamie and I to have your back. Let's think this thing through."

"Down," Jamie cried as he dropped to the ground between them. "Get down. Our ticket in may be coming right to us." He circled behind the tree trunk and disappeared while Parrish pulled Tess closer to the shadow of the big tree and waited.

Wendy Fortix hated the way the air hung heavy and breathless as she hiked away from the Marketplace. She was going to need a bath before she got even halfway to Geneva. She'd be able to smell herself soon: another reason to despise those Lane girls. Her backpack dragged at her shoulders. A spot near her neck started to burn. *Should've padded the straps better*, she thought. Thank God she'd known enough to throw some aloe into her bug-out bag. Marco'd never seen the need for such niceties, insisting on guns and ammo and water and not much else. He'd always depended on her for the civilized touches, the nicer things.

Putting her head down, she watched for snakes as she pushed through a thicket of saw palmettos. Snakes! She hated them. She hated it all: sweat and

B.O. and snakes and no clean water for bathing and no one to bring her butter for her bread. She felt the bitter tears burn their way into her throat, let rage engulf her as she headed into the heaviest of the tree line.

When the man reached out and grabbed the strap of her backpack she screamed. Not a snake. Worse. It was a man—or close enough. The freckles on his nose ruined the stone-cold look in his eye.

She lashed out, swinging wildly, wishing for her pistol. He jerked the strap, pulling her off balance and onto her side. He put his filthy boot on her neck, not hard enough to choke her, but enough to make her stop squirming.

"Stay down, or I'll drag you back to those Amazon killers myself."

The jumpsuit she was wearing was a steely blue; there were smears of old grease on the knees. The woman wearing it had rolled up the arms and pants legs so she wouldn't trip, so the sleeves wouldn't hang down over her hands. The backpack told them what they needed to know; she was bugging out.

"Well, Benny," Parrish said, reading the name off the front of the mechanic's jumpsuit, "I didn't realize that Sears was still making emergency calls."

When the woman twitched, Jamie jerked her to her feet, squeezed her elbows together.

"I know your name," Tess said. "You're Wendy Fortix, Jerome's mother. You were there, at the top of the stairs."

Wendy looked at Tess with keen brown eyes, her black hair tied back, knotted up in a paisley strip of cloth. The white streaks in her hair, winged back into the knot at the nape of her neck. She looked neat and tidy and a little crazy.

"Who are they? Those women?" Tess asked. "What did you do to them to make them come looking for you?"

Wendy Fortix laughed.

"Do? What did we do to deserve your intrusion into our home? Let me go, you silly girl. You are already dead. All dead." Wendy looked at Parrish, her eyes turning venomous. "They want something: the place, the people, revenge, spare parts? What's the matter with you? Why do you ask idiot questions?" She looked back at Tess. Her look turned speculative. "Such a darling little idiot, you and my new daughter-in-law."

Tess resisted the urge to slap the sly look off the woman's face. "You need to shut up. You're not the high and mighty queen any more. Let's go."

Jamie pushed Wendy toward the parking lot. Tess pulled the dethroned queen's backpack off.

"Go through that," Parrish said, his voice as flat as the way he looked at the woman in Jamie's strong grip. Parrish seemed stronger than before, not as flushed. Tess tossed him Wendy's bottle of water.

"You, drink that."

Jamie raised his eyebrows at the way she'd mimicked Parrish's tone. "Nice," Jamie said, "You've almost got the hard case, big boss attitude down, Tess."

"Oh God, you sound like the Three Stooges."

Parrish marched to Wendy, pushed his face against hers. "No, but we are survivors of the Florida/Georgia Machete Gangs. You might want to make a note that we still have all our arms and legs. If you want to keep your nose, you need to shut your mouth, like the lady said."

There was no mistaking the quiet death in his voice. No one moved for a long, drawn-out moment. Wendy finally shrank back.

Tess had heard Parrish sound annoyed, frustrated, even seriously angry, but this . . . this was something else. He sounded deadly, a death dealer wielding a machete.

Tess closed her mouth and bent over the confiscated backpack.

"Hey, look here." Tess held up a Ruger target pistol. "It's not as good as the one I lost, but it'll do." She ransacked the bag. When she had finished she tossed it under a thatch of wild sweet potato vine. Parrish didn't look at any of them when he took point as they headed back toward the mall and its occupiers.

CHAPTER 50

INSTEAD OF HEADING straight to the parking lot, Parrish led them in a circle around the building, far enough into the tree line to stay out of sight. He saw that there were more guards stationed at every entrance now; it was the old Marketplace but under new, deadlier management. The lone woman watching the swamp buggy looked like their best bet at slipping inside. He recognized her as the cackling guard from before. He hoped she was still a bad shot. He was sure that she'd spotted them as they circled the mall, but hadn't sounded the alarm for some reason.

Jamie pointed and said, "Definitely the weak link."

Parrish heard Wendy sum up the situation pretty accurately. "Maybe the one they left with that vehicle is a moron? A lot of that going around these days—broken brains, can't deal with reality anymore. Weak minds can't be trusted in the inner circle." Wendy studied Tess. "That man who made the speech, some kind of family? Right? That's why we're going back. Interesting. He seems real stable." She smirked.

This time Tess didn't hold back and slammed a fist into Wendy Fortix's mouth. The woman didn't even gasp. Parrish tried not to be impressed with the punch or Wendy's lack of response.

"Tess!" he warned.

"Sorry. You need to teach me how to shut her up before she gives us away," she lowered her voice to a whisper she thought no one could hear, "or I kill her."

"You think I don't know how to take a punch?" Wendy kept right on pushing her luck, honing in on Tess. "You think I haven't been afraid?" She licked the blood from the corner of her mouth. "Are you afraid? Why? Why would you be worried? That boy, the red one, Jamie, says they were only shooting the men and older boys . . . They won't shoot you. Looks like an army of ticked off females. They'll like you. Me too. We should dump these two." She finally took a breath. "How pretty you are Tess. Those big gray eyes, your curls and that smooth tender skin. So perfect. They'll like you a lot."

Parrish caught Jamie's eye.

Jamie stopped walking, drew two hunks of cloth out of one of his pockets, wadded it up, and stuffed it in Wendy's bloody mouth. He wrapped the whole package with an old necktie from his pack.

"That's how you do it."

"Thanks. I'll make a note," Tess said.

Wendy's eyes spit dark fire.

It was easy to see the worry that settled over Tess's face, but this was the world now. He wanted to tell her that and would have, if he wasn't so deathly tired. The world was a battlefield and the only balance of power was carrying the biggest stick or having the biggest bargaining chip. He hoped that Marco Fortix's widow would be good enough, because they were seriously outgunned.

The swamp buggy guard should have taken her shot at them when she'd had the chance. Parrish recognized good training and discipline but knew slow reflexes when he saw it. The Amazons had left the girl outside for a reason. They'd banked on the other women doing their jobs, leaving this semi-broken girl in the most secure location they could. One look at her vacant eyes was all he needed. She'd probably forgotten what she was supposed to shoot at.

Jamie had her trussed and tossed in the front seat of the monster truck after a short, brutal wrestling match where he'd gotten a bloody nose, and a look that should have killed him. She wasn't going to be complaining anytime soon, not being tied up the way she was and out cold.

Using the swamp buggy as cover, they moved closer to the main building. It was good luck when the sky turned black and filled up like a bag full of drab, filthy cotton. A great rush of wind belted across the parking lot with rain in its breath. Dirt and debris pushed whoever had been watching the entrances back—another stroke of luck. The storm finally exploded.

Parrish looked over at Tess, the clenched muscle in his jaw visible beneath the flush across the ridge of his cheekbones. She suspected that he was moving through each moment with sheer force of will; still he managed a cocky grin when the rain slapped down. He'd been right again to wait for the weather to turn. But she'd been right to veto the idea of Jamie or Parrish being the one to walk into the adrenaline fueled nest of man killers.

Parrish nodded to her.

She walked alone into the big entrance to the mall with her hands held high.

"I'm here for my people."

A tall woman, her face still covered with a black bandana, looked at Tess with bright blue eyes. The others circled Tess, a loose necklace of bristling menace. They walked her down the hall into the atrium. It was unnerving not being able to read the little quirks and movements of the women's faces under the bandanas.

The only hints of what the woman next to her was thinking were eyes that had narrowed to slits. Out of the corner of her eye, Tess saw smears of what might be blood on the atrium cement, splatter on some of the blanketed storefronts. But no bodies, where were the bodies? Tess had expected more carnage. There was a deadly quiet inside the building. No one wandered or stared.

"I said, 'I'm here for my people.'"

The woman with blue eyes waved back the others that drifted forward, their hands white knuckled on their weapons.

"No."

The woman's voice snapped like the crack of a pistol shot. They stepped back. Outside, rain slapped against the blocks and patchwork boards covering the gaps, big and small, all over the building. The roof of the atrium started to drip.

"Ell, there's a problem with one of the—" said a short, solid woman wearing a greasy ball cap over her headscarf and carrying what looked like a fillet knife.

So the blue-eyed leader had a name—Ell.

"Go on. Figure it out," she said, softer this time, sounding tired. "I'll handle this."

Greasy ball cap backed away, staring at Tess. She pointed the tip of the knife in Tess's direction, drew an invisible circle in the air.

"Go!" Ell ordered, watching as the woman slunk away.

Ell visibly straightened her spine before she swung back to look at Tess. Her look was more curious than worried. "It can be hard for them to settle down after . . . well, after." She swiped sweat from her forehead and sighed.

"Listen, I don't have any sides to take in all *this*," Tess said, holding her empty hands out, palms up. "Don't want to. Don't need to. Just need my family, and we'll be gone and that's all. They were here to trade. That's all the business we had with this place. We'll never be back."

Ell nodded once, turned, and then walked to the bottom of the escalator steps. She sagged and sat, her hands braced loosely on her knees. In slow motion, she reached up to unwrap the twist of black cloth from around her head. Her hair, a smooth, cool brown hacked short, clung to her head like a damp cap. With a final flick she pulled the scarf free and raked a hand through her wet hair.

Tess gasped at the scar on the woman's face. It pulled her face off balance, dragged at the corner of her eye. Someone had done a very poor job removing the brand she must have had once and stitching her back up. And it was too bad too. It had been a very pretty face . . . once.

She raised her eyebrows at Tess's gasp. "Now, why don't I think that you're telling me everything there is to know? Like why the generator isn't working. Those lights, you wouldn't know anything about those lights, right? Or what might have happened to the man who ran this place? A man named Fortix."

Tess shrugged and made a show of studying the darkened Christmas tree lights at the top of the escalator. The upper balcony looked like a cave of shadows as the storm raged. Water dripped, splashed, and ran in rivulets down the walls.

"Maybe they shorted out? Are you sure they ever worked?"

Ell barked a laugh. Somewhere a child screamed.

Beyond the Strandline

"Pretty sure," she paused. "You are a terrible liar. You know what else I'm pretty sure of? I'm pretty sure you're going to tell me all about the Christmas tree lights and a bunch of other stuff before this is done." A pistol shot, ricocheted and echoed from the far end of the hallway "But for now . . . well . . . I've got some stuff to do, some . . . let's call it cleanup." She used the scarf to mop the back of her neck. "*This*," she said, pointing to a stain on the concrete, "is one of the problems with being a bunch of women. We insist on cleaning up our messes." Ell tipped her head and studied Tess while another woman walked over and whispered in her ear. The newcomer gave Tess a glare.

"I don't know who your family is," Ell offered. "I mean which ones."

"There was a man," Tess began, gulped, "a dog, and two kids. They were here in the beginning, before –" She hardened her voice. "Before the shooting started."

Wind wailed through the open entrance of the atrium and the rain blew in nearly horizontal. A sheet of plywood flew off of one of the gaping holes overhead. It was a tropical storm if they were lucky and, if not, then it was a hurricane. Gwen and the others would have their hands full back home, Tess thought. Home. It sounded farther away than the moon.

It was getting harder not to grab Ell by the throat and shake her. *Keep it together, Tess. Give Parrish and Jamie a chance to find them. Be a decent distraction.*

"I'm Tessla. Tessla Lane. My family used to be—" She was ready to tell this woman more than her name if it kept her focused.

"Shut up. I don't care who you used to be." Ell raised her hand, cut Tess off. "Juno here is going to make you welcome. Aren't you, Juno? Seems I'm needed elsewhere. Something about one of our guards getting herself so rudely tied up. Your handiwork, I suppose. Seems excessive if you were going to just walk in here and surrender."

"She made me nervous. I didn't like the idea of her shooting me in the back."

"Golda? Her name's Golda—we think. And you might have a point."

When she smiled this time, only one corner of her mouth quirked up. "She can't tell us much, but then she hasn't been able to tell us much of anything since Marco Fortix cut out her tongue. Apparently, her raving got on his nerves. Juno, take Miss Tessla here to Margo and whoever is helping her."

Juno's eyes, muddy brown and weary, turned toward Tess. The woman's yes came muffled and dull from behind the bandana she wore. There was blood on her cargo pants.

Ell walked away, heading toward the end of the mall where the gunshot had sounded, presumably to check on the woman Jamie had knocked unconscious—a child with no tongue.

The sound of the storm had made it hard to hear anything inside the Marketplace, but in a sudden quiet lull, Tess heard someone crying from behind one of the quilts. Tess shut down the dread she felt when the crying suddenly stopped. Silence was worse. Juno gestured her to move forward.

They pushed her to the center of the building, under the escalator, against the far wall; the Amazon women had created a staging area inside the open space under the balcony. Two other women were there, breaking down their weapons, going through boxes of supplies and food. They pushed Tess onto a stacked pile of canned black beans.

With a jolt, Tess finally realized where she was; it was the basin where the fountain had once poured water into the shallow, pretty stream of the old Oviedo Mall—Ally's fountain. The wall next to the fountain had been boarded up with layers of random planks and hunks of wood that rattled with the blasting wind and rain. She strained to hear anything above the wailing wind and clanking wood.

After watching Tess walk into a den of lionesses, Jamie and Parrish, dragging Wendy, doubled back to move the horses as close as they could to their escape route—if things went well they would need to move fast. Near the hanging pole, a massive overgrown hedge made as good a blind as any to stash the jittery horses. Jamie worried about leaving them in the wind, but there was little choice, now that the storm had arrived, groaning and screaming its way through the hardwoods around the Marketplace.

Spooked, the horses pawed and shied at the thrashing, pounding storm, but Parrish didn't plan on them having to stand there long.

Beyond the Strandline

It was a plan—in and out—find ZeeZee and her father and the kid, Stone; do it in a hurry while Tess scouted out the situation and distracted. Gather up Tess, be gone. That was the plan. As plans went, it sucked and they all knew it.

They tied Wendy to the hanging pole while they tended to the animals. Served her right. It felt right, making her have to stand beneath the dead kid and have to watch the way the wind tossed the girl's body back and forth. They'd hung a child from a rope for God's sake. It was a small enough punishment to have to look at what she'd been a part of, at what her husband had allowed to be done.

Refusing to look up at the corpse, she watched them with snake's eyes through a drenched, black web of hair.

The wind clawed and screamed. Parrish dragged Wendy free from the pole, pulled her gag off; no one could hear her now.

"Come on. Let's go see how those women feel about a kid killer."

Bending her head, she let her hair fall forward, and then flopped the wet mess out of her eyes, slapping Parrish in the face with the sloppy drenched ends.

"Sorry for that." She pretended to examine his face, glanced at the bloody, soaked bandage on his shoulder. "You aren't looking too sharp. Somebody should see about that . . . little problem with your arm there. Gangrene is nobody's friend these days. Let me go, and I'll be able to help. I've got military grade antibiotics. Still good. Probably. And I've got a lot of experience with nursing."

Jamie called, "Come on. Time to move. The rain has slacked some."

"Move," Parrish said. "And you can keep your *nursing* to yourself. I've seen the results of your care and compassion." He glanced back at the girl's body melting away in the rain.

In and out, find ZeeZee and Jon and the kid, then gather up Tess. It might have worked if they hadn't stumbled over the bodies in the loading dock of the old Sears store. They'd been dragged then dumped there. The storm had slowed down housekeeping chores for the new owners of the Marketplace, it seemed. They hadn't been able to drag the bodies far.

There weren't as many dead as they'd expected, but still they had to check—to be sure that Jon Lane or Stone weren't here, already dead and stacked up like so much firewood. Jamie crawled over the side of the dock, began flipping over corpses.

"No Jon. No Stone," Jamie called out, breathing through his teeth.

"Oh, look what they've done." Wendy sounded more annoyed than sorry. "And that smell. Butchery."

"Looks like leftovers: old men and a couple of bigger boys," Jamie said. "Absolutely no girls."

"Let's move. We got lucky there's no one posted here . . . Tess must have them convinced she's all there is. We got lucky." Parrish's voice faded to a hiss. "Stay down." He slammed back against the wall, behind a cement pillar, dragging Wendy next to him.

Two women appeared, lugging the body of a frail old man. They dragged him to the edge of the bay, counted three, and tossed. Their eyes popped open above their scarves when they heard a grunt and a curse from the heap of dead men. They stumbled back, tripping, and fell into the women behind them, the ones with their guns still slung over their shoulders. The ones holding ZeeZee Lane by one thin arm.

Jamie was up and over the edge of the loading dock like a gazelle leaping a fence. He had the smaller of the first two women in a bear hug before the others could react. He dragged her over to Parrish, used her as a human shield, pressing a knife to her throat. In the struggle, her headscarf came loose and fell to the floor. Someone had carved letters finside a scabbed over heart on the skin of her shaved head, The wounds were new, still raw. She looked about fifteen, no older than Ally or ZeeZee. Jamie didn't blink.

"Your guns. We'll take them."

Parrish pushed Wendy out in front of him, put his pistol to her head and said, "This woman helped Marco run his slave market, and we're pretty sure you'll want her in one piece. Get your boss. Now."

CHAPTER 51

THEY EXPECTED TO be shot on sight: Jamie and Parrish, two armed men in a den of women with good reasons to hate them. Instead, they marched into the center of the old mall behind four Amazons and Wendy Fortix, with ZeeZee dragging up the rear, carrying a confiscated rifle.

When ZeeZee saw Tess tucked up on a pile of beans, she bolted the last ten feet and threw herself on top of her sister. Jamie and Parrish walked the other four women and Wendy to the staging area, their rifle barrels hemming them in as efficiently as knitting needles working on a hat. The word of mouth alarm sounded all over the building. Women came running to find their friends at the mercy of Jamie and Parrish, two men. It wasn't to be tolerated.

Relief and something else flooded Parrish's face when he saw Tess. Jamie gave her a quick, bright grin.

"ZeeZee, where's Stone and Father?" Tess whispered, trying to get her sister to focus, ignoring the hostage crisis growing all around them—with them as the hostages.

Her sister looked at her without blinking. Her lips moved: too low to be heard beyond the circle of their arms or the roar of the wind outside. *Safe*, she mouthed. ZeeZee put her hands on either side of Tess's face and smiled. Good enough. Father and that boy were safe, for now.

It was enough to make Tess relax her grip on her sister's slender arms and give her a quick squeeze. Father was all right. Somehow he was all right. He was together with Stone and that fool of a dog. Okay, if eyes were the windows to the soul, then ZeeZee's eyes were billboards of reassurance.

Tess gave her sister a nod and then looked over at Parrish and Jamie. Neither one looked any too happy at the growing standoff around them.

"They had ZeeZee," Jamie said. "Or we—"

"Where's the boss?" Parrish asked, cutting Jamie off, barking at the Amazons. "We don't need to be here any longer than we need to. Get her, the one in charge."

Outside, a screaming whirlwind moved through the tree line beyond the parking lot. The wind continued to tear and pick at the patched walls. It poured through holes in the ceiling, gusting through the long hallways. A loose board started to flap and bang somewhere.

One of the women with Tess pointed at Parrish with the barrel of her rifle. She was a solid, athletic woman, built like a softball player. Her tired eyes stayed fixed on Jamie, daring him to give her an excuse. Tess watched Parrish shift his weight, struggling for balance against the pain in his arm. The bald girl shoved back into his bad shoulder, smashing against his wound with her elbow.

He fell to one knee and grunted, grabbing for his shoulder; his eyes hazed with pain. Tess grabbed the pistol out of his hand, covering his fall. Everyone scrambled, shifted as tension picked up. Tess yanked on the bald girl's shirt collar, dragged her back into the circle. Parrish bucked up to his feet, shivering. He trained his rifle on another of the women.

"Back off," Tess said, when the others pressed forward.

"I'm here for my sister and then we are gone. We don't need anything else. Fair trade." She pointed to Wendy, arms still tied behind her back.

"Tess," Jamie called, shaking his head. He pointed to the balcony overhead and the ring of rifles pointing down at them. He reluctantly put his hands in the air.

From somewhere in the dripping darkness above them, there was a gasp, a muffled scream, and then someone yelled, "R.J.!"

Tess looked up, trying to reassure herself that she'd heard someone call out a name, maybe a nickname, but there was nothing to see: just more covered faces, red-rimmed eyes, and death at the end of a half dozen gun barrels.

Mistaken, she had to be. No one sentimental enough around here to be yelling out nicknames, maybe she'd imagined it.

"Sit down, little girl. You're quite done giving orders." One of the four women they'd captured had spoken. Her diction was perfect: clean, concise, and educated. She sounded like someone's English teacher.

The woman closest to Jamie pulled the rifle from his shoulder and turned it on him, indicating to the others that the balance of power had shifted once again. Her voice sounded hoarse and rusty. This one was nobody's teacher. Whispers flew among the women, spreading through their ranks impossible to overhear. It was like a secret language.

The other women taken prisoner by Parrish and Jamie, shifted back to the Amazon side of the equation without a word, not a taunt or insult or curse, nothing. They stood quietly, after stripping Parrish and Jamie of their weapons, including the knives strapped to their shins. The others had already taken Tess's tomahawk and the Ruger she'd found in Wendy's backpack.

The English teacher grabbed a rifle and took charge, keeping up a cheerful chatter as the men were searched. "We don't have any argument with you. Yet. Although I've got a feeling one of us isn't going to forgive and forget being tied up at her post in the swamp buggy."

She nodded up to the people looming above. The guard they'd tied up was among them, the one the others called Golda. Her dazed look was both unsettled and menacing.

The guard continued, "Don't mind Golda. Ell just wants the flesh traders." The teacher waved the barrel, indicating the invisible residents of the Marketplace. She grabbed Wendy Fortix by the arm. "We just need to make sure Ell is done with you before we send you . . . on your way."

The hesitation in her statement told Tess all she needed to know.

The teacher tightened her grip on Wendy, apparently very aware of the prize she held in her hands. She and a few Amazons walked off to find Ell with Wendy, the old Queen of the Marketplace, in tow. They left Parrish, Tess, Jamie, and ZeeZee surrounded by more armed, veiled women. They tried to quietly reassess the situation without alerting their new babysitters, but no one seemed to care when they talked to each other.

"Parrish your shoulder is bleeding again." Tess pointed at the damp splotch of blood that wet his upper sleeve. "We need out of this." She could see the muscles of his cheek clenching as he ground his teeth.

Jamie whispered, "This storm might be working for us. Okay?" He looked at ZeeZee who took a breath and nodded at the sound of churning wind outside. The pelting rain pushed the guards at the entrances back away from the gaping doors.

The wind grew to a roar and then a scream and then a howl and finally a freight train. The air pressure dropped. Several people covered their ears, including ZeeZee. She slapped her hands over her head just as Jamie dragged her back away from the plywood in front of them that suddenly bulged inward and then disappeared out into a mad twist of rain and wind.

Parrish threw himself on top of Tess when the freight train slammed against the side of the atrium, ramming the trunk of a huge oak tree through the hole left by the missing plywood.

The branches of the tree swept the two guards next to the wall off their feet and shoved them halfway to the escalator. Plywood peeled away in layers. Cement blocks tumbled. The wind swirled over them in a maddened explosion of leaves and dirt. Blinded but suddenly on her feet, Tess grabbed Parrish's hand and dragged him through a gaping hole in the wall. She glanced back to make sure Jamie and ZeeZee were close behind. Better to take their chances in a tornado then to wait for the silent girl soldiers to figure out what to do with them.

"Along the wall, stay close to the building until we can get across the lot to the horses!"

The worst of the tornado skipped away around the corner of the building. Rain still pelted them, but the worst of the wind seemed to have disappeared with the twister. There was a break in the blinding rain. Behind them someone screamed; there were shouts, and a rifle shot. Parrish pulled Tess down to her knees.

"Run. Think zigzag. Don't be predictable. Use the wrecks, the wagons. Now. Go!"

Beyond the Strandline

Tess watched Jamie drag ZeeZee nearly off her feet as they dodged potholes brimming with filthy water and upended hay wagons. He helped her jump over a downed tree trunk as big around as a drainage culvert. Tess ran to catch up.

The wind slapped at them when they reached the hanging pole. The horses were gone, the child's body ripped away.

"That woman. The woman you had with you? What happened to her? Why did they take her?" ZeeZee said.

"Because she's Wendy Fortix, Jerome's mother. Forget her!" Tess held out her hand to ZeeZee. "We're gone!"

"Hurry," Jamie shouted over the pounding rain. "Let's get out of this muck. Hopefully the storm will keep them tucked up at the Marketplace, but let's not find out."

Parrish stayed silent, the muscles of his jaw clenched to knots.

The rain acted psychotic, one minute driving straight down into the dirt, kicking mud up to their knees, and the next minute slashing at them almost sideways. It stung their skin like pinpricks.

"Not a hurricane or we wouldn't be able to stand up," Parrish gasped out.

Like a slap, a gust of wind pushed them back. Putting their heads down they plowed along the old road between Main Street and the Marketplace. The wind kicked up a notch, enough to make walking a serious challenge.

"The big church. Head there. Some of the walls might still be standing," Parrish shouted.

Dragging and struggling and fighting their way to the old downtown of Oviedo, they collapsed into a ruined corner of the big church on the hill. The blocks kept the worst of the wind and slashing rain off of them, but there was no way to be dry.

Exhausted, they huddled close. The men pushed Tess and ZeeZee into the center as they crouched over the top of the two women. By the time Tess noticed what they were doing, getting all protective and macho, she was too tired to object, especially when Parrish whispered in her ear.

"Quiet. If I don't lean on you, I might fall down. Let me pretend for a minute that I'm taking care of you."

It wasn't long before the fevered heat from his body turned to icy tremors and shaking. Turning, she put her arms around him, willing what strength she had left into him. Next to her, ZeeZee's whispered prayer seemed appropriate in the shadow of the ruined church.

By morning the sun was back, pouring light over the ruin left by the storm. Trees formed interlaced pieces of a giant puzzle.

"We need to go. They'll want to know what we know about the area, maybe, or the resources around here, or God knows what else. I would. I'd want information. I can't believe they'll be okay with us just walking away," Jamie said.

"What about Father?" ZeeZee's blond hair was caked with mud. Bits of leaves and sticks were glued to her shirt. Next to Tess, Parrish stared at ZeeZee with bleary eyes. It was hard to tell what color his skin was under the layer of mud and filth left by the storm.

"Tell me what you can." Tess threaded one arm through the crook of ZeeZee's folded arms. ZeeZee relaxed just enough to smile at Tess.

"Stone knew all kinds of ways into the Marketplace, all kinds. We just walked right in. And inside there's about a hundred little rooms and spaces behind all those curtains. He knew them, those hidey-holes. But there were no men around, just the ones they'd killed, old men, broken men; I think the strong ones had already left before those—"

"Amazons. That's what Jamie calls them."

"Yeah, Amazons. That works," she paused, "When we saw Father, I made Stone take me to try to get him back. And then the Amazons came for us when the shooting started . . . I got separated. Stone pushed me into a pile of rags. I don't know after that. I don't know what happened. I just know that Father and Stone got away."

ZeeZee fidgeted, doing funny washing motions with her hands. It worried Tess, but now wasn't the time to figure out what was really going on with her little sister.

"If I know Stone, they'll be halfway home by now," Tess said. "Can you walk?" She looked at ZeeZee, but the question was meant for Parrish.

She kept the question quiet, not wanting to frighten her sister. Jamie already knew how dangerous the situation was with Parrish. He knew probably better than she did.

Parrish nodded and let Tess pull him to his feet. When he staggered she gasped and then Jamie was there, his arm under Parrish's good arm.

Jamie looked at her. "Keep ZeeZee moving. I'll help Parrish home."

There it was again: that word, "Home." They were going home.

"What about Wendy and your horses?" Even now, tenderhearted ZeeZee worried and fretted for people, for animals, for things beyond her control.

"The horses can take care of themselves and Wendy may not have made it through the night back at the Marketplace . . . with any luck. Zeez," he reassured. "I'm pretty sure that Stone knows what to do to get your father back to the S-Line. Let's just get *us* back to the S-Line too."

Tess knew Parrish was bad off when he dropped his head and didn't look up again. Jamie smiled at her then, but she knew a broken smile when she saw one. It took longer than normal to navigate the labyrinth of broken and downed trees between Oviedo and home. At one point, Jamie handed her a rifle, so he could use two hands to steady his friend.

"Hey!" She held it up, recognizing it. It belonged to Parrish. She could tell from the scratch on the stock, a lightning bolt. "How did you get this? They took our weapons. They took my tomahawk. How does this make sense?"

She stopped and stared at the AR-15 in her hand as if it would talk and tell her how it had come to be there.

Jamie stopped too, eased Parrish to the ground to let him rest for a minute.

"ZeeZee, take a break." He rubbed at his neck, handing ZeeZee a small handgun from the back of his pants. He stretched. "It was there in the pile near the ammo. I snatched it and a pistol or two on our way out during the storm. I've got no idea why it was there, because I can't see the girl soldiers being that clumsy. No way. But they were there in plain sight."

Parrish looked up at them.

"They weren't clumsy." Parrish collapsed onto a downed palm trunk, his feet in four inches of standing water. "It was on purpose. They wanted us to have a weapon, well, at least one of them did. Someone was helping us. They wanted us gone. There was one girl acting strange up on that balcony, couldn't describe her if you put that gun to my head. Maybe green eyes? But there was . . ." He stopped when his voice started to shake and caught his breath. "Someone helping us."

"Okay, I'll take your word for it. I was too busy running for my life," Tess said, staring at the rifle. "We'll take it. I don't care who she was or why she did it. We'll take it." She handed the rifle back to Jamie, suddenly sad and worried that its rightful owner was too far-gone to carry it himself.

"Good enough," Jamie said. "How about it old man? Ready?"

Parrish tried to nod. Failed.

CHAPTER 52

At Van Arsdale, they'd veered off 426 toward whatever the storm might have left of Jamie's pump house and corral. Jamie lowered Parrish to the ground to let him rest, behind a stack of downed trees, just off the main road.

All along the road, water—gray, dank, murky—partly hid the tangled branches of collapsed trees. The body of a feral dog floated where the ditch had turned into a pond. Not Stone's dog, though. That dog was still out there somewhere with Stone and Tess's father. That's what she would believe until . . .

The world between Oviedo and the S-Line had reverted back to a kingdom of water moccasins and bullfrogs. Mosquitoes would explode out of the standing water left behind by the storm in a matter of hours. The air would turn to the sludge of heat and humidity and evaporating water as soon as the sun hit.

But they were here and away from the Marketplace, and they were alive.

"Take us back to the S-Line through the back . . . door, Jamie." Parrish didn't have the energy to lift his head when he spoke. He sat, sprawled out, in the only dry lump of sand for a mile, his back pressed against the shattered trunk of another royal palm tree, the color of his face mimicking the pale skin of the palm. She'd watched him sip rainwater from the big glossy leaves of the magnolia trees. If only they'd thought to fill their canteens during the storm.

"But it's going to take us longer to navigate the backwoods trail, especially now when half the world is under water. And you need to get back."

"What we need is to become invisible, as soon as possible," Parrish said, gulping air, "and stay that way. Besides, I'll manage."

Jamie glanced over at Tess, jerked a shoulder.

"Probably right," Jamie said, sounding agreeable. "Especially with that swamp buggy contraption running around—don't know where they're getting fuel, but I'm pretty sure they'll have thought it through." He slapped at a deerfly on his neck. "Come on." He reached for Parrish. "Either way, you need Gwen."

"Tess?" ZeeZee grimaced when she jumped down from the downed tree trunk where she'd perched like a skinny bird. There was mud to her knees; it streaked across her face and caked her hair. The only shiny thing left on her was the handle of the pistol Jamie had given her.

"Yeah?"

"They got away. I saw Dad and Stone get away." She sounded more hopeful than sure. "Tess."

Tess could feel the weight of her sister's need to be reassured, to believe. "Sure. They're already home, waiting for us."

"No, not that," she said. There was a look in her eyes that Tess recognized: weary horror. It made her look older, less fragile, less like a little girl. "Why? Why are those women like that?"

Tess stalled, checking what little gear her captors had allowed her to keep. "Which ones? Those Amazons or the filth at the Marketplace?"

"Both. Those women shot old men and boys, just killed them. Would have killed Stone and Father if they could."

"Yeah," Tess said. She walked to ZeeZee and wiped a streak of mud from her cheek. "They would have. I guess the wolves come in all shapes and kinds these days. It's why Grandpa made the S-Line—for us. He saw what it would become. Somehow he knew."

Tess watched Jamie help Parrish climb a pyramid of jumbled tree trunks.

"Come on. Let's go home."

Cattle had grazed the land—once. Now, the jungle and clumps of wiregrass clogged the open spaces. Standing water formed temporary ponds and swamps. Some of the muck Jamie made them trudge through, some he skirted. Before an hour had passed, Tess couldn't have found her way back to the

Beyond the Strandline

Marketplace, let alone forward to the Strandline. It would be another two or three hours before they hit the river, he told them; maybe then she would have a clue as to how close they were to home and safety.

It was cooler when they hit the heavier trees of the hardwood hammock. Huge limbs littered the forest floor and tangled in knots over their heads. Jamie didn't hesitate before plunging into the gloom and shade. The ground was drier here. There was less standing water to navigate, but the storm had moved through the huge old oaks and maples like a gardener pruning with a giant machete. It had changed the terrain so much that it worried Tess how often Jamie seemed to hesitate.

"So, how long?" Tess finally asked. Jamie tried to look reassuring before he trudged on, but never bothered to answer her question.

Parrish had finally managed to do most of his own walking without help, but she could tell he had settled into the strategy of just putting one foot in front of the other. When he stumbled on a twisted lump of a massive live oak root and went down with a grunt to one knee, Tess reached out.

"Hey, lean on me. How 'bout it?"

Instead of looking at her he sagged against her side.

"Yeah, okay," Parrish muttered.

His cracked lips started to bleed. All this water, and he was dehydrated—too dangerous to drink any of the storm runoff—not enough clean water left puddled in the big magnolia leaves.

"Water, water, everywhere, nor any drop to drink." The refrain from the poem ran through her head in a depressing loop. Maybe they should stop and take the time to boil some water before they all went down with dehydration.

"How much longer?" Tess asked.

Jamie looked back at her over his shoulder. When ZeeZee walked ahead of him through a clump of flattened palmettos, he called to her, "Straight on, due north from here."

"Not long now—" he began. ZeeZee's scream cut him off.

Tess left Parrish and blew past Jamie to get to her sister.

She blasted into a small clearing, one of those bare patches of sterile white sand where the ground stayed barren and empty, a sandy island in the middle of an ocean of green. At the center of this one, a sinkhole had collapsed in on itself. The rain had soaked the sand above and below, softening it, washing it away, and eroding great patches of ground. The feral hogs had been digging into the pit. The pigs, smelling the bodies below, had plowed the ground like mini bulldozers, increasing the size of the sinkhole. ZeeZee was trying to scramble up the side of the collapsing pit that served as a makeshift, mass grave. Tess could not reach her.

CHAPTER 53

"Come on, kid, don't look. Look up. Look here." Parrish held out his hand, ignoring the dull thudding that had become his head, hoping she'd refocus on him. Adrenaline surged through him, giving him enough energy to take charge. When Tess tried to reach down to her sister, he waved her off.

"Don't, Tess. The sides of the pit are collapsing. The limestone's collapsed underneath. Let me talk to her. Just give me a minute."

Parrish sent Jamie to watch their backs with a look. Parrish turned back to the panicked kid, trying to catch her eye. If only he could make her look up.

But he couldn't. She was beyond seeing him, hearing him. He'd seen it enough times, that frozen inability to look away when the nightmare was too real, too slammed in your face to ignore. She was in the terror zone.

The stink of death rolled over them: fetid water, rotted bodies, and decay.

"Come on, Zeta, look here. Look at me."

Finally, ZeeZee dragged her eyes from the body at her feet. Her face was the color of the flesh that still clung to the child's exposed corpse.

"I fell. I just walked where Jamie told me and I fell." It was the whine of a wronged child.

Parrish inched farther over the edge of the hole.

"There are dead people down here." It was a whimper.

"Parrish," Jamie said. Stress and shock lanced through his voice. "We've got company."

Parrish glanced at Tess and saw it in her face. She looked at him, her eyes almost black in the sudden darkness of a stray, lonely storm cloud that coasted across the sun.

She mouthed two names. "Father. Wendy."

"Zeez, give Parrish your hand. Let him pull you out," Tess said, not looking at her sister any longer, focused on the woman holding Jon Lane close enough for Tess to see the tears on her father's face.

"I'll fall and land on them. I don't want to touch them. I'll fall and touch them." The rabbit caught in the headlights look was back again. "Why are these dead people here?"

ZeeZee was still beyond being able to understand that Wendy Fortix stood at the edge of the clearing, holding her father, with Tess's tomahawk balanced at the notch between his neck and his shoulder, a killing spot, and the sinkhole, another kind of killing spot. It was a place where he and Jamie buried the anonymous dead, the ones that died from starvation and exposure, the ones that died out here in the woods. They buried them without words or ceremony in the soft ground of the sinkhole so that no one had to dream about who they might have been, or how they might have come to be nothing more than the rattle of bones under a blank sky.

The kids were the worst. Parrish had found the last two cuddled up together in the hollow of a lightning blasted oak tree, bone thin, maybe four or five—lost, forgotten, dead. It still happened—less and less now—but even now it still happened.

"Why are they here?" ZeeZee still fixated, couldn't know how dire the situation had become: Wendy holding her father's life in her hands, the sand in the pit about to swallow her down. All she could see was the corpses.

"Parrish!" Jamie said.

"Yeah, I hear you."

"You'd better hear him, because I'm about done chasing you around this disgusting wilderness. God, the smell alone," Wendy said. "I had an oasis, a sweet- smelling free zone in all this rotting stink."

Parrish struggled to keep his focus on ZeeZee's blond head. Under her feet, a lump of clay and sand crumbled.

ZeeZee wobbled at the edge of the widening hole. A child-sized skeleton rattled and rolled, drawn to the center of the pit like a rabbit to its den, sucked down by gravity and geology.

Beyond the Strandline

Tess heard Parrish gasp when he tried to reach down for ZeeZee. She fell to her knees next to him. The crazy idea that she could lower Parrish down to her sister with one hand and yank the tomahawk away from Wendy with the other bloomed in her brain. She was close enough to her father to smell sweat and blood, hear his whimpers. She watched Wendy press ever so gently against his skin. Blood dripped.

"I'll drop you, you witch," Jamie shouted from behind.

Tess shook her head at Jamie, trying to get him to stand down. "No." Tess kept her voice steady and reasonable.

"She's right!" Parrish barked back at his friend. "Help me here."

Jamie frowned at them both but obeyed. When he started to help Parrish, Wendy shook her head at him too, and Tess watched his jaw harden, his eyes narrow with anger. Jamie wasn't one to like being ordered around.

"Move again, and I kill him," Wendy ordered. "The gun, toss it in the woods, that puddle works fine for me."

"Please, Jamie," Tess said.

Jamie glanced at Tess, gave her a quick nod, and then did as Wendy commanded.

"Dad, where's Stone?" Tess said. "Where's the kid?"

He tried leaning away from the pain. "He went on. I went back—for you, for ZeeZee."

Wendy, as tall as the man she threatened, pressed harder with the tomahawk. "If I slip or bear down, you'll bleed out in three minutes."

"Tessie." Jon Lane sounded like a man drowning.

"Yeah, Tessie. How do you like the fallout now? Pebbles in a filthy pond. Thanks to that well-timed thunderstorm, eluding those crazy bitches at the Marketplace was hardly a challenge. And who do I stumble upon on my way out to visit your lovely, safe home but Mister Jon Lane, speechmaker and hostage taker? Now I want my son. I want Jerome."

Wendy glared where Parrish balanced at the edge of the pit.

"Still doesn't look too chipper, that arm of yours, champ . . . looks like it hurts. Sure hope you good people have some antibiotics put aside, and that they're still effective. They should be sealed up in foil packets, individually.

That's how the military did it. Nothing like them. That's what we had going, you see. We got what people wanted, and then we traded for what we needed—better than gold—medicine, perfume.

"Too bad, because I still had some back . . . well . . . I almost said home. Had a man last year die from an ingrown toenail. Infection. Gangrene. Septic. Screamed for a week. Didn't have the good meds then. Crazy. Just so, so crazy. Crazy times."

ZeeZee squealed.

"Again, thanks for the concern," Jamie snapped out. "But right now we're too busy for your crazy."

Parrish's world swirled out of control when a wave of nausea climbed up his throat. "Jamie," Parrish gulped. "I need your help."

ZeeZee's squeal turned to crying.

"I don't have your idiot son," Tess screamed, turning to face Wendy. "He's not here. You'll have to come with us and get him."

"You. Will. Get. Him. Now!" Wendy snarled, lifting the tomahawk, she showed off the bloody edge. Jon Lane took a breath.

"Tess, get your sister. No more deals." Her father's quiet voice cut them all off. She met his eyes, and remembered her mother. Feeling cold to her feet, she understood. She nodded when he smiled.

Wendy's demands dissolved into incoherent grunts as her father pushed back against her hold on him and reached for the tomahawk.

Tess crawled closer to Parrish, looked down into her sister's blue eyes. "Come on. I'll pull you out."

Parrish reached over to help. Jamie stepped between them, reached down and anchored their legs.

"Don't you fall in too, or I'll have to leave you both," Jamie said.

There were grunts and shuffling behind them, blurs of a struggle. "Hurry, hurry, Parrish," Tess said.

"I know. I know."

ZeeZee clung to the ragged side of the sinkhole, fingers and toes scratching to stop her slide. She kept her face smashed against a layer of gray clay and lifted her arms. There were claw marks through the layers of dirt. The void at the bottom of the sinkhole shifted, trembled, gave way. The bodies' of the dead children disappeared. Dirt rattled down into a black cavern.

Together they pulled ZeeZee over the rim of the hole.

CHAPTER 54

THE SINKHOLE SETTLED. In a matter of minutes it had doubled in size.

There was a roaring in Tess's ears. It was panic for ZeeZee—the hammering of blood—the sound of angry screaming from Wendy Fortix, and her father's grunts as he struggled with the woman holding the blade to his neck.

Tess dragged her sister farther away from the collapsing edge of the sinkhole.

Parrish groaned once and then nothing. Jamie scrambled for his rifle.

"Stop that! Stop fighting me," Wendy shrieked. "Do you think I won't cut your fool head off?"

"I think you won't, if I cut this one first," Ally called from the far side of the clearing, her voice flat and final.

"Ally!" Father sounded sad enough to cry. The tomahawk settled back into the groove of his neck.

It was Ally with Jerome. She held a skinning knife under his right ear and pushed the grim-faced boy farther into the clearing, nearly to the edge of the sinkhole. It was hard to know if Ally saw the pit or anything beyond Jerome and his mother.

"I've got this, Jamie," Ally spit.

Jamie, up to his knees in the puddle where he'd thrown his rifle, blinked water out of his eyes and clenched his jaw at her comment.

"What are you doing? How'd you find us? You were supposed to stay back. Stay home." Tess said. ZeeZee trembled in the dirt next to Tess, curling into a ball.

"Those Doe Kids are everywhere playing hide-and-seek, peeking. They told me you were coming. They showed me. Heck, I'm sure Stone and his buddies are still out there right now, making sure we are enjoying our games. It's all fun and games. Now I'm playing the game, right Wendy? Right? Mom-in-law? What a fun game, hide-and-seek and marry-the-captive-slave-girl."

"Oh, now, Dear, we have our little customs and rituals, everyone does. I thought you looked very pretty at the ceremony."

Jerome choked out, "I tried to tell her . . . how lucky she was. How good I could make it for her."

A curse, the sound of splashing water, drew everyone's attention back to Jamie. Wendy yanked Jon sideways, so she could keep her eye on the young man who radiated rage.

Tess watched the hate wash over Ally's face in waves, watched Jerome gulp when Ally pulled the ugly short-barreled pistol from the back of her jeans and shoved it into his backbone with her right hand. All Wendy could see was the knife in the girl's left hand—not the gun, not the real threat. Of all of them, Ally was the best shot with a pistol, but it didn't take much skill when the shot was point-blank. The knife was nothing next to the gun hidden from Wendy's view.

"I butcher animals, you idiot. I know how to do it, so that it's quick. Right, Tess? You need to step away from my father," she said to Wendy. She sounded almost polite—almost.

Tess looked at Jamie whose hands had gone to tense knots. He glanced down at the dripping rifle in his hands. Parrish pushed to a crouch next to the sinkhole. Tess could see the way his hands trembled, the way he clenched his fists against his knees to try and stop the shaking.

From her belly Tess pushed up to her knees. ZeeZee stayed curled on her side, breathing hard.

"Look at me, Honey. You're tough. But you don't want to do this." Tess called to Ally. But Ally was in another place, remembering maybe. Her unblinking eyes saw only Wendy. Her hand held the knife, white and bloodless. Tess whispered, "Parrish, stop her. The gun."

Tess called over to Ally, "Sweetie, just look at Parrish."

There was more screeching from Wendy, followed by the sudden steady drone of conversation from her father. He was using his most soothing, persuasive voice. The physical struggle hadn't gotten him far, so he'd reverted back to his old common ground, let's all be friends tactics.

Parrish stumbled to his feet, holding his hand out to Ally. "Ally, give it to me," Parrish said. "You don't want to do this. Believe me. You don't want this."

Trusting Parrish to handle Ally, Tess pulled ZeeZee upright. They both faced Wendy. Jamie used the moment to quickly raise his rifle and aim it at Wendy. She swung toward the movement like a snake striking; the tomahawk slipped and hit bone, Father's collarbone. He screamed and fell.

Without even blinking, Ally raised the pistol from behind Jerome's back and shot Wendy Fortix dead. She fell like a rag doll.

Jerome barely peeped when he stumbled forward and collapsed to his knees, balancing at the edge of the sinkhole, a hand against his neck where Ally had cut him, not a killing cut, just a knick. Ally hardly looked at him.

She looked at the gun in her hand as if she expected to find an explanation for what had happened. Jamie reached over Wendy's body to pull Father to his feet, pressing his hands on the slice across Father's collarbone.

"Tess." Ally sounded like a child. "I . . . just wanted to go to see the fountain." Her sister turned bleak, tormented eyes toward her.

"I know. I know."

Ally looked down at Jerome weeping at the edge of the sinkhole. "What? Shut up, you worm. I don't understand why *you* should be crying. You brought this all on yourself." She unconsciously rubbed a hand across the healing brand on her cheek.

Tess watched Ally look back up at everyone in the group, one by one, and then finally rest her gaze again on the softly weeping boy at her feet. Confusion, rage, disgust, and fear flowed through her face almost simultaneously.

"Stone came back without Father or you or ZeeZee, and I thought . . . I thought. He has to go." She waved the gun in her hand at Jerome. "I wanted him to . . . just go . . . away. And the kids, Stone, they knew. They watch everything, everywhere."

It unnerved Tess, thinking of the children tracking them, watching them, even now: so many scores to settle; so much out of control emotion.

Beyond the Strandline

"You stupid, bitch," Jerome shouted. He was on his feet and hurling himself at Ally. "She was going to let you stay, protect you, give you—"

Ally fell back, dropping the gun. His hands closed around her throat. His tears mixed with his curses as she clawed at his hands. Tess scrambled toward her sister as the edge of the sinkhole gave way. She could feel the sick flop of her stomach as she fell sideways. From the corner of her eye, she saw ZeeZee jump free of the collapsing pit.

Blindly, Tess reached out, clawing for balance, feeling herself fall . . .

"I've got you." It was Parrish's voice. His hand gripped her arm. "Jamie, help. I can't . . . hold . . . her."

"Help Ally! Get her!" Tess screamed. "Don't worry about me."

Jamie and Parrish pulled Tess away from the edge. She bolted toward Ally and Jerome. Her father sat in the dirt breathing hard through his teeth, trying not to faint.

As Tess reached her sister struggling with Jerome, a bullet hole bloomed in his temple like a sickeningly sweet flower; the side of his head dissolved as the bullet exited. He looked at Ally with a stupid, blank face. His mouth formed a wordless "Oh."

Ally—panicked and horrified—shoved at the bloody ruin of Jerome Fortix as he fell on her.

Tess reached her and helped her shove, pulling her sister into her arms. Words were impossible as shock thrummed through both of them. There didn't seem to be enough oxygen in the whole world. Ally's soft blond hair was spotted with flecks of blood and other . . .

Tess's brain shut down. Not yet. She'd think later. Right now, she hugged her sister fiercely.

Looking up, Tess stared across at Ally's mirror image. ZeeZee held the gun she'd used to shoot Jerome Fortix carefully, correctly. She ejected the maga, slipped the safety on and ignored the body at her feet.

From the shadows, the scouting party from the Marketplace watched the drama play out.

"Good enough," said the only woman without a scarf over her face. She smiled. The scar on her cheek pulled her mouth out of balance, turning it into a lopsided grimace. "Let's head back."

"Ell, are you sure we shouldn't draw some lines in the sand before we go?"

The half dozen women turned to their leader and waited.

"No. They won't be tempted to welcome us to their neighborhood anytime soon or bother visiting ours. That suits me fine."

"Ell, you might want to get back up here. Check this out," a short woman with cold green eyes hissed. Her perch in the oak was high enough to give her a decent view of the clearing, especially with her military grade binoculars. The woman they called Ell joined her in the fork of the big tree; Ell took the binoculars and focused.

Ell watched the older man, who'd managed to drag himself to his feet when he heard the gunshot, blood staining the front of his collared shirt, bend down and start to roll the body of Wendy Fortix toward the widening edge of the sinkhole. The girl who had shot the woman walked around the hole. She started to help the man shove at the body. They tumbled it into the sinkhole and watched it disappear. The man wrapped his arms around the now crying girl.

On the other side of the pit, the other girl, a twin to the first except for her unmarked cheek, walked around the pit and helped the older girl, Tess, shove the body of the dead boy in with the woman. Neither girl shed a tear. The unmarked girl pushed the pistol she'd used to kill the boy into the waistband of her pants and then wiped dirt from her hands onto her jeans.

Tess ignored the others and then went to help the young man, the one with dark hair, to his feet. He looked ill, injured. He staggered against her. When he looked into Tess's face there was a softness, an open affection, and something else. He smiled sadly at the pretty girl next to him with curly hair, and the woman behind the binoculars knew.

Her fingers cramped around the binoculars as she whispered, "Ryan. It's R.J."

The name moved through her memory like the last wisp of a fleeing storm cloud. Couldn't be. Her mind refused to accept the possibility.

The green-eyed woman next to her nodded, and then whispered so the other guards couldn't hear. "I told you. I told you it was him. I saw him at the Marketplace before the tornado. He's alive."

One of the other guards noticed their hushed conversation and called up to them.

"What'd you say, Ell?"

"Forget it. Nothing." She shook off the feeling that washed over her. It was like trying to jog underwater. "They've finished this up for us, for now. Neat and tidy. I'd have done the same thing. We're done here."

The boy with red hair braced an arm around the sick one's shoulders—no, not the sick one—R.J. He sagged against his friend. Tess turned a worried face to the others, said something. Ell watched them gather themselves together, shake off the horror of what had just happened, then start off into the green shadows of the deeper jungle lining the river.

"Nothing more to see here," she said, dropping lightly to the ground. She gave the signal to the others to move out.

CHAPTER 55

THEY PUT PARRISH on Grandfather's cot on his stomach, near the kitchen, near the boiling water and hot broth and sterile strips of cloth. Next to the peroxide and the willow bark tea. But it wasn't enough, and it wasn't going to be enough. Anyone could tell that.

Hadn't Wendy Fortix told them about the man who'd died from an infected toenail?

And the panther attack had been so much worse: dirty claws, the filth of the riverfront, not stopping to rest, not taking care of the wound. Now he lay on the cot like a man made of white, bleached bone. When he took a breath the sheet covering him barely moved, just like a dying man.

Gwen had given him valerian so he could sleep. That and exhaustion had worked—for now, but it wouldn't work forever. The pain would become too much. He wouldn't be able to handle it. No one could.

Tess had helped Gwen soak the bandage off and gasped when she saw the way the infection had exploded. Gwen's stitches had all but disappeared into the swollen tissue around the gash.

The way everyone tiptoed around the longhouse and cast those quick embarrassed peeks at her grandfather's cot was beginning to make Tess angry enough to . . . well, if she hadn't been so tired, she'd have thought of something nasty to yell at them. She raised her hand to brush the hair back from the side of his face.

"Hold him still. This is going to hurt."

"What are you going to do?"

Gwen held the pot of nearly boiling water with a potholder. Steam rolled up. Gwen had to turn her face away from the heat.

Beyond the Strandline

"You aren't going to pour that on him. My God."

Gwen's eyes narrowed against the heat and mist. She looked at Tess.

"There's an antiseptic, garlic, in this to help clean the wound. I don't know what else to do. It's infected. He's going to die if we don't do something drastic, and then he may still die."

Parrish moaned. His eyes flickered open.

"Tess?"

"Here. I'm here. Do you know where you are? Who's the president?"

He almost smiled, but didn't try to answer her. Tess couldn't blame him. He dragged air into his lungs, and she watched as his jaw clenched against the pain and fever.

"I know it's bad," he began, "I know . . ."

With one hand Gwen pulled the sheet back and down to his waist. Over the muscles along his ribs, through the meat of his side, a set of puckered scars marred the smooth skin.

"Tess, don't keep me here," he said, and then gulped. "Not here. When it gets bad. The boys, Ally, and Zeez, they'll be frightened."

"Stop it."

Ignoring her, he looked up at Gwen. "Do it. I won't move. Fast, before she can argue."

She poured the hot water over his shoulder. The smell of garlic filled the longhouse.

He screamed and went as still as a dead man.

"Wendy Fortix, she talked about antibiotics, something about wrapping them in foil. I don't remember all of it. He should never have come after us," Tess said.

Gwen pushed a protein bar into her hands and gave her a "get real" look. She almost laughed. Power bars. Protein bars. Hard tack. They were Gwen's answer to everything.

"Thanks. I'm going back. I have to, to get any antibiotics I can find, and then I'm out. I'm not staying around for dinner." Tess checked the chamber of her grandfather's Glock, the gun Ally'd used to end the Fortix threat. She shoved the gun into its holster on her hip. "I'm taking one of Jamie's horses."

"But I can't imagine Wendy Fortix being able to store antibiotics that would still be effective. Not after this long. Don't go, Tess."

Tess met the older woman's eyes.

"I can't do nothing. And Wendy seemed so sure." Tess looked at the unconscious man on the cot. "And if there's any chance—"

"Tess."

"I'm going."

It was a morning that reminded her too much of that other morning, when ZeeZee had first come to tell her about Ally. She ran her hands through her tangled hair. Good enough. Her hunting vest felt heavy, loaded up and ready. She slung an empty backpack over her shoulder. Hopefully, she'd have medicine in it when she came back from the Marketplace. Something.

"Gwen, don't let them worry about me. Keep them busy. It's going to be woman to woman at the Marketplace. I'll be fine."

When the older woman snorted, Tess pulled her close and hugged her.

"I know. Thank you. I don't say it enough. I know that."

Gwen pushed her back and looked hard into Tess's eyes.

"You. Hurry. And come back—safe. I love you and this family, and I don't say that enough."

CHAPTER 56

THE MARKETPLACE WAS an armed camp. The swamp buggy was still there; they were using it to pull vehicles to the edge of the parking lot. Three armed women watched the perimeter from the elevated bed of the big vehicle. They were taking no chances with having only one guard anymore. All the other entrances had three guards.

The parking lot itself had been cleared of all those ratty wagons and broken-down trucks. The women and children who'd surrounded the building were nowhere to be seen. The wrecks were being pulled to the edge of the parking lot and parked end to end, a barrier of sorts, the beginnings of a walled encampment.

Whatever else the Amazons were about, they certainly seemed to be expecting trouble.

Doesn't matter, she told herself. The truth of it was that she'd come "hat in hand," hoping to appeal to whatever humanity the group still believed in. The truth of it was that Tess was prepared to sign away her soul to get what Parrish needed.

Holding her hands high and stepping between the bed of a hay wagon and the hood of a rusted Nissan pickup truck, Tess stepped into the clearing of the parking lot.

The quiet was unnerving inside the building. The generator was still off, the lights still out. At the top of the escalator, the darkness was cut only by the gaping holes in the roof and the flicker of candles.

"I need to see the boss." They'd taken the Glock, patted her down, and took her vest and backpack. Slick and disciplined. Everything they did screamed military tightness, and it didn't take insignia and uniforms for Tess to understand that there was a back-story here, and it came from a militia mentality.

Most of the women walked around without their head wraps—every face screamed with scars.

"The boss?" One of her guards, her face still covered, laughed. She was shorter than Tess, her hair completely covered. Her pale green eyes reminded Tess of the water in a tide pool.

"I like that," Green Eyes said. "We should call Ell: *The Boss Lady*. Hey, what do you think about that?" She nudged her companion with one shoulder. Tess recognized the dazed look of "Golda," the guard they'd tied up from before. She didn't laugh.

Tess looked for the woman she'd traded Epsom Salts for lip balm, but came up empty. The tables had been cleared—more mopping up, more downsizing, maybe? More like someone had been ordered to take inventory. It was pretty clear that the Marketplace was closed for business until further notice.

At the top of the frozen steps the woman called Ell waited. They walked Tess up to her. The girl with the green eyes held Tess by the elbow, pinching her hard.

"They said I should have drawn lines in the sand when it came to you and yours. I blew them off." Ell looked tired when she waved Tess's guards off. When they still hesitated, she barked, "Go! I hardly think this girl is going to slip a shiv between my ribs. Are you?"

"I don't know how I could. They took everything. Fresh out of shivs." Tess held her hands up, palms forward.

Ell took a look at Tess, up and then down. "No, I don't know how you could. Go!" As the guards turned to walk down the escalator, Ell reached for one of the women. When the guard looked back, she hesitated, not wanting to leave Ell's side. It was Green Eyes. Her look shown with soft worry and concern, even a hint of panic.

Not complete savages then. Ell and the woman hugged like friends.

"I'll be fine, Britt. You just keep everyone moving along. It'll be fine." The green-eyed guard, "Britt" apparently, started to move back down the escalator. Golda simply turned back, snorted, and spit at Tess's feet.

"I don't want trouble with you or the Marketplace. I promise. In fact," Tess hesitated, "I need your help."

Ell raised her eyebrows. The skin around her eye puckered and pulled. Tess wondered if it still hurt, all that scar tissue.

"Come on."

It was a lovely space. There were pillows on the rocking chair, actual pillows, with those little stitches that made crosses. What had Grandma called that kind of sewing? Cross-stitching?

Tess reached out and ran her finger over the raised knots in the center of one of the cross-stitched flowers. There was a blue-cushioned end chair opposite the rocker.

Someone had walled off a small sitting area in one of the movie theater spaces.

"Sit down, Tess. Don't be afraid. I'm in charge now," Ell said, pouring water into a delicate china cup. She pushed the cup into Tess's hand. Ell looked around as if she was just now noticing her surroundings. "Nice stuff if you can steal it. Looks like Wendy Fortix liked nice stuff. Too bad it's all other people's stuff."

"I'm not afraid," Tess began. "Really, really worried." She sipped the water, thought about Parrish's chalk white face.

Ell looked around the space, seeming uncomfortable for a minute.

"Yep. I get that. The worried part."

Ell looked at Tess with startling blue eyes. Tess noticed that her hair looked clean. She'd had time to wash.

Tess fought off the feeling that she should wipe her face with the sleeve of her shirt. Forget it.

"Yeah, about that. Listen, I don't need to know what you're about or what you're hoping to accomplish here at the Marketplace. I just need something I think Wendy may have left behind."

"And here I thought you were just passing through."

"Okay, so we're both sitting on facts best left alone. I'm trying to tell you that I'm not here about you taking over this place."

Ell sat back in the rocking chair, not rocking. She waited and watched Tess.

"What I need to know is if Wendy left any medicines, antibiotics. Maybe something she knew how to make in her workshop? Or even a stockpile that she'd tucked away. It's a big favor, I know."

Ell tipped her head at Tess. "Someone is hurt badly? Someone you care about. Your sister? Was she hurt? One of the women that live with you?"

Something about the way Ell focused on the females in her family sent warning bells off for Tess. There was no mention of brothers or men.

"Yeah. My sister."

"I don't remember any of my people mentioning your sister being hurt or injured."

Tess put the cup back in its saucer, carefully. "No, it happened after we . . . left here."

"And you knew that the Fortix woman might have antibiotics because?"

Lying. It was one of those social skills that people perfected from long association with other people they couldn't or wouldn't trust. Tess cursed her isolation. Grandfather should have given them some lessons in lying.

"Listen. Does it matter? I really need that medicine."

She was on her feet, hands clenched. Ell tipped her head and watched her. She didn't seem surprised by Tess's outburst.

"Ahhh, not your sister then. Someone else. Someone very important to you," she said. Her eyes narrowed. "Someone more important than a sister. A mother?"

"I don't know what you want me to say to you." Tess walked to a small bookcase and stared unseeing at the collection of odds and ends: a glass bottle, a ceramic dish, a decorative thimble and a pincushion. "I see what you've got here. All these women. The scars that you hide. The brands. You shot the men, the boys. I know what you did."

Ell sighed and then smiled her crooked, pulling smile.

"A man. You want medicine for a man. The one that came with you, the dark-haired one I bet. How bad is it?"

"He's dying. Without antibiotics, without . . . something . . . he's dead. He will die."

Beyond the Strandline

Tess turned away from the bookcase and perched on the edge of the cushion of the bright blue chair, hands clasped in her lap. Ladylike. Controlled. Ha, that was some joke. If only she knew what to say to break through this women's suspicion.

"I don't know what your group is about, but I can guess. My sister, Ally, they took her, the people here, and burned a brand into her face. She's pregnant because of this place and Marco Fortix. She's fourteen years old. And now someone, *a man*, that has done nothing but tried to protect us from our own stupidity is going to die, because I haven't done absolutely everything I can think of to stop it."

"Do you know what will happen if I let you come in here and take aid and comfort to the enemy?"

"The enemy? You don't even know this guy. He's just some guy that got swept into the madness when he was only a kid. Some of these girls with you aren't much older."

"Golda, one of the girls who didn't want to leave me with you, before, on the escalator. I spoke sharply to her. You remember?" Ell reached for the pitcher of water, filled the teacup.

Tess felt itchy. More talk. Seriously? Couldn't they cut through this bull and get to the point? Why did Ell care to explain herself? She had all the power, and they both knew it.

"I'm going to tell you about Golda, although she wouldn't thank me. She was eight when the civilized walls came tumbling down. Eight. Her family was slaughtered when a biker gang came through their little farm. What they didn't kill or eat, they took. Golda was one of the things they took. Gang-raped and used for trade and barter, for entertainment, and she survived—survived after a fashion, and then found her way into the loving arms of Marco Fortix, who shut her up for good. She's one of the reasons we're here. She endured worse than hell at the hands of men. Always men."

Tess heard her grandfather's voice again.

The S-Line is an oasis. You can't know what it must be like out there beyond the line, Tess.

She met Ell's eyes, refusing to feel guilty because her life had been different.

"We killed them all and the pigs they forced her to live with. Do you understand? We. Killed. Them. All. And taught her how to be a very good shot. Broken does not mean harmless."

Cold didn't come close to what was in the other woman's eyes, but she had to ask.

"And the scarves? Why hide?"

Ell stood up, stretched her arms over her head, clenched and unclenched her fists.

"You've seen the scars," she said and then waited for Tess to nod. "The scars make us victims. The black scarf makes us warriors. Not complicated. It's a simple world now. I can't help you. It was men that burned, cut, or bled us. We're not here to help your man. We don't forget who did this to us. We won't forget. Ever. Don't come back. I'll let you live, but don't come back."

CHAPTER 57

FOUR AMAZONS WALKED Tess to the edge of the parking lot, handed her the vest, the Glock, but no backpack, then gave her a shove toward the path back to the ruined Main Street of Oviedo.

"Hey, maybe I'm not from that direction. Maybe I'm from up north. You don't know." Tess pointed over her shoulder to the north.

A muffled snort dismissed her.

"Sure. You're from one of the Pine Flats Clans." The woman's voice sounded husky through her head covering. "Go. Don't come back. She won't like it."

Tess felt the weight of failure settle on her shoulders.

"Yeah, I get that. Too bad there isn't anything I've got that Ell wants."

They might have smiled or smirked. It was hard to tell. Tess had to admit that without being able to see their faces or read their reactions it was easy to feel unsure and intimidated. Hard to judge your enemy when you couldn't see their expressions.

She held out her empty hands to the women. "Please, there's medicine. I know there is. Please."

They stood shoulder to shoulder, a wall of soulless disapproval.

She was going to fail. Parrish was going to die. She took a step toward the guards. The shortest of the four women, the green-eyed woman Ell had hugged at the top of the escalator, Britt, raised her rifle and pulled the trigger. The round exploded past Tess, deafening her. She stumbled backward, hit a chunk of loose pavement, and fell backward.

"Go! Now!"

Tess made it as far as the ruins of the church on the hill. The storm had finally brought down the last of the three crosses. Bleached bones littered the ground like toy pick-up sticks waiting to be collected by some giant hand.

They made her sad. They'd been easy to overlook before when they'd been so worried about getting Parrish back to the S-Line.

What had he said? That there was no one around who cared enough to bury them?

The humidity came down on Tess like bricks: oppressive, heavy, and choking. The storm was gone, but water still filmed everything and festered under the sun in slowly evaporating puddles.

The exhaustion hit her on Main Street. Those bones on the ground were too real, too much of a reminder. Tess collapsed against the wall where they'd hidden from the storm. Back again, to where she'd started, too much like the bones. The end never changed, did it?

Parrish was going to die. They'd have to figure out where to bury him so that he wouldn't be an anonymous pile of bones under a too-heavy sky.

Tess thumped backward into the blocks and then turned to press her forehead into the wall, her fingertips tearing into the rough, crumbling stone, her knees grinding into the wet ground.

"Grandpa," she said before she thought. "How do I change the end of the story?"

Nothing, except the sad thrumming of a tree frog. The tears that tore out of her throat threatened to gag her.

"God, I can't watch him die, and I won't pray for some lame-assed strength to be able to. I can't do it."

"Then don't."

The backpack thumped against her leg. Shocked, Tess jumped up from the grime and damp.

It was the one who'd taken a pot shot at her, the one Ell had called Britt. Tess knew those eyes: hard, cold, green ice. Behind Britt, the horse Tess had ridden to Oviedo stamped and snorted.   The girl was alone. The backpack felt heavy against Tess's leg. It was loaded.

"Most of the pills are sulfa based. Foil wrapped. The expiration dates on this stuff is mostly bogus. It can last for decades. Did quite a bit of research on the shelf life of antibiotics in all my spare time." The girl rolled her eyes then shifted off the balls of her feet, relaxing her fighting stance. "Shut your mouth, Tess. It's not an attractive look. Besides, you need to move." She yanked on the horse's lead rope. "Found this guy tied out back. Wouldn't want anyone to eat him."

"Why are you helping me?"

The girl shook her head, jerked one shoulder up.

"None of your business. Get up and get out. Help him. And don't come back."

Parrish. His name exploded into Tess's brain. She slung the bag over her shoulder. It sagged down her arm with the weight of its contents. The horse danced back when she reached for the reins. Spooked. He'd had a bad time of it. Well, hadn't they all. She threw the backpack into the saddle, looped one of the straps over the saddle horn.

Britt stood and watched Tess struggle into the saddle, never offering to hold the horse, to help. Tess felt her staring. It took her a minute to settle the horse, calm him. She turned him toward home and Parrish and . . . maybe, a miracle.

Looking over her shoulder, Tess said, "Thank you. I just—"

The girl bent down and picked up a stick, walked to the side of the horse. Reaching up she made a big show of latching the front pocket of the backpack closed, gave it a pat, and then pointed with the stick.

"Go. And, Tess, some of the stuff in that bag is penicillin. Don't give it to him. He's allergic. It'll kill him." She raised the stick in her hand and slammed it down on the horse's butt. He bolted for home.

The horse knew the way, at least to the crossroads of Van Arsdale and 426. Tess let him have his head, once she'd gathered the reins and settled into the animal's mad escape from the church on the hill. Because of the storm, the path was a complicated puzzle of downed trees and standing water. She let the horse pick through the tangle of it, kept her head down to try to keep from being swept out of the saddle by a low-hanging branch.

It kept her busy, trying to stay in the saddle when the horse dodged around deadfalls and debris. She was grateful. It kept her from worrying about what she might find back at the S-Line or what she'd heard from the girl with ice for eyes back at the church.

CHAPTER 58

THE AGONY HAD arrived. He knew that it would. He'd seen it: the raging, screaming process of death by infection. Gwen had done what she could; he got that. But there was nothing to stop the jackhammer throbbing in his shoulder, not now. The garlic and boiling water phase was done; he was almost glad.

He wasn't going to do it to Tess, make her have to watch and listen as he screamed his way into delirium and nightmares. Didn't he have a plan? Sure.

He thought about the .357 Magnum under the floorboards of the fishing shack. Hadn't he always known that it would end badly, one way or another? The face of Orlando floated next to the cot. He remembered Orlando, that boy who'd killed his brother and sister and then himself. He was a disembodied head. They'd found a headless ghost to torture him with after pouring acid on his shoulder. No! Not headless, because Orlando watched him with those huge, dark eyes.

Parrish tried to make the boy understand. "You know. I know you do. You don't wait and let the world pick you to pieces like a crow picks the eyes out of a skull."

He gasped when the throb became fire. He struggled back from the edge of screaming, trying to focus on the boy's pretty caramel face, his soft brown eyes. There was blood trickling from the corner of the kid's mouth. Parrish reached out, trying to wipe the boy's face with his fingertips. Fire. Fire. And more hot irons under his skin.

Rebar. That's what it was. Hot rebar. They were shoving it into the gaping wound. The stitches had come out. The wound flapped wide.

Beyond the Strandline

Hot rebar was a nice touch. Wasn't that what they'd been using to torture Orlando's baby brother with when Parrish held that baby down? The guy they called Richmond Parrish making it easier to torture the little boy.

Tess crashed through the screen door. She held the backpack in front of her like an offering.

"Gwen! Somebody! Anybody, I'm back!"

It was late but not close to dusk. There was still the hot breathlessness of late afternoon weighing down the day. The lazy, hazy hours, that's what Grandfather had called it.

"Gwen!" The longhouse was empty. That couldn't be right; they wouldn't have left him by himself . . . not unless. Oh, please . . . no. A grinding moan from the cot drew her like a mother hearing a child's cry. No child. Parrish was covered with a light, summer sheet, his head turned to the wall of the longhouse, hands hanging loose to the concrete floor.

Tess pulled the sheet down, tried not to gag at the lump of oozing flesh his shoulder had turned into. It was hard not to see the radiating lines of red that flared away from Gwen's neat stitches.

Parrish mumbled, "Orlando." The place? She reached out and brushed back his sweat-soaked hair. His lashes sparkled. He'd been crying. It was too much. She dragged the backpack open. It was stuffed with individually wrapped pills in aluminum foil; fancy official chemical names marked the packets. The girl, she'd said to use the sulfa drugs. Right. Some of the printing had worn off the packets.

How much should he get? How would you know? Think, Tess, think.

When she was little, the antibiotics came in pink liquid that you kept in a fridge.

He said, "Please, I'm sorry. I'm sorry I didn't want to die but I will. I will now."

"Okay, that's enough of that," she said, touching his bare shoulder, shocked at the heat under the palm of her hand. "Parrish, you have to help me now."

"I won't. I won't make her sad. I won't." He shook his head, rubbing his face against the linen pillowcase. "Too many . . . crying . . . all the time. Have to . . . Shut. Them. Up."

"Parrish, wake up. You have to swallow this. You have to be awake."

The screen door slammed. In the corner of her mind she registered the sound. Someone had fixed the screen door.

"Gwen?"

"No, Tess, it's me."

Her father stood back, looking at her as if he hadn't seen her in years. He tilted his head and studied her.

"You cut your hair."

She reached up and touched the snarl on her head. "What?" He'd obviously regressed since their brush with death at the sinkhole. She didn't have time for this. "Forget it. It doesn't matter. Help me." She poured water from the clean pitcher, boiled and sterile, meant for drinking. Easier to dissolve the pills in the water, pour it down his throat. How many did she dare give him to start?

"What are those? How did you get those? From where?"

"Later, I'll tell you later. They're antibiotics," Tess said. "Sulfa drugs. Only give him the sulfa, he's allergic to penicillin."

"He told you that?" He sounded skeptical as he pawed through the saddlebag.

"No. No, he didn't."

He ignored her odd answer, picked up a packet, read the contents on the packet, tore it open and handed the capsules to her.

"These," he said, handing her a fistful of pills.

Surprised by his certainty and by the comfort his certainty gave her, she dropped the pills into a cup and watched them dissolve. Where had this sudden clarity come from? Had he been shocked back into reality, seeing Parrish so bad off?

"Help me." She reached down and shook Parrish, hard. He screamed at the jarring. Not waiting for her instructions, she watched her father swing Parrish's feet off the cot while she shoved up next to the semi-conscious man. Between the two of them, they were able to brace Parrish upright sitting next to him on the cot. He lashed out and caught her on the cheekbone with the back of his hand.

"Oh, Tessie, are you okay?" her father asked.

She rubbed at the lump on her face and shook off her father's concern.

"Okay, maybe now we're even," she said, shaking the sluggish man. "Parrish, wake up. You have to or you'll choke."

He started to pant, head hanging. After a minute, he nodded.

"Tess? Let me die."

"Quiet."

She pressed the cup to his mouth. But he was unconscious again. Too much liquid poured out of his mouth, down the front of his chest, wetting the front of the bandage.

"No. Swallow. You have to swallow."

The next thing she knew, her father was on his feet. He hopped over the cot, pulled Parrish's head back by his hair, and told her, "Pour it down his throat. Now."

Jon reached around and ran his hand hard over the spluttering man's throat.

She looked at her father.

"How did—"

"Your sisters. They came home weighing three pounds apiece. They never did like taking their medicine. Your mother and I . . ." he stumbled over the word *mother*, paused, started again, stronger this time, "Your mom, we had a system. Ally was always harder to convince then ZeeZee."

Parrish hissed, "Geez, what . . . did I . . . ever do to you? I don't want to stay here. Take me to the fishing shack. I'll be less of a problem there."

"Yeah, okay. We're on that." She nodded over his drenched hair at her father, who nodded back. Together they helped settle Parrish back onto his stomach.

"Seriously, Mr. Lane, help me get out of here. I don't want to bother anyone."

"The shack's full of kids right now. No room for you, I'm afraid." Father smoothed the sheet back over Parrish's back.

"I'll get Gwen," her father said, then nodded at Tess. "You're going to give him more in two hours. Overwhelm his system. And then . . ." he stopped at the screen door. "And then we'll see."

"Yeah. And then?" She looked up from smoothing out invisible wrinkles in the sheet. Her father looked at her with a crooked smile.

"Then you'd better pray."

Yeah, prayer sounded about right. She reached down and stopped Parrish from clawing at the cement under the cot. She held his hand in her lap and wiped blood where he'd scraped his fingernails down to the quick.

They poured lava on his shoulder and poison down his throat over and over and over and over and he couldn't remember what came after that, more pain and pain and pain and . . . he tried not to scream when the lava flowed through him, but he did. He knew that he did. And that was embarrassing. Darby would be embarrassed for him. She always knew when her little brother was unhappy. But that wasn't right either. Darby was dead. But Tess wasn't.

Because she was alive and there, to hush him, comfort him. He wished she'd stop.

It made him feel worse to have her there.

"Parrish," she whispered. "I brought medicine. Real medicine. They had it at the Marketplace. It's going to be okay."

"Tess," he said. His voice sounded like rusty nails in a bucket. "I can't." He sucked in hard, stiffening against the pain.

His hand clamped around hers until she thought bones would crack, his or hers.

"Can you drink some more for me? We need to get it into you, the medicine."

"No. Don't waste it on this."

"Shut up and take the medicine. Are you really going to let a cat kill you?"

There was a muffled coughing sound from the pillow, not a laugh but close.

Beyond the Strandline

The screen door whined as someone pulled it open.

"I'm here," Gwen said. "Come on. I'll help you."

Tess looked up at her.

"Sleep," Gwen said. "I'll get Kilmer to help me with Parrish. Check the backpack if you have to have something to do. I'd rather you slept."

"Me too." Tess dragged the filthy backpack to her platform. She wanted to obey Gwen and just sleep, could feel the demand for sleep in her bones, but she needed to wind down, keep her brain busy for a while, keep her imagination under control. Tess reached for the backpack and watched as Gwen gathered up the treasure trove of foil-wrapped medication she'd pulled free and started sorting through it. She clucked like a happy hen over a clutch of beloved eggs.

Crawling up onto her sleeping platform, she sat, turning her back on Parrish and Gwen and the generous gift from a stranger who had been shooting at her one moment and then tossing salvation at her feet the next. The backpack was mud caked and worn, mended at the corners. Tess ought to know; the backpack belonged to her.

Tess ran her hand over the neat stitches she'd made with dental floss, best repair thread in the world. Gwen's trick. Good stuff, dental floss. Gwen had brought sacks of the stuff with her when she and the boys had arrived. A donation from the dentist she'd worked for—before. Tess wondered if the dentist was still fixing teeth, probably not, probably had a new line of work, if he'd lived.

Opening the backpack's front pocket, she was surprised by the feel of paper under her fingers. More medicine? She pulled the homemade envelope out. It was glued shut with a paste of flour and water. The girl had done a good job. The edges of the envelope made from heavy brown paper were neat and sharp. Tess wanted to hold it up to the light, see what she could see, but didn't want Gwen to notice. She turned it over in her hands, stared at the name printed on the front: Ryan.

Who the heck was Ryan?

Tess tucked the envelope under her pillow, strangely comforted by not having to look at it anymore. She slept.

CHAPTER 59

The scratch of a match, a precious match, shocked her awake.

"Parrish," she said and had her feet on the ground before she finished saying his name.

At the end of the longhouse, close to her grandfather's cot, Stone lit the hurricane lamp. He set it on the stove. The lamp made a half circle of light on the floor, outside the circle the darkness was total: no moon, no starlight, and no light inside. The longhouse glowed at one end. The rest was still and empty except for the softly blubbering snore of the dog who'd climbed under Tess's bunk.

Where was everyone else? Where were they sleeping, the Doe Kids and her sisters and Kilmer and Jess T? Oh right. Down at the fishing shack. Isn't that what Father had said? There were too many cobwebs in her head.

Stone stepped out of the glare of the lantern light.

"Everyone is sleeping in that shack by the river or in the barn."

"I remember. You read my mind. I couldn't think if I'd heard that right." The quiet was suddenly as stifling as the darkness. "Why is he so quiet? He isn't . . ." She let the sentence drop when she saw how still the body on the cot had grown.

"Why didn't anyone call me?" She collapsed onto her knees next to Parrish. He was so still. The quiet fell around her and felt as solid as a velvet curtain.

She laid her head next to Parrish's against the scratchy linen of the sheet on the cot and listened to him breath. It was quick and shallow, but he'd stopped moaning. At least there was that. She'd heard him earlier even in her sleep, and knew that he'd been struggling desperately for control.

"He's sleeping a little bit easier. I gave him more of the medicine."

"Where are my sisters?"

"The barn. All the boys are at that shack, and the girls are in the big barn. I think that medicine woman is trying to take the wildness out of us."

She could hear the smile in his voice even in the darkness.

"You call her the medicine woman? Really? You know her name is Gwen, right?"

"Yes, but we like to give new names, because the world is different now. New."

She considered the idea for a moment. "Yeah, because the world is different now. I like it. It's a nice idea."

Suddenly curious about the leader of the gaggle of abandoned children she prompted, "People call your group the John and Jane Doe Kids." She caught his quick frown. "Children with no names. It's the name they gave to bodies they couldn't identify. Did you know that's how my grandfather thought of you?"

He jerked his thin shoulders at her.

"Yeah sure. But I don't like it. Those are names for people without names, but we've given ourselves new names, and that makes us real."

Tess slanted a look at Stone's shadowed presence in the dark. "It does. You're right."

"Sometimes it's better not to remember the old things, I think."

"Why?"

"Because there's no going back to it. No changing it. There's only forward."

She considered that.

"Sure. I see your point."

Parrish's breathing changed, became something more like the sound of wet sandpaper tearing. Quick horror swept through her.

"No. No," she said, reaching down to touch his chest. "Help me. Let's get him on his side. Stone. Help me! Get pillows from the other beds."

She rolled Parrish onto his good side.

"Parrish, wake up. Listen to me. Come back!"

He took a deep, shuddering breath and moaned when she had to push against his bad shoulder.

"Please . . . wake up."

Stone brought the pillows and helped prop him on his side. Parrish whispered something.

Tess bent to hear the dry, cracked sound of his whisper.

"Get Gwen," he rasped. "She has . . . a way . . . to make it stop. Ask her."

"What are you talking about? What does Gwen have?"

"Morphine bombs. We talked about it. In the beginning she told me, for when it gets to be too much."

Parrish wasn't making any sense. Delirious.

Stone stepped into the ring of light. Their eyes met and she saw that he understood, was shaking his head.

"Morphine bomb?"

Parrish gulped back a cough.

She pushed at the pillows, trying to keep him from rolling onto his stomach. "What do you mean, 'for when it gets to be too much?'" Still looking at Stone, whose eyes were empty holes of black in the low light, she snapped, "Hush now. What are you thinking? I'm pretty sure Gwen did not offer to 'end you' with morphine. Besides, you seem better."

"Yeah, okay, maybe," he muttered.

"You're arguing with me, aren't you? You have to let the antibiotics work, that's all. Morphine? Why would you think that way?"

"What did you give him?" she shouted at Stone.

There was a flush of red on Parrish's neck now—a rash.

Stone stepped back into the light and held up the torn foil wrappers that littered the picnic table.

"Show me." She snatched one of the wrappers out of the boy's hand. "Erythromycin. Cin. This is penicillin. I thought you knew what you were doing! He's having a reaction to the penicillin. Get Gwen. Go."

"I'm sorry. I . . ." He backed away from her and then hustled out of the longhouse.

She sat on the floor and took Parrish's hand.

He inhaled sharply.

"Tess, don't."

"Don't what?"

"Don't try to hold on to me."

"Why? Why would you think that way?"

"Because I've," he stopped to wheeze, "done terrible things."

"So you're going to make us do terrible things to you? No. I won't let you die."

She watched a smile flutter over his face. The hollows under his cheekbones were deeper, his eyes sunken in shadow. She reached for his hand.

"You're right. Hand me a gun."

"Now that's the Parrish I know and love."

Love. She'd said it without thinking and realized she meant it. She felt his fingers tighten on hers.

"I would tell you not to . . ." he said, then gulped, "not to bother, but I know how stubborn you are."

"Right. So save your breath."

He squeezed her hand and didn't let go.

Later in the night, there was fuzz in Parrish's brain, or was it cotton or wool? The right word was hard to catch. It was hard to settle on one word to describe the way his thoughts rolled around, drenched with fog and pain. Maybe, not so bad as before. Maybe. Except that his chest hurt, and it was hard to shake the vague feeling that he'd said things that might be considered . . . What? What had he said? The fog shifted and swirled and there was less fog. A little less. Maybe.

The fog had been nice in its own way: no hard questions or sharp memories, just oblivion. The faces of the dead and broken faded. Oblivion, it might be nice, not hurting anymore.

Then someone was pouring water down his throat and he was drowning, which seemed a terrible way to die. He tried to curse, thought he heard Gwen and Tess yelling at him to drink, drink, drink. Water burned his nose. *Go torture someone else*, he thought, and then slipped under and into the fog again.

Later, someone's fingers slipped through his, had gripped him tight. Tess. He knew without looking; it was Tess holding his hand—a solid, clinging weight that brought him back, kept him tethered to the pain. For a minute it made him angry, but then he remembered the smell of her hair, her skin, and knowing that she wouldn't let go. Her fingers threaded through his and pulled him back—back to her.

He squeezed her hand and hung on.

CHAPTER 60

"Tess?" Sometime between the fog and the ache in his shoulder, he called her name.

When he opened his eyes, their clasped hands filled his view. It was a knot of fingers resting on the edge of the cot. He blinked and tried to focus beyond the sight of her gripping his hand to see her face next to the wall of pillows they'd built around him.

She was asleep and drooling, sitting on the floor, her face pressed against the edge of his cot. He smiled.

"Tessla."

Her eyes fluttered open, sleepy and unfocused. He flexed his hand and enjoyed the feel of her long fingers slipping through his. His shoulder still ached, but the fire wasn't as fierce. Sometime in the night the fog had blown away too. He took a deep breath.

When she lifted her head, he laughed at the way her hair had flattened out on one side and sprang out into spiraled spikes on the other side.

He watched awareness flare into her face, wakefulness, and then her quick gray eyes clouded over with concern, but for what? For him, he realized. Worry for him.

A filter of morning light grew inside the longhouse.

"Parrish, how bad is it? Do you hurt?"

"No," he gulped. "Not like before. How long have I been out?"

She cocked her head. Sunlight made a halo behind her lopsided hair. "Three days and don't BS me. I have a crick in my neck."

She put her hand on his forehead, stared at his eyes, and then stood up to check the bandage on his shoulder.

"I don't know. I'll have to check with Gwen when there's more light, but it seems better," she said, pausing. "She was here, after Stone gave you . . . well, never mind. It really seems better than before. You seem . . ." She sat back on her heels, exhaled, and then hung her head.

"Tess, it's better," he said. He reached out to brush back her wild curls and sucked in a breath. It must be better, because he'd forgotten and used his bad arm.

"What's wrong?" Two frown lines made her look serious and worried.

"Nothing. Wrong arm. Forgot."

"You're always doing that." She ducked her head again, hiding her eyes.

"What?" He loved the way she could make him want to smile. "Hurting myself?"

"No, you goof," she said and then reached up to finish brushing back her hair, "my hair. Touching my hair. You do it all the time."

It was true.

"Your hair." The light in the longhouse set the tips of her curls aglow—sunshine through honey. "I think that's when I knew I would end up staying . . . no matter how hard I tried to leave."

"My hair kept you from leaving? Are you hallucinating?"

"No." He tried pushing up off of the cot. The air shimmered and swam and dipped. He was damned if he was going to faint in front of her. "Help me. I need to . . . sit up. I need to know I still can." His shoulder still throbbed, but less. "I won't be sitting up too long. Trust me." He swung his legs to the floor. She wedged herself under his good arm. She sat next to him, her arm around his back. They sat side by side.

"Don't move," he said, "or I might fall down."

"You are better. You're sitting up. But you're obviously not well, because you just admitted to needing my help."

He laughed and then regretted it. His shoulder hurt. He caught his breath and then relaxed against her side—content to breathe the air she breathed, to smell the soap she'd washed with.

"What did you mean about my hair?"

"I told you." He shifted, trying to be more comfortable. "Your sister brought me your braid after you'd cut off all your beautiful hair, so you could save Ally, so no one could grab you by your hair. I thought it was the bravest thing I'd ever heard. I think I knew then that I couldn't leave."

She looked at him with those storm-filled eyes of hers.

"You think?"

"And then you saved that idiot dog."

Blinking like an owl, she shook off her surprise when he mentioned Stone's dog. That's the way they all thought of the mutt now—Stone's dog.

He reached for her hand, raised it to his lips, and kissed her open palm.

"Or maybe it was when you threw that tomahawk at me on the trail home, or . . ."

She smiled and cupped his scruffy cheek.

"I knew when you shaved that first time."

Laughing, he bent down to find her willing mouth with his own.

An hour later, she poked and pushed and rearranged the pillows. He didn't have the heart to tell her that she wasn't helping and it only hurt when she prodded. The screen door slammed shut. Gwen hurried toward them.

"Tess, you're hurting him. Here. Here, take this and back up." She handed a pail of water to Tess.

"Thank you for coming that night when he was talking crazy."

"The crisis was mostly over by the time I got here, and you were both asleep. Sorry about having to wake you up, but I think pushing the water through him flushed the last of the penicillin out." She pulled a glass thermometer from her medical backpack and shook the mercury down.

"Why didn't you use that before, or did you?" Tess asked.

"No point. We were going to know soon enough if the infection was going to kill him." She shoved the thermometer under Parrish's tongue. "I didn't want this one to chomp on the glass when he was half out of his head and break it. I don't have a replacement."

He looked at Gwen with a grumpy frown. "You don't have to talk about me like I'm not here, thank you very much." Gwen shrugged, waving away his complaint.

"I'm so sorry about the penicillin, Parrish. It slipped by me. Stone was just using the packets I set out for him. It was my fault—the allergic reaction. We got lucky. You are one tough guy." She looked at Tess and then shook her head in apology. "I knew you were allergic. I'm so sorry."

"Penicillin?" Parrish said. "How did you know I was allergic to penicillin? I don't remember telling you that. *I* barely remember knowing that."

Gwen looked surprised at his question. "It was Tess. She knew. Didn't you tell her? You must have."

Parrish looked over at Tess, who squirmed uncomfortably as he glanced at her. "Sure, I must have told her."

CHAPTER 61

SAMANTHA THE GOAT was still a pushy prima donna, kicking at everyone but Tess or Parrish, when he bothered to help out with barn chores. But the milking didn't bother Tess. Milking goats was one of those mundane, routine rituals that allowed her to think, kept the others from bugging her, and gave her a few moments to herself.

Father had offered to take over the chore. He'd been doing a lot of that lately; volunteering, stepping up, keeping Ally and ZeeZee busy and out of trouble. Tess was still getting used to having him be more like a father than a bystander. It was nice.

She patted Samantha's side. "Don't get me wrong. I like it. But, between you and me, I'm still skeptical. My dad's being a father and Parrish . . . well, I miss him you know. Don't tell. Just between us girls."

"Okay. My lips are sealed too."

Startled, Tess swung around on the milking stool.

Parrish looked good, a little thinner, maybe, but good. His cheekbones cut more sharply across his face and cast deeper shadows than before. He'd pulled his hair back from his face, which highlighted the spark of gold in his eyes. Must be getting ready to get back to work. He leaned an elbow on a slat of wood.

He looked good standing there so unsure of himself when she didn't say anything.

"Hey," he said.

"Hey."

Samantha stamped. She was out of feed and ready to be done with the morning milking.

Tess lifted the brace of the stanchion and let the big milk goat jump down. She turned to Parrish. "Haven't seen you around lately." More like three days, six hours, and . . . she pulled her wind up watch out of her overalls, checked the time—eighteen minutes. She'd been trying to be patient.

As soon as he'd been able, he'd taken himself off to the fishing shack. He and Jamie had turned it back into a "Guy's Only" haven of guns and gun oil and hunting gear. That was the rumor. They had Stone and the other boys whirling around them like grubby satellites.

"True," he started to say, but saw her frown and stopped. Standing up straight, he faced her. "Just trying to get my breath back and straighten out some . . . stuff. Been hunting. Got a bit behind on that. Hunting, you know. It's all about food."

"Is that supposed to be an apology?" Tess picked up the milk bucket. "Walk with me if you want to talk." She headed out of the barn. He grabbed her arm, took the bucket out of her hand, and set it down.

"No. I don't want to walk and talk. I want to stand here and look at you."

He ran a fingertip down her cheek and along the line of her jaw. She hadn't forgotten what it felt like for him to touch her. She'd tried, telling herself that he had too many secrets, too many ways to disappear from their lives, no matter what he'd claimed in a fever.

She closed her eyes.

"It was you." His lips were at her ear.

"What?" She opened her eyes. All she could see was him—looking at her, studying her, solemn and serious.

"I've been ready to be done with all of this . . . pain . . . for a long time— for a long time . . . until you. You saved me, Tess."

When she started to say something, he took her shoulders, pulled her closer and said, "Just let me say this. When I was sick I could feel you, holding me. I felt it. It was you."

He stepped back and pulled a strand of tiny polished shells from his pocket.

"I needed time to make this."

Beyond the Strandline

In the center of the string was an oval of white abalone. He'd carved the delicate petals of a rose in the surface of the shell.

It made her smile. Jewelry. He'd given her jewelry, her first and only jewelry. She looked up at him. "I don't know what to say. It's really beautiful. It's jewelry."

Suddenly, he jammed his hands in his pockets and seemed almost shy.

"I remembered what you said about the shells . . . on the beach."

It took her a minute to make the connection. "In the strandline on the sand. Sure, I remember."

"Yeah." He stepped back, took the necklace out of her hand, and tied it around her neck. His fingertips lingered on her skin. "Because you and this place are the best of what's left. I know that."

Tess reached up to touch the cool white rose around her neck. Her fingers trembled. She looked into his face and saw a light like a fever in his eyes. He bent his head to hers. He seemed so intent, so focused, that it frightened her.

"I need to tell you something."

"Now? Really?" He smiled.

"Really. You haven't been around much, or I would have said something sooner. But you seemed distracted. It doesn't matter." She shook her head, shrugged off her worry. "Don't you want to know how I knew about the penicillin? How we got it? How I knew?"

She felt him stiffen and step back.

"I must have told you."

"No, you didn't. But someone else did."

Tess pulled the wrinkled envelope out of the pocket of her work overalls and handed it to him. He looked at the name on the envelope and went pale.

"Sit down. It's okay. You know, you're still getting better. There was a girl from the Marketplace. She gave this to me, and the medicine that saved you. But I wasn't sure about the name."

"The name?" he said, sounding stunned, empty.

"Parrish, are you all right?"

"Yeah, sure." He tore open the crumpled paper and pulled out a handwritten note.

She watched him read it and then run his hands over the writing like a blind man reading Braille. He looked through Tess, turned, and started to walk away.

"Parrish!"

He stopped, turned back. Tess saw something dark and bleak creep into his face, his eyes.

"It's not my name, you know that right? Parrish, it's not my name," he said, looking at her to see if she understood. "Richmond Parrish, it's where I was born. No one used their own names. It was easier that way. Cleaner, somehow."

She bit her lip, thought about the conversation she'd had with Stone about the importance of new names. What did he want her to say?

He held the note out in front of him. "My name is Ryan Summerlin. I was born in Richmond Parrish, Virginia. My sisters' names were . . ." He paused and considered. "No, not were . . . *are* . . . My sister's names are Brittany and Ella. I had another sister but . . . she died. Darby died." He turned away. "But not Brittany and not Ella."

"How did the girl . . . know you?" But she knew the answer. "Your sister. That girl is your sister, and they called the one in charge Ell. Ella. They knew you. They had to know. It's why they helped us."

Outside the barn, the wind started whipping through the tops of the trees. Leaves rattled. Clouds skittered overhead. The light faded from the sky. Rain splattered in the dust outside the barn, kicking up mud.

He walked to the entrance of the barn where he stood silhouetted against the cloudburst.

"Those women, they shot all those people. They told me to stay away. That if we stayed away . . . we'd be safe." She waited, holding her breath. "What will you do?" She was tempted to try and touch him. She didn't.

She watched him take a step into the rain and then hesitate. Turning, he looked back at her and held out his hand. Tess moved toward the man and the storm.

CHAPTER 62

MOST OF THE Doe Kids couldn't remember having cake. When they'd heard that Gwen was making a birthday cake for Ally and ZeeZee's fifteenth birthday, they arrived before the sun came up. They were there, sitting at the picnic table and the extra table Jess T had made out of planks of cypress and four oak stumps. Tess laughed when she saw them. Stone's dog dozed at the end of a clothesline they'd used to tie him to a tree at the edge of the clearing.

"It's going to be a while before the cake's ready, gang."

No one budged.

"Oh, never mind. See you at the party."

They were still there when Gwen carried her Crazy Wacky Chocolate Cake from the longhouse with one of the last of the emergency candles shoved in the middle. Gwen beamed over her creation: a cake made without eggs or milk or butter, a secret recipe from her great-grandmother, and a reminder from the past that the world should never be without cake.

Blake and Blane danced next to her like giddy marchers at a parade. Everyone clapped. Jess T and Kilmer started up a baritone version of "Happy Birthday" that made Tess wish for her grandfather's beautiful tenor voice.

Ally and ZeeZee sat in places of honor on a bench Father had dragged from the longhouse for the party. Parrish helped Stone pass around a crazy collection of plates and saucers the Doe Kids had been collecting for the event—pilfered from who knew where. Jess T had been telling them stories of other birthday parties where the plates had all matched and the Mommies had served something called ice cream.

Ally and ZeeZee blew out their candle.

Everyone brought gifts for the twins: Tess had made them new rabbit-fur bags; Parrish cleaned and oiled and polished two matching SIG Sauer pistols that no one had known about. He'd found them in their grandfather's things, making him even more convinced that there was a treasure trove of weapons out there somewhere. The Doe Kids brought bits and pieces of things they found in the woods, pine knots and eagle feathers. Gwen baked a cake. Father gave them both hand-stitched journals made from his precious stash of paper. And then Kilmer and Jess T presented them with beautiful patchwork saddle pads.

"Wow. Those are really beautiful," Tess said, as she reached for one of the hand-stitched pads. "Goliath is going to look pretty darn spiffy when you use these, girls."

"Well, about that, I'm not sure even these saddle pads could fancy up that old stumpy grump of a mule," Jess T said. It was a long speech for him.

"These are still so gorgeous," ZeeZee said, hopping up to give Kilmer a quick hug and then Jess T. "Aren't they Ally?"

But Ally wasn't looking at her sister. Instead she looked to the far side of the clearing where Jamie and Stone led two of Jamie's white horses. The horses danced at the end of their lead lines like mythical creatures from a dark magical forest.

"ZeeZee look!" Ally cried, holding her hand out to the mare that Stone led. Her other hand cradled the tiny bump of her stomach. The horse sniffed at her hand, smelling cake. "Look at what Jamie's done for us."

"Oh, Parrish, did you know about this?" Tess said while the children admired and chattered excitedly.

Parrish walked over to shake Jamie's hand, saying, "Nice way to outshine us all."

Jamie laughed, shrugged, and said, "A boy horse and a girl horse. I just thought that the girls could start a nice little herd of their—"

The horses jumped and reared at the sound of the *pop, pop, pop* of rifle shots. Jamie's face faded from pleasant good cheer to stunned confusion as the stain of blood on his shirtfront spread like a flooding tidal pool. He looked down and then up and then at his friend.

"Parrish . . ."

Children screamed. People scattered. Kilmer pushed over the picnic table, started throwing kids behind it. Parrish caught his friend as he collapsed, and Tess scrambled to see where the shots had come from. In the gloom of the hardwood hammock near the longhouse, Tess caught the glimpse of the shooter, a girl with a riflescope still trained on the clearing. The Amazon dropped softly to the ground from a fork in a tree, turned, and disappeared from view, heading in the general direction of Oviedo and the Marketplace Mall.

An odd, guttural sound echoed and crawled and finally whispered as she ran from Tess's sight and the gory results of her revenge. Laughter. It was that girl's, that Golda's, insane laughter.

Broken doesn't mean harmless. Ell's voice misted up from the bloody ground.

When Tess turned back to the scene of the birthday party it was to see the stricken look in Parrish's eyes and to listen to ZeeZee quietly weeping in the dirt next to Jamie.

Ally stared at Tess, dry-eyed and bleak, the brand on her face an obscene warning.

After . . .

THE SLOW BROWN water slid by—a slippery, wet ribbon. Tess watched a pinecone bob and twirl past. It was easy to imagine that some poor squirrel, upriver, with butter fingers and bad luck had lost its treasure. It happened. Treasures slipped away, no matter how hard folks worked to hold on to them.

Kneeling, she patted absently at the small lump of dirt on top of the Indian burial mound, bones on top of bones. She had finally remembered to ask Ally the name of the little girl they'd buried here, next to the river. Moss. They'd called her Moss, like the Spanish moss that floated from the oak trees overhead—a growing, fresh tree lace that decorated every corner of the Strandline Ranch.

Wondering if the little girl called Moss would have liked the lantana and fern bouquet she'd brought and would continue to bring for as long as she could, Tess placed the flowers at the foot of the grave.

"We won't forget you. I promise," she said, glancing over at her grandfather's grave.

Pushing to her feet, she thought, not for the first time, how much she liked the spot they'd picked to start the graveyard of the S-Line. Not too shabby. There was plenty of room for more graves when they needed them. Time would tell. It wouldn't be the worst thing, she realized, to wind up here under the oaks and tree lace.

She didn't have to turn around to know that Parrish was still there, watching her, protecting her, waiting to escort her back to the longhouse.

When he finally touched her, running the tips of his fingers down her bare neck, she shivered—a tiny earthquake of sensation. His hand came to rest on her shoulder. He stood behind her, a solid wall of support, of comfort.

Turning, she let go, moved into his arms, and cried: for a little girl she'd never known, a grandfather she should have thanked, and for a world they would never see again.

Recipes, Notes, and Other Observations
by
Gwen Dunn
The S-Line Ranch & Oasis :)

Year Seven

For: Blake and Blane and the girls. Just wanted to jot down some things I've figured out—Just in case . . . and for the future because there is a future. Please don't doubt that!

Fly and Bug Spray: Different bugs, different oils, different herbs. The mix changes, depending. This summer the mosquitoes haven't tormented us like last year (been pretty dry, no rain). But the Noseeums are miserable. They're driving us nuts not to mention Goliath.

<u>Directions for bug spray:</u>

Spray bottle half full of water (boiled)

Fill with witch hazel to top

Add (Essential Oils): 30-50 drops of a combination of Citronella, Clove, Lemongrass, Rosemary, Tea Tree, Eucalyptus, Cedar, Catnip, Mint

Note: Essential Oils are not going to last forever. Substitute with fresh or dried herbs. Peppermint, Spearmint, citronella, lemongrass, catnip, cloves (anything mint)

Important: Don't let Jess T cut down the citronella grass on the south side of the barn. He thinks they're weeds. They're not.

Boil Water and add dried herbs (experiment with combinations) 3-4 TBSP; mix and cover; let cool; strain herbs out; mix with witch hazel (1 cup) (1/2 tsp of vodka as a preservative-optional) cider vinegar (1 cup)

*** (In a hurry, I use 1/2 C. witch hazel + 1/2 C cider vinegar + eucalyptus oil)

Miss Tuggs gave me this next one. Nice lady. Sometimes, I wonder how she weathered all this. I wonder how a lot of people weathered all this . . .

<u>Four Thieves Bug Spray: An Old, Old Recipe</u>

Apple Cider Vinegar; Sage, Rosemary, Lavender, Thyme and Mint; quart jar with airtight lid

1. Vinegar and dried herbs in jar.
2. Seal tight. Shake well each day for 2 to 3 weeks.
3. Strain the herbs out.
4. Very strong; dilute with water to use on skin.

June: Finally found my aloe vera soap recipe. Soaps from storage are running out, although they lasted the magic seven years. Colonel Kennedy planned on a Biblical seven years of lean (Genesis 41) and here we are still living lean. Time to make soap.

Find soap mold. Check storage shed.

ALOE VERA SOAP RECIPE:

7.5 oz "mineral" water
3 oz lye (caustic soda)
1.5 lbs extra virgin olive oil
0.4 oz beeswax

1.8 oz aloe vera juice (remember to show kids how to harvest the aloe pulp)
0.18 oz mint essential oil

CarefulGloves and Goggles**

1. Pour water into saucepan. Add lye SLOWLY, stirring gently until it is dissolved.
2. Use the thermometer heat to 120 degrees and 140.
3. Heat olive oil to between 120 and 140 (in separate pan) stirring in beeswax slowly.
4. Remove olive oil from heat. Add lye mixture to olive oil. Stir slowly. Don't splash.
5. Stir every once in a while (every 15 minutes until it thickens and congeals.)
6. Stir in aloe vera juice, and essential oil. Stir for one minute with a spoon or whisk. (Don't make foam)
7. Pour into greased soap mold. Tap out any air bubbles.
8. Cover with a towel, let stand 2 days. Uncover and let stand for another day.

Hardtack good enough for civil war soldiers, good enough for us . . .

4-5 cups of flour
2 cups of water
3 tsp. of salt

Mix. The mixture should be dry rather than wet. Roll it out (1/2 inch thick). Shape into rectangle; then cut: 3x3 inch squares, poke holes top and bottom. Bake for 30 minutes @ 375 degrees, flip, bake for 30 minutes more. Let dry and harden for as long as it takes. Store in airtight bucket.

To eat: soak in water/milk (15 minutes) fry in buttered skillet.

Emergency Toilet Paper: "Cowboy Toilet Paper"

Mullein and borage both look alike, but I like Lamb's Ear because you can do other things with it. (I've heard it called 'woolly woundwort. Gets about 12 inches tall, perennial, flowers spike up to about 18 inches. I'll make a sketch when I get a chance.)

Birthday Cake-Wacky Cake (no eggs, milk, or butter, my Little Gramss recipe) for when the hens are molting or it gets too hot and they're not laying. [Reminder: Let Tess know that the big brown hen has started hiding her eggs again.]

Ingredients –

- 1 1/2 Cups flour (all-purpose)
- 3 Tbsp. cocoa (unsweetened)
- 1 Cup white sugar
- 1 tsp. baking soda
- 1/2 tsp. salt

- 1 tsp. white vinegar
- 1 tsp. pure vanilla extract
- 5 Tbsp. vegetable oil
- 1 Cup water

Mix first 5 ingredients; make three depressions (two small, one big) Add vinegar to small depression, add vanilla to other small depression and oil to big one; Pour water over and mix until blended smooth.
 Bake 35 minutes. Frost

HAPPY ALMOST AUGUST BIRTHDAY ALPHA AND ZETA, FIFTEEN YEARS OLD

About the Author

LINDA L. ZERN is an award-winning author who has written children's chapter books *(Mooncalf, The Pocket Fairies of Middleburg)* and an inspirational book *(The Long-Promised Song)* serving as both writer and illustrator. A collection of the author's humorous essays *(Zippityzern's: A Collage)* is available at Amazon.com. When she is not writing fiction she is growing and training flowers, butterflies, grandchildren, rabbits, chickens, and police horses. *Beyond the Strandline* is a work of young adult fiction with action, adventure, survival, romance, grid collapse, and a "prepper" backdrop.

Connect with Linda Online

Facebook (Author Page):
https://www.facebook.com/LindaLZern

Twitter
https://twitter.com/LindaLZern

ZIPPITYZERN'S BLOG (Linda L. Zern)
www.zippityzerns.blogspot.com

Linda L. Zern Website
www.zippityzerns.com

AMAZON AUTHOR PAGE FOR LINDA L. ZERN
www.amazon.com/author/lindazern

JOIN THE BOOK CLUB FUN:

To be part of the "Hidden in Plain Sight" BOOK CLUB and discussion group, concerning the lives of Tess and Parrish and all things Strandline - Follow the link . . .

http://www.zippityzerns.citymaxcom/hidden_in_plainsight.html